Sixty Saints for Girls

ST. BERNADETTE

Sixty Saints for Girls

Joan Windham

with illustrations by
Renée George

Christian Classics, Inc.
Post Office Box 30
Westminster Maryland 21157

First American Printing, 1990
Second American Printing, 1992
Third American Printing, 1993

Printed in the U.S.A.

Contents

Preface

This is not a real Preface such as I imagine one to be. It is an Apology. So very many Girls of all ages and Countries, English, American, Canadian, South African and so on, have written to me during the past years asking for their names to be included in the next book. I have done my best to find the Saints and to make their Stories but I have been so terribly long about it that I am afraid that the people for whom they were written are now past the age of wanting to read them! If this is so, then it is my fault and hence my Apology to them all.

Perhaps these Girls may now have Daughters bearing the same Names and so all will not be lost. I do hope so.

J.W.

St. Anne

This is a story about the Mother of Our Lady, and although there are hundreds of stories about her, I chose this one because it is my Favorite, and I hope you will like it too.

When Anne was quite young she married a man called Joachim and they were Quite Rich. As they had no family and had Too much money for the two of them, they did a very Sensible Thing. They divided their money into Thirds. One part they gave to the Temple of God in Jerusalem, one part to pilgrims and the Poor, and the third part they kept for themselves.

After years and years they still did not have any children and they wanted a Family very much. Now in those days the Feasts of the Temple were not exactly like the Feasts of the Church because of course all the Christian things hadn't happened yet (but they were just going to). But the Feasts were kept and people used to take presents to the Temple for different things. Sometimes it was money, sometimes two pigeons, or a lamb or some fruit. And the Priest in the Temple used the things to live on and to make vestments and mend the roof and all that, in the same way as our church Collection is used nowadays. They used the lamb's wool for clothes and vestments and sometimes they sold the presents and used the money. Well, Anne and Joachim wanted a child so much that they decided that Joachim should go with a present to the Temple in Jerusalem for the Feast of the Dedication, and pray that God would give them a child.

"And say that you will give the Child to the Temple for God if He sends us one," said Anne.

Now Jerusalem was a very long way off and Anne knew that Joachim might be away for weeks and weeks. He wanted to take some lambs for a present to God in the Temple, and lambs take a long time to take anywhere when everyone has to walk and rest and be fed and all that. However, Joachim set off with all his paraphernalia (which is miscellaneous articles of various kinds), and he thought that on the way back he would visit his Flocks and Herds that were feeding and being looked after miles and miles away.

"So I might be even longer than we thought," he said to Anne, "but don't worry, my dear wife, I will come back, and I hope God will answer our prayer."

"Goodbye, my dear husband," said Anne, "come back soon!" and she stood by the door and waved them all goodbye.

After weeks and weeks of slow traveling (because of the lambs) they got to Jerusalem the day before the Feast Day, and after a Good Night's Rest Joachim washed the two best lambs until they were as white as snow. They really did look lovely and Joachim was very proud to be able to give God such a beautiful and valuable present. But when he came to the Temple the priest who was there receiving the presents was quite Abominable to him.

"Aren't you Joachim?" he said.

"Yes, I am," said Joachim.

"How dare you come to the Temple?" asked the priest in a Grand and Sneering voice.

"I came to pray to God on this Feast Day," said Joachim politely, "and I brought these two lambs."

"Well, you can take them away again," said the priest rudely. "God doesn't want presents from *you!* He must be angry with you or He would have blessed you with Children years ago! I don't know what you've done, but you must be a very Sinful and Wicked man. Go away!" Of course none of this was true, but poor Joachim was so upset that he nearly cried. He took his two lambs and went slowly away. He couldn't understand why the priest had been so horrid. "He may be right," he thought; "after all, priests usually *are* right. Perhaps God *is* angry with me and I didn't know it."

He walked away out of Jerusalem and he thought:

"What will poor Anne say? She will not like having a Wicked Husband. I don't think I can go home yet until I find out what terrible thing I must have done."

So he went to visit his flocks and herds on the mountain side, and all the time he was so upset and worried that his Shepherds and Herdsmen could scarcely recognize him.

"What *is* the matter with Joachim?" they asked one another. "He looks so Sad and Thin that he isn't like himself any more."

Joachim stayed with his shepherds and herdsmen for months. He wondered and thought and thought and wondered and was so sad and confused that the others thought he must have Lost his Wits. (Wits are what keep you alive and brisk in your mind. Joachim wasn't brisk any more.)

"I do hope he finds them again," said the Shepherds. "He used to be as Sharp as Two Pins."

"He hasn't even got the Sense he was Born With," said the Herdsmen; "he doesn't even seem to Sit and Think. He just

Sits." And because they all liked Joachim very much, they didn't bother him but gave him food at the proper times and made him lie down in the Dry and the Warm at night.

But all this time Anne was getting very Fussed and Bothered.

"It's all very well," she said to her maids, "he said he might be away for quite a long time, but this is a *Very* long time and I am afraid my poor husband must be Lost or Ill or Dead."

"Cheer up, Madam," said one of the maids, "it is only a year and a half!"

"*Only* a year and a half!" said Anne. "I thought it might be four months and a half at the Very Longest!" and she went out into the garden with her Sewing. She sat under a laurel tree in the Shade and she thought about Joachim and about the Temple and the Lambs and the Baby they didn't have.

"I *do* wonder what can have happened to my poor Joachim," she thought. "I am so very lonely without him." She sat and looked at the garden and she saw a bird picking up caterpillars and grubs in her beak to take to her babies in their nest.

"Every wife has babies except me," said Anne, "even the birds." Then she heard one of her maids laughing with a herdsman:

"She never had any children and now she hasn't even got a husband," she giggled. "*She* isn't much good! I think I'll give Notice and go to a proper Family."

Anne began to cry. After a few minutes she dried her eyes and blew her nose and began to tell God how bothered she was about Joachim, and God was sorry for her and He sent two Angels, one to Anne and one to Joachim and He gave them both the same Message. And this was the Message:

"If you both go to the Golden Gate in Jerusalem you will

find each other again. And you will have a baby soon and you must call her Mary. When she is old enough you must take her to the Temple, just as you promised, because I have something *very* important for her to do when she grows up."

Joachim and Anne both started out at once and after a week or so they both arrived together at the Golden Gate in Jerusalem. They were so pleased to see each other that they laughed and cried and hugged each other and then they sat down and Anne said:

"But, my very dear Husband, what a silly old thing you were not to come home and Tell me about that horrid priest! Fancy going away and being miserable all by yourself!"

And Joachim said, "But my very dearest Wife, I thought you might believe him and think that I was really a Wicked and Sinful man."

"What nonsense you do talk!" said Anne, and she brushed some dust off Joachim's sleeve. "You look Thin and Tired, darling, let's go home and settle down again." And that is what they did.

After a time the Angel's message came true and they had a baby girl and they called her Mary. Anne loved her very dearly, and taught her to read and write and sew and garden and cook and look after the house. Then, when she was still quite a little girl, Anne took her to the Temple in Jerusalem to give her to God. Mary saw the Temple and knew that God was there. She ran up the fifteen steps to the Temple and there she stayed with the other girls, making vestments and doing embroidery and polishing the gold and silver things on the Altar until it was time for her to get married. (What was her husband's name?)

Anne and Joachim went home very happily together. God had kept His promise to them and they had kept their promise to God and all was as it should be.

St. Anne's Special Day is July 26th and hundreds and thousands of people are called after the Grandmother of Our Lord.

A Legend of the Flight Into Egypt

When Our Lord was nearly two years old He was living with Our Lady and St. Joseph in their house in Bethlehem. (It was the same house they were in when the Three Wise Men came to see them, bringing presents to the Baby Lord.)

Now, King Herod was very, very angry when he heard that there was a new King born in Bethlehem. *He* wanted to be the most Special and Important King in the Land, and if there were *two* kings they would have to share Importances, and he didn't want to do that. So he Summoned his Councillors and he said:

"As those Three Wise Men haven't come back to tell me where the new baby King is, I suppose they must have gone home another way. So do any of you know where he lives, because I want him Killed? When I asked the Wise Men they *said* Bethlehem, but now they have tricked me once, that might be a trick too."

None of the Councillors knew *exactly* where Our Lady and St. Joseph lived, but one of them said:

"My brother heard the Three Wise Men talking about Bethlehem, Your Majesty, so I suppose they *must* be somewhere near there."

"The only Thing to Do," said horrible King Herod, "is to kill *all* the baby boys that are Two Years Old and Less than Two Years Old, because He is *sure* to be one of them, and then I can still be the most Important King."

The Councillors thought this was Rather a Bad Idea, but they didn't say so in case King Herod had them killed too; as he did, if people didn't always agree with him.

So Herod sent for one of his Officers.

"Take your Soldiers," he said, "and go to Bethlehem and kill *every* little boy there is who is Two Years Old or Less than Two Years Old. It doesn't matter who they are, rich or poor, kill them all, and start first thing tomorrow morning."

That night, while the soldiers were Packing Up ready to go to Bethlehem, God sent an Angel to St. Joseph, who was asleep, and the Angel said:

"Get up *quickly* and take Our Lady and the baby Jesus and go to Egypt! Herod is sending his soldiers to kill all the little boys tomorrow, so go *now,* and stay there until I come and tell you that it is all right again."

So, in the Middle of the Night, St. Joseph went and woke up Our Lady, and, while she was packing up a few clothes and some food (they couldn't take very much because of carrying it), and dressing the baby Jesus, he went out to the stable to get his big Donkey. It was a very big Donkey, like a pony, not like the little seaside ones, and it had a dark-brown stripe all the way down its back from its head to its tail, and its name was Pharaoh because it came from Egypt. St. Joseph usually called it Flopears because its ears were so big and floppy, and Our Lady called it Softears because they were so soft to stroke.

SSG-B

Well, St. Joseph woke up Pharaoh (who wondered why they were going out in the Middle of the Night) and put on the saddle so that Our Lady could ride when she got tired. Then he hung two big baskets, one each side of the saddle, to put the food and clothes in. Then he led Pharaoh round to the door and told him to wait a minute while he went in to help carry out the bundles for the baskets.

"Are you ready?" he asked Our Lady, "because we *must* hurry; it is nearly tomorrow, when the soldiers are coming."

"I'm just coming," said Our Lady, and she popped two wooden animals that St. Joseph had made for Jesus into the basket just as St. Joseph was carrying it downstairs. She picked up Jesus and wrapped a shawl round him and hurried down, and found St. Joseph putting rags round Pharaoh's hooves so that he would not make a noise on the stony street.

They walked all the night and by the morning they were miles and miles away from Bethlehem and on the way to Egypt. It takes four days to walk from Bethlehem to the nearest bit of Egypt, so they had to sleep on the way. Once they came to a Shepherd's Hut on the side of a hill, and the Shepherd let them spend a night there, but mostly they had to walk over Hot Dusty Desert. St. Joseph was carrying their water in a goatskin and he was getting very worried about whether they would have enough water to last them out, because it was *so* hot, and they kept getting *so* thirsty, and Pharaoh drank such a lot at once, when it was his turn.

At last they saw two Palm Trees sticking up out of the sand.

"Good!" said St. Joseph. "There must be some water there or the trees wouldn't grow. Now we can rest in the shade, and I will fill up the goatskin."

Pharaoh pricked up his floppy ears and began to trot, because *he* wanted to rest in the shade, too.

But, under the Palm Trees, there was a Band of Robbers, who had got there first! They were all asleep (because they had been Robbing all night), except the Two Youngest, who were Keeping Guard. The names of these two were Dysmas and Gestas.

When Dysmas and Gestas saw Our Lady and St. Joseph coming towards them, Gestas said:

"Look! Let's Rob these people! They've got some big bundles and a strong donkey. If we take their water, too, they will die of thirst and then they can't tell anyone. Let's wake the Others and make an Ambush."

(An Ambush is when people hide behind things and Pounce Out on you.)

"No, don't let's," said Dysmas. "They don't look very Rich and we've Robbed quite a lot of people lately, and the Lady looks very tired. Let's Warn them instead."

"Well!" said Gestas, "I *do* call that a silly idea! What's the good of being a Robber if you don't Rob?"

"Well, if I give you my share of last night's Robbings, will you let them go?" asked Dysmas.

"All right, I suppose so," said Gestas.

So Dysmas ran out to meet Our Lady and St. Joseph and Warned them. Our Lady thanked him very much and St. Joseph said:

"We are very short of water. Do you think you could fill our goatskin for us without waking the Others?"

Dysmas went to fill it, and when he came back he looked at the Baby Jesus and said:

"I love your Baby, he is the sweetest one I have ever seen. What is his name?"

And Our Lady said:

"His name is Jesus, and some day He will reward you Himself for what you have done for us today."

Dysmas couldn't think what she meant. "I don't suppose I shall ever see them again," he said to himself as he watched them going out of sight.

But, when Our Lord was grown up and was Crucified, you remember the two Thieves who were crucified at the same time? Well, one was Gestas and the other was Dysmas! And Dysmas was the one who asked Our Lord not to forget him, and Our Lord said to him:

"*Today* you shall come to Heaven with Me." So he had a very Special reward, after all, didn't he? because he was the *only* person (except Gestas, the Bad Thief, who doesn't count because he wasn't looking) in the Whole World who has died looking at a *Real* Crucifix, not just a statue of one. He hung on his Cross, looking at God Himself crucified on *His* Cross, and so he forgot his own pain and just loved Jesus until he died, and then went to Him in Heaven. And if you can think of a more perfectly lovely way to die than that I would like you to let me know.

When the Holy Family got to Egypt, they found a very cheap house to live in at a place called Heliopolis, near Cairo. It had to be a cheap one because St. Joseph had earned all his money in his Carpenter's Shop, and they'd had to leave that behind! (I wonder who looked after it for them?) Anyway, Our Lady had brought the Gold and the Frankincense and the Myrrh that the Wise Men had given to the Baby Lord, so she sold these (they were very valuable) and then they had enough money to live on. The Wise Men would have been very glad if they had known how useful their presents had been.

They had only been in Egypt a few months when the Angel came back and said:

"It is all right now, King Herod is dead, so you can go home again."

So they packed up all their things once more! We do not know how they went back. There wasn't such a hurry this time, so perhaps they went back by Sea, in a Boat. It would have been nicer for them, not so hot and dusty as the Desert, and no Robbers and Ambushes and things. But when St. Matthew was writing about it, he didn't say.

But they never got back to Bethlehem after all! Because on the way they heard that King Herod's son Archelaus, who was now King, was just as horrible as his father, so it would be safer to live far away from him! So St. Joseph said to God:

"Where is a good place to go that will be safe for Jesus and Mary?"

And God said that he'd better go to Galilee, because another of Herod's sons ruled there (as the Prince of Wales rules in Wales), and this other son, called Herod Antipas, didn't bother much about his subjects.

So they went and lived in a town called Nazareth, in Galilee, and St. Joseph had a new shop to be a Carpenter in, and he made more little wooden Birds and Animals for the little Jesus to play with until He grew big enough to learn to be a Carpenter Himself.

Now, there is a Special Day belonging to this Story, too,

and I will give you three Guesses whom it belongs to. Our Lady? No. St. Joseph? No. Not even Dysmas the Good Thief, because he has his own Special Day. Well, it belongs to all those little boys who were killed in Bethlehem. What Lucky little boys they were, weren't they? They had very little time to wait before Heaven was opened for them, and they had no chance of Denying Our Lord, as some of them might have done if they had grown up and been there when He was Crucified. And they were Martyrs, too, because they died for Our Lord's sake, although they couldn't help it. So they are called the Holy Innocents, because they were too little to sin, and their Special Day is the 28th of December, quite near Christmas, when Our Lord is little, too.

Sts. Martha and Sarah

Once upon a time there was a woman called Martha and she had a sister called Mary and a brother called Lazarus. I am not going to tell you about the things that happened to them that you can read for yourself in the New Testament, but I shall tell you a Story about what happened a good deal later. You do just remember, don't you, that Martha was the busy housekeeping one of the two sisters and that Our Lord raised their brother Lazarus from the dead?

Well now, some time after the Resurrection of Our Lord, the Story is that Martha and her sister Mary and their brother Lazarus and a few other Christians left Palestine in a ship. They had all been teaching about Christianity (which was a New Thing), and already some people were trying to get rid of the Christians. So these few people sailed away from Palestine and thought they would go somewhere quite different and start a patch of Christianity there. And when it spread a bit they would move on and do the same thing somewhere else.

The ship they sailed on was going first to Marseilles in France, and the Christians thought that they would land there and let the ship go on without them. And so they did.

As soon as they had found somewhere to live they started preaching and teaching. Martha and Mary and Lazarus and their maid Sarah stayed in Marseilles, but all the others moved on in little clumps in different directions. Martha used to tell the French people a lot of little family things as well as Christian Teaching. She told them the sort of things she used to cook for Our Lord when He stayed in their house and the things He said and what colors He liked best to wear. She told them, of course, all about her brother Lazarus, and how once he was dead for three whole days. After a time, when they found that people liked their stories and were kind to them, they separated and went different ways so as to spread Christianity more quickly.

Martha went to teach the people who lived between Arles and Avignon. (You remember the town that has a bridge that people dance on?)

One day she saw crowds of people running up the road to

her cottage and she went out to see what it was all about.

"What is happening?" she asked the first people who came up her garden path.

"It's the Dragon!" they panted, and they looked behind them with frightened faces.

"The *Dragon?*" asked Martha. She had always believed there was no such animal.

"It lives along the river," said the people, "and it has killed a lot of our sheep and cows before now, but today it has been killing people!"

"How very sad!" said Martha. "But why do you come and tell me about it? I should have thought it would have been better to tell the Police or the Soldiers or someone."

"Yes, perhaps," said a man who was standing in front of the crowd. "But we had an Idea."

"What Idea did you have?" asked Martha.

"Well," said the man, "we thought it might be a good way for you to prove that Christianity is true. If your God has any power, let him show it to us now. Come with us, Martha, and see if your God will save us from the Dragon!"

"Let me see, now," said Martha. "Of course God will save you if you believe that He will, because nothing is impossible for Him. But He always said that you must have Faith. Have you got some Faith?"

The people said that of course they had, or they wouldn't have come to ask her help. So Martha, who had a Kind Heart, said she would go with them straight-away. She thought she wouldn't tell them just yet that their faith wasn't exactly the kind she had meant.

So Martha and the people went along the bank of the river

Rhone until they came to the flat gravelly part where the Dragon lived. When she was in the middle of this flat part she knelt down and so did everybody else.

"What shall I do now?" said Martha to God. "You know I'm terrified of Dragons."

"It isn't a real dragon," said God very quietly to Martha. "Real Dragons aren't big enough to eat cows and people and things. This is the Devil pretending to be a Dragon to frighten all the Pagans away from here, so that you will have nobody to teach about Me."

"Thank You very much for telling me," said Martha very quietly to God. "Shall I make the Sign of the Cross?"

"Yes," said God.

So Martha made a big Sign of the Cross and walked up to the Dragon, who stood quite still and shivered with fright at the Sign of God. It was so frightened that it couldn't move at all, although it did try to open its mouth at Martha. Martha took off her sash and put it round the Dragon's neck, and then she called the people to come and kill it quickly before it began to move again, and they did. Then everybody cheered and said that Martha had most certainly proved that Christianity was true, and they all became Christians that very day. Martha had a lot of work to teach them all they needed to know and believe, but she managed it all right in time.

Later on a big City was built at that very place where the Dragon lived, and it is called Tarascon, because Tarasque is the French word for dragon. (We might have called it Dragontown or Dragonville or something.) Of course St. Martha is the Patron Saint of the city.

St. Martha's Special Day is July 29th, and although there are fourteen or fifteen other St. Marthas, this was the first one. As well as being Patron Saint of Tarascon she is the Patron Saint of Housewives (why?), and I know a Hospital in London where the Housekeeping Sister is always called Sister Martha, even if her name is Rose or Helen or something.

There is another saint in this story. Do you remember Martha's maid called Sarah? Well, she is really Saint Sarah, and she is the Patron Saint of Gypsies, but I can't find out why. When I do find out I will write you a story about her. I just mentioned this so that all the Sarahs won't feel left out.

St. Penelope

Once upon a time there was a little girl called Penelope and she was six years old and she lived in Italy. Her father was a very busy man and her mother had a lot of committee meetings, and so Penelope used to go about by herself much more than is usual for such little girls. They were a Pagan family and so were lots of people in the Town. She loved to slip out of the door on Market days and wander about the cheerful stalls. The Fruit Stall she liked best because, as well as there being all the different colored Fruit and Vegetables, the Fruit Woman always gave her something to eat. Just one thing, but how delicious! The Jewelry Stall was lovely too, and so was the Stall where they sold birds in cages and kittens and puppies and tortoises. Penelope made a lot of friends in the Market, but she loved the Fruit Woman best.

One day she went down to the Market and found that a lot of her friends had not put up their stalls.

"How funny," she thought. "I hope they're not Ill or anything," and she walked around looking at the Stalls that were there, but somehow she didn't quite like to ask what had happened to the others. Presently she left the market and wandered down a side street, and whom should she see coming out of a little house but all her Market Friends with the Fruit Woman!

"Hullo, love!" said the Fruit Woman. "Whatever are you doing down here? It is too far from home for you to be by yourself."

"I think perhaps I might have been looking for you," said Penelope. "Why haven't you got your Stall up?" The Fruit Woman looked at her friends and they shook their heads.

"Why are they shaking their heads?" said Penelope. "What won't you tell me?"

"Well, love," said the Fruit Woman, "I'll tell you, but it's a Secret."

"I'm good at secrets," said Penelope. "I never tell them, not even other people's!"

"All right," said the Fruit Woman. "Well, this is Good Friday, see, and that is a day we don't work but go to church instead."

"Why *Good* Friday?" asked Penelope. "Why is it better than any other Friday?" So the Fruit Woman told her about Our Lord and about Christmas, and Easter and Whit Sunday. Penelope couldn't bear her to stop. It was the most Interesting secret she had ever heard. "Go on!" she said. "Tell me some more!" At last the Fruit Woman said that she really must go home and that she would tell her some more another day. "But remember it's a Secret, love, or there will be terrible Trouble, because we are Christians, you see."

Well, Penelope went to the Market as often as she could, and in between selling things the Fruit Woman told her more and more. About Our Lady and the Sacraments and about Mass.

"Can I come with you to your Church?" asked Penelope. "Oh *please* let me, I will be as quiet as nothing at all!"

"No, love, that I couldn't allow," said the Fruit Woman. "There would be the most dreadful things happen if anyone found out where we go. Anyway, we go to different houses every time so as to be more Secret."

One day Penelope went down to the Market quite early and saw that the Christian women's stalls were not there. She trotted off down a side road and there, just in front of her, was the Fruit Woman! Penelope hurried along and managed to get into the house just behind her. No one noticed her particularly because a lot of children were going in with their Mothers. Penelope sat down in a dark corner and watched everything. Some of the things the Priest was doing she understood because of what the Fruit Woman had told her, but some of the things puzzled her a lot. She came out of the Church with everyone else and hurried home without any of her friends seeing her.

Soon after this a Persecution of the Christians started and the Fruit Woman and her friends didn't come to the Market any more.

The Persecution got worse and worse and everyone talked about it. Penelope's father was quite excited when he came home one evening because one of his office boys had been a Christian all this time and no one had known!

"Just imagine!" he said. "None of us had an idea that the wretched boy was a Christian. Anything might have happened!"

"What might have happened, Daddy?" asked Penelope.

"Well, anything at all," said Penelope's father. "You never can Tell with Christians."

"*I* think they're very nice people," said Penelope, forgetting about the Secret.

Her father and mother both looked at her.

"When have *you* ever seen a Christian, Penelope?" asked her Mother.

Penelope remembered the Secret. "Oh," she said, "I saw some in the Market, but they aren't there now."

"Good riddance," said her father, "but what else do you know?"

"Nothing about *people,* only about *things,*" said Penelope. "Very interesting things they are, *I* think!"

When her father and mother found that Penelope really did know quite a lot of Christian things, they were worried. After Penelope had gone to bed they had a Talk.

"It's your fault, my dear," said her Father. "I didn't know you allowed her all over the Town by herself, it's madness!"

"I don't *allow* her," said Penelope's mother, "I didn't know she did! It's all your fault because you won't let me have a Nanny for her!"

"Well, one thing I do know," said Penelope's father, "and that is she won't go out any more!"

So he had a very high wall with no door in it built round a house, and in the house he put Penelope and thirteen maids to look after her. (People seemed to do that to their daughters quite often in those days. St. Barbara was one and St. Christine. Even Rapunzel-Rapunzel-let-down-your-hair, but she wasn't a Saint, only a Fairy Story.)

Little Penelope was quite happy with her thirteen maids. They did the gardening and the cooking and the cleaning and the washing, and nobody went in or out. Food and things used to be left on the top of the wall by the errand boys, who climbed a ladder. Then one of the maids climbed a ladder from inside and took down the baskets. But it was all too High and Difficult for Penelope.

After a while Penelope began thinking about the Fruit Woman and remembering all the things she had taught her. She wished so very much that she had learned more, and one day she began to pray to Our Lord, whom she didn't know. She prayed a lot and for a long time until one night, when she was asleep, a wonderful thing happened! Her Guardian Angel came to see her!

"It's quite all right, Penelope," said the Guardian Angel, "don't be afraid of me. You have never heard of me, I know, because the Fruit Woman didn't have time to tell you about me, but I am your Guardian Angel."

"Oh," said Penelope, "do you know the Fruit Woman?"

"Yes, I do," said the Guardian Angel.

"Oh well, it must be all right then," said Penelope. Then she remembered her manners to a visitor. "Won't you please sit down here," she said, "and tell me what I can do for you?"

"Well, it's really what I can do for *you*," said the Guardian Angel. "God sent me to say that He has heard you praying about being a Christian and He thinks, in the circumstances, that you are quite Old Enough even if you are only Six. So He said that I must come and teach you all about it myself, as there seems to be no one else."

"Thank you!" said Penelope. "How very kind of God. The Fruit Woman said He was."

So Penelope learned all about everything from her Guardian Angel, which was not a thing that happens every day, is it? When she knew quite a lot the Angel said:

"Now I think it is time for you to be Baptized, Penelope, and I will arrange for a priest called Father Timothy to come here somehow, and from then on he will Take you in Hand himself."

In a very short time after that the Roof began to leak, a thing it had never done before, and one of the thirteen maids sent for a builder to come and mend it. So, a few days later, up the Outside Ladder came a workman with a bag of tools. He stopped on the top of the wall and waited for the maids to put up the long Inside Ladder for him to climb down. Then he said:

"Where's the leak, Miss?"

"It's right at the top of the house in Penelope's room," said a maid. "Penelope is a little girl that we look after," she said. "I'll take you up."

So up they went to Penelope's room where Penelope was sitting doing a jigsaw puzzle.

"Good morning, Miss," said the Workman, winking at Penelope. "I've come to mend the leak."

"Oh yes," said Penelope, "it is a very wet leak; it sometimes Actually Drips and it has made a huge damp patch on the ceiling, hasn't it?"

"It has indeed," said the Workman. "All right, I won't keep you, Miss," he said to the maid. "I'll just mend it and then I'll be down for a bite to eat!"

"All right," said the maid, and she went downstairs.

The Workman got out his tools and climbed on the chest of drawers; Penelope watched him.

"Penelope," said the Workman.

"Yes?" said Penelope.

"Do you know who I am?"

"A workman," said Penelope, "but I don't know your name."

"It's Timothy," said the Workman, and he gave the ceiling a bang with his hammer and some bits fell down.

"Is it?" said Penelope. Then she remembered the Angel. "*Timothy,* did you say?" she said, all excited.

"Yes, *Father* Timothy really," said the Workman, getting down off the chest of drawers. "I've come to baptize you, little Penelope, and I'd better do it first before anyone comes."

So he baptized Penelope and made her a Christian. Then he went on mending the leak because he had been that kind of workman before he was a priest. Then he told Penelope he would come and see her whenever he could and would bring her Holy Communion. Then he went away over the wall with his bag of tools.

Penelope sat and thought for a long time, and the longer she thought the happier and more excited she became. At last she began to dance round her room.

"I'm a Christian! Hooray! Hooray!" and she began to make up a song about it just as you do. She danced round the house singing, and whenever she came to the Hooray part of the song, she knocked down a pagan idol and broke it. "Hooray!" she sang and bang went a statue off the mantelpiece. "Hooray!" and crack went another as she swept it off a windowsill. It was a wonderful feeling, and she had just broken the whole lot when the maids finished their snack and came out to hear the Last Smash.

"*Penelope!*" they shouted. "You naughty little girl, *stop* it, Penelope!" and some of them ran to get her father.

When he arrived he was furiously angry, and he did a most extraordinary thing, even for an angry Pagan. First he whipped Penelope (well, any Angry Father might do that), but then he tied her to a Wild Horse and was going to set it free to gallop away into the Wilds where Penelope would starve. And all because she was a Christian. Just as he was going to let the horse go, it turned round and bit off his hand! And then it stood still, with Penelope tied on to its back, and waited while he bled to death. A most amazing state of affairs altogether. Penelope's mother started crying, because what with one thing and another she thought there wasn't going to be anybody left, and all the gardeners and maids came running and shouting and milling about, and what with this and that there was an Absolute Pandemonium (which, I believe I have told you before, means that there were devils all over the place and I should think that by this time there probably were). The most surprising thing of all, to my mind, was that the Wild Horse still stood quietly, with Penelope tied on its back.

At first Penelope was so frightened and surprised and sad and bewildered (and *that* means to feel as though your brains were lost in a wilderness) that she did nothing. Then she began to be very sorry for her poor mother, who was crying sadly. She couldn't untie Penelope because she was afraid of the Wild Horse and so was everyone else. So Penelope said to God:

"Dear God, I'm a very new Christian and I do hope you know that Father Timothy baptized me this morning." (Of course God did, but Penelope wasn't quite sure.) "So, dear God, please will You make my Father better because I truly didn't mean to make all this Upset in the Family, although I am *very* glad I'm a Christian."

And God loved little Penelope, who had had such a lot of things happen to her when she was Only Six, and so He quickly mended her Pagan Father's hand and he came alive again and all the people cheered. When the Pagan Father was told he had been Actually Dead he was very surprised. "I thought it was a dream," he said, "and I thought the Horse bit off my Hand."

"It *did!*" said the people.

"Your hand was lying just *there*," said the Gardener. He pointed to the place with his toe.

Suddenly they remembered Penelope, who was still tied on to the Horse. Her father untied her and lifted her down and the Wild Horse galloped away into the Wilds.

Well, as soon as the Father could, he and his wife became Christians and so did Three Thousand other people who heard about it all. And so Penelope thought it was worth it and she thanked God all her life for His very great kindness to her.

St. Penelope's Special Day is on May 5th and hundreds of girls are called after her. This story was made for a Penelope whose other name is Susan, but her birthday isn't on May 5th. Is yours?

St. Ursula

Once upon a time there was a Princess called Ursula, and her
father was the King of Brittany in France and they were
Christians.

Now Ursula was only Fifteen years old, but she was very
clever and she knew all about Stars and things and how to Rule
countries. So, of course, heaps of Kings and Princes and Dukes
and Marquises and Earls and Viscounts and Barons and things
wanted to marry her so that she could help them to Rule
their Kingdoms and Principalities and Duchies and Marquis-
ates and Earldoms and Viscounties and Baronies and things.
But she didn't marry any of them, partly because they weren't
Christians and partly because she didn't want to get married
anyway.

One day there was a terrific Fanfare of Trumpets in the
Palace Yard. Ursula popped her head out of the window to see
what it was all about, and there was an Important Ambassador
going in to the King's Throne Room!

"I expect it's about me again!" sighed Ursula. "I'd better
wait until he's finished talking before I go down."

In a little while someone opened the door. There was the
King.

"Ursula!" he said. " 'Pon my Sam, I don't know what to say
to that Ambassador chap downstairs!"

"Why, Daddy?" asked Ursula, "whose Ambassador is he?"

"He has been sent by the King of England," said the King of Brittany. "Prince Conan of England wants to marry you and no two ways about it!"

"But the English King isn't a Christian!" said Ursula.

"I know, m'dear," fussed the King of Brittany, "but he's an Important sort of King and we can't afford to Affront him. He'll send over an Army, and I don't want his ill-mannered English soldiers all over the place."

"Well," said Ursula, "I'll go down and talk to the English Ambassador." So she tidied her hair and powdered her nose and went downstairs with Great Dignity. (Dignity means elevation of mind based on Moral Rectitude, which is Proud but not Vain.) She walked carefully up the long red carpet to the chair with the Ambassador on it.

"Good afternoon," she said politely. "Can I help you in any way?"

"No, no, my good child," said the English Ambassador pettishly. "I'm waiting for the Princess Ursula. And I hope I don't have to wait too long!"

"*I* am the Princess Ursula!" said Ursula, making herself very Tall. "In Brittany, Ambassadors stand up when they speak with Princesses!"

"Oh Dear!" said the English Ambassador, getting out of his chair very fast, "I beg your Highness's Pardon!"

"Granted," said Ursula, bowing her head kindly. "What did you want me for?"

"Well, it's our Prince Conan," said the English Ambassador. "He's set on marrying your Highness, and what he'll do to me if I go back without you I don't dare to Contemplate!"

"What's Contemplate?" asked Ursula, who didn't know that word.

"Regard with continued Attention," said the English Ambassador.

"Oh," said Ursula. "But I don't want to marry Prince Conan."

"Couldn't you Reverse your opinion?" asked the English Ambassador.

"Well," said Ursula, "I *will* marry Prince Conan, but only on Three Conditions."

"*Thank you,* your Highness!" said the English Ambassador. "What are the Conditions?"

"*First* that Prince Conan must be Baptized," said Ursula, "and *second* that he must give me Ten Girls for Ladies-in-Waiting, and each of those Girls must have a Thousand Girls for Maids-of-Honor. *And* I want a Thousand Maids-of-Honor for myself!"

"But that's Eleven Thousand and Ten girls!" said the English Ambassador.

"I know it is," said Ursula, "and the Third condition is that he lets me (with all my Girls) travel about for three Years so that we can visit lots of places where Saints lived and go to the Holy Land."

"Aren't you asking Rather a Lot?" said the English Ambassador. "I'm sure that our Prince Conan will never agree to all that!"

"Well, then, I won't marry him!" said Ursula. "Good afternoon!"

And she turned round and walked with great Dignity along the narrow red carpet and up the stairs again.

"Well?" asked the King of Brittany, who was sitting on the Top Step waiting for her. "What did you say?"

Ursula told him what they had said.

"But my good child," said the King of Brittany, "he'll never do all that!"

"Well, then, I needn't marry him!" said Ursula. "I don't really want to very much."

"But supposing he *does* do all that?" asked the King of Brittany. "What will you do then, eh?"

"I'll go to England with the English Ambassador," said Ursula, "and while I am traveling about with all my Girls I will make them all into Christians. Then I'll go back and marry Prince Conan, because he'll be a Christian by then. And all the Eleven Thousand and Ten girls will get married and have Christian Children and all England will be Christian in No Time!"

"Well that *is* a Good Idea, 'pon my Sam it is!" chuckled the King of Brittany. "I must say, Ursula, that you've got some sense in that head of yours!"

So the English Ambassador sent a messenger to the King of England, and he told Prince Conan, who sent a message back saying:

"To our Ambassador in Brittany. Tell the Princess Ursula that I will obey all her Requests.
                    "Signed 'Conan P.' (P. for Prince)"

So Ursula went to England with the English Ambassador, and there to meet her at Dover were Eleven Thousand and Ten Girls! There were Tall girls and Short girls and Dark girls and Fair girls, and Blue-eyed girls and Brown-eyed girls and girls with Curly Hair and girls with Straight Hair and Shy girls and Jolly girls, but they were all Young and none were Ugly!

They were all beautifully dressed in Silks and Velvets and Reds and Purples and Golds and Blues and Silvers, and they all stood in Rows and waited for Ursula.

Next day Ursula and her Eleven Thousand and Ten girls all collected in a field and Ursula told them about Our Lord and the Sacraments. She explained so well, and the Holy Ghost told her such a good way of saying it, that all the Eleven Thousand and Ten became Christians at once and were Baptized in a Stream that, very Luckily, was in the field.

Then they all packed into a Fleet of Ships to start on their Pilgrimage.

"We don't want any Sailors and things," said Ursula, "we will manage it all ourselves!"

And they did! The only thing was that they started to sail South to Rome, but by some mistake they went North up the river Rhine and landed at Cologne in Germany, which was all very Surprising. (It was the place where they make Eau de Cologne.)

When they saw where they had got to they thought that it was Rather Funny, but they all got out and rested on the River Bank and Ursula had a Dream. She dreamed that an Angel came and told her that although they would get to Rome in time, they would all come back to Cologne and be Martyred. "*All of us?*" asked Ursula. "Yes," said the Angel, and then Ursula woke up.

So they got back into the Fleet and went on up the River,

and everyone ran along the River Bank staring at all the Ships with Girls for Sailors! They sailed on until they came to a place called Basle and then they got out and walked. It took them Ages, but they walked over the Alps and down Italy until they got to Rome, where they wanted to see the Pope. But the Pope had heard of their coming and he was so pleased with them that he went out to meet them with a Procession!

When Ursula told him about the Angel the Pope said:

"I would like to be a Martyr too!"

"So would I!" said all the Bishops and people in the Procession.

So they all went back with Ursula and Eleven Thousand and Ten girls, up Italy and over the Alps to Basle. There they all squashed into the Fleet and sailed down the Rhine to Cologne, where Prince Conan was going to meet them, because he was tired of waiting for them in England.

While they were sailing to Cologne some of the Girls said:

"Why should *we* be Martyrs as well as Ursula?"

And some of the Others said:

"We'd Much Rather go back to England. It's Horrible and Frightening to be Martyrs!"

When Ursula heard about this she made them tie up their Ships. Then she got out on the Bank and told them that it was really a very Good thing to be Martyrs.

"Because," she said, "when you die Ordinarily you will be almost sure to have to go to Purgatory anyway for a little while, and perhaps for a long while."

"Why do we?" asked one of the Girls. She hadn't been a Christian very long so she wasn't Sure of her Facts.

"Because very few people are Good enough to go straight to

Heaven," said Ursula, "but very few people are Bad enough to go to Hell. So Purgatory is only to make you Clean and Tidy ready for Heaven. But if you are killed because you are a Christian, God makes up to you for the Frightening and Awful time you've had for His sake, and so He lets you go straight to Him in Heaven."

The Eleven Thousand and Ten girls all thought that they wanted to be Martyrs after that, and they all prayed that they would be Brave. It is easy enough to *say* you'll be a Martyr, but if someone tries to kill you very Slowly or something, then you would Rather Not Be, unless God helps you. What do you think *you* would do?

Well, while the Ships were sailing down the River to Cologne in Germany there were two Roman Generals (not Christians) who were commanding the German Army, and their names were Maximus and Africanus, and they soon heard about Ursula and her Eleven Thousand and Ten girls.

"What about all those girls?" asked Maximus.

"*What* about them?" said Africanus.

"Well," said Maximus, "if they all come and stay in Germany they might get married, and what with them and all their Children they'd Convert Germany, and that would never do!"

"No, it wouldn't do at all," said Africanus, "because what would become of *us?*"

So they sent a message to Maximus's cousin Julian King of the Huns, and the message said:

"Please, Cousin Julian, can you very Kindly send another Army to Cologne, because Eleven Thousand and Ten of the Enemy are arriving in a Fleet of Ships!"

Well, of course, Julian King of the Huns thought that the Enemy was a great Army, and so he sent his Fiercest and most Barbarous Soldiers to wait in Cologne.

"And mind you Slaughter the lot of them!" he told them as they marched off. (Slaughter is to Kill like Pigs.)

When the Huns saw Ursula and the Girls and the Pope and the Bishops and the Procession all arriving and Prince Conan Meeting them as he said he would, they couldn't believe their Eyes!

"Is *this* the Enemy?" they said to each other.

"Of *course* it is!" said Maximus and Africanus crossly. "Now hurry up!"

So the Huns rushed at them all and Killed them as fast as they could. But when they came to Ursula they thought that it was a pity to waste anyone so Pretty, so they saved her and took her back to Julian King of the Huns.

"Don't cry," said Julian when he saw her. "You marry me and be Queen of Germany and never mind about all the Others being Killed!"

"No!" said Ursula. "I *won't* marry a Pagan who has just killed all my Eleven Thousand and Ten friends *and* the Pope and the Bishops and Prince Conan. I couldn't, could I?"

"You could quite easily, if you stopped being a Silly Christian!" said Julian, who liked the Devil very much. "Why don't you worship Satan instead?"

"Because he isn't God!" said Ursula sensibly.

"Well, I'll shoot you with my Own Hand then," said Julian King of the Huns. "Be a Good girl, now!"

Then Ursula said very quietly inside her:

"Please, God, will You make me Brave, because I don't *want* him to shoot me? I'm frightened and I want to go back home to Brittany."

And God said to Ursula (quietly so that Julian wouldn't hear):

"Would you really Rather go home, Ursula?"

And Ursula said:

"I want to go home because I'm afraid of being hurt. But I-myself-inside-me don't mind what happens to my body if only You, Kind God, will help me to do what You want, and what *I* want really."

"You-yourself-inside-you is your Soul," said God. "You are a Brave Girl, Ursula, and I will help you to be Braver!"

Then Ursula said to Julian King of the Huns:

"Even if you *do* shoot me with your Own Hand, I would rather be Wounded and die Slowly than even *Pretend* to worship Satan!"

So Julian King of the Huns shot her dead and she went to God and found all the Eleven Thousand and Ten girls and the Pope and the Bishops and the Procession and Prince Conan waiting for her.

"Did you think I wasn't coming?" she said to them. "I'm sorry I'm late."

"No," said the Others. "God told us what was happening and so we prayed for you to be Brave!"

"Was I Brave enough?" asked Ursula.

"Yes, you were," said God.

St. Ursula's Special Day is October 21st, and heaps of people are called after her. (Did you know that "Ursula" means "Little Bear"? So it's rather a Funny name, really.)

St. Susan

Once upon a time there was a girl called Susan and she had a brother called Victor and they lived together in a very small house indeed, because they were very poor. Victor used to go out to work every day, and Susan kept house for him and did other people's sewing whenever she had time, and that made a little extra money. They had three hens, a puppy, and a very small garden with vegetables in it. It was too small to have flowers as well, so Susan used to pick flowers from the roadside to put on the table at mealtimes.

One day, when Victor was out at work, Susan was sitting in the sun on the doorstep doing her sewing. As she sewed she heard a horse trotting very far away. The sound came nearer and nearer until at last, right down the road, she saw a man on horseback. As he came nearer still she put down her sewing and watched him, until at last she saw that it was the Prince himself and she stood up and curtsied as he went by (as you would do and as I would do, that is, if you are a girl; boys bow). The Prince, who was a Pagan, turned and looked back and then he turned his horse round and went back. Susan looked so Pretty standing in her cottage doorway that he Fell in Love with her all in a moment, and wanted to take her back to his Palace at once.

"Thank you, your Royal Highness," said Susan, "but although I am Honored, I have to stay and keep house for my brother Victor; he has no one else. And, as yet, I do not know you, and so I must decline." (Which is a polite way of saying No.)

"But I am the Prince!" he said. "You can't just refuse to come. Are you engaged to be married to someone else or something?"

"No," said Susan, "I'm not. But I expect I'll get married some day!"

"No, you won't," said the Prince, "not if you won't come home with me now."

"I'm sorry, your Highness," said Susan, smiling politely, "but I can't do that."

The Prince was so angry with her that he said, "All right! If you won't look at me with kindness and love, then I'll see that you don't look at anyone else!" And he called his minions, who had been riding a short way behind him, and told them to make Susan Blind then and there, and they did.

When Victor got home from work and found what had happened to Susan, he was in Despair. He was so Sorry and so Furiously Angry that he just walked round and round and round the cottage; he couldn't think or speak. At last he calmed down a little and made up his mind what to do. First he went in to Susan again and put her to bed and made her a very special Egg Flip, with an egg from one of their three hens, and he put it in a cool place. He next went to a neighbor and told him what had happened. The neighbor was terribly sorry and asked what he could do to help.

"Could you spare me a little wine?" said Victor. "Susan needs something to Strengthen her and I could put it in a

Special Egg Flip I've made and that would Nourish her too."

"Of course I will," said the Neighbor, and he gave Victor some wine in a cup. It was Red and Beautiful wine made from his own grapes and was very strengthening. Victor took it home and put some of it into the Egg Flip and took it to Susan.

"There, darling Sue," he said, "drink this up and it will Strengthen and Nourish you."

"What is it?" said Susan, because she couldn't see and she wanted to know what it was before she tasted it. So Victor told her and Susan drank it all to please him. She had a terrible pain in her eyes.

Then Victor set off to see the Prince. He found him having supper and he did not Stand on Ceremony but went Straight to the Point.

"I've come about my sister, your Highness," he said.

"Oh? Who is your sister?" said the Prince, and he went on eating his Roast Goose.

"Susan," said Victor.

"Oh, yes, pretty Susan," said the Prince. "Well, she's not so pretty now, is she? That will teach her not to insult Princes!"

"You are a wicked, selfish and cruel person," said Victor, "and if an honest Christian girl can't sit in safety on her own doorstep without being pestered by the likes of you, then it is time someone killed you off and we had another Prince," and he turned and marched out of the Palace.

The Prince and his minions were so Absolutely Astounded at Victor's speech that they didn't move for a minute, but they just stared at one another, and by the time someone thought of catching him, Victor was out and away! He was going to call in at the Church on the way home to ask the priest to come and see Susan when he heard the Prince's minions chasing after him.

"Kill the Christian!" they shouted. "Kill the Christian for Treason!" (Treason is doing something bad against the Queen or President. It is an Imprisonable Thing to do nowadays.)

Victor began to run toward the Church, but just as he got to the steps up to the door, the Minions caught him and killed him. They killed him mostly because he was a Christian. If he had been a Pagan, they would have taken him back to the Palace. So Victor was a Martyr and he was buried near the Church.

It was lucky that, before he was killed, he had told the neighbor about Susan. Because the neighbor's wife looked after Susan very kindly. But she was very ill and her eyes hurt her Too Much, so in a very short time she died, which was lovely for her because God had Victor all ready and waiting to meet her in Heaven. The neighbors buried Susan with Victor under the floor in the Church.

Now comes a very Interesting part of the story. God did not want people to remember about Susan and Victor and nothing at all happened for Eight Hundred Years! No one remembered them at all by that time, and no one knew where they were buried or where they had lived or even that there had ever been such people!

Well, eight hundred years after they died, some workmen were mending the church. They had some of the floor up and they were digging around and they found two very old skeletons in the remains of two coffins.

"I wonder who they were?" said one workman, whose name

was Edward James.

"There's no name or anything anywhere," said another man, whose name was Richard Valentine.

"Well," said Edward James, "we will have to move them because of our work."

"There's an empty Marble Tomb in the Churchyard," said Richard Valentine, "I wondered about it yesterday. We could put them in there for the Time Being."

"All right," said Edward James, and they kindly put the two skeletons into the empty tomb and went on with their work.

Now, in this Town where they were mending the Church there was a Blind Woman who always had a pain in her eyes. The Parish Priest, whose name was Father Andrew, was worried about her because the doctor couldn't help her and there did not seem to be the right kind of people to look after her. One day after Mass he was praying for all his people and he said to God:

"You know, dear Lord, I am very bothered about the Blind Woman. She's *so* patient and kind that it does seem a Shame Doctor Jeremy can't help her. So, dear God," said Father Andrew, "please would *You* do something about it? Even to find a proper person to look after her would do, but if You *would* make her eyes better it would be a wonderful thing."

God didn't say anything to Father Andrew, but that night He sent him a Dream. And this was the Dream:

He dreamed that somebody told him to take the Blind Woman to the Tomb of a Saint who had just been found in his Parish.

When he woke up he said to himself:

"But that *can't* be true! I haven't got a Saint in my Parish. And if one had just been found, surely I would know about it," and he got up and went to say Mass. As he was going home to breakfast he saw the two Workmen.

"Good morning!" he said.

"Good morning, Father Andrew," said Edward James and Richard Valentine; and then Edward James remembered the Skeletons. "Father," he said, "do you know what?"

"No, what?" said Father Andrew.

"Well," said Edward James, "Richard Valentine and I found two old Skeletons of people yesterday and we put them in that Tomb over there. We didn't know what we ought to do with them. Was it all right to do that?"

"Yes," said Father Andrew. Then he remembered his Dream and he went to look. "I *wonder*," he said to himself. "I really do wonder!"

After breakfast he thought he would go and see the Blind Woman. "I'll just take her to the Tomb in *case* my Dream was true," he thought, and he did. When they got to the Tomb, he took the Blind Woman's hand and put it on the stone.

"Now ask God if He will please Bless you," he said, "because I had a Dream last night and it *might* have been about you!"

So the Blind Woman did and the pain in her eyes stopped at once!

"There!" she said. "I feel so very much better, Father. I wonder who these people were. Tell me about your Dream." So Father Andrew did and while he was telling her the Blind Woman began to see, and by the end of the story she could see Perfectly Well. So she and Father Andrew both thanked the Saint whose name they did not know and they went home.

After a few days people began talking about a Young Man who was sometimes in the Church. A lot of people saw him and each time he told them the same thing. He told them about Susan and the Prince and said that Susan would always pray for Blind People very specially because she had been Blind herself. When people remembered to ask him who he was, he said he was Susan's brother Victor! So that is how we know what really happened to St. Susan and St. Victor.

St. Susan's Special Day is on February 9th and hundreds and hundreds of people are called after her and can have her for their Special Saint. But Blind people all the World over can have her for theirs even if their names are Gladys or Rose or something. St. Victor's Special Day is February 9th too, so that he can have it with his sister.

✓St. Agatha

Once upon a time there was a girl called Agatha and she lived with her rather rich family in Sicily. (Sicily is a small island at the bottom of Italy. If you imagine that Italy is a leg and a foot kicking a ball, then Sicily is the ball.) Agatha and her family were Christians, and, as so often happened, they were all arrested by the Governor's minions and tortured. Her father and mother soon died, but Agatha was young and strong and she stayed alive. The Governor was a horribly cruel man. He went on torturing Agatha for a Whole Month to make her stop being a Christian. She was so terribly hurt that even the Pagans were Shocked.

"If you go on like that," they said to the Governor, "even our own gods will turn on us." And they followed him about the streets in a Mob, telling him to kill Agatha properly and have done with it. But the Governor did not like being told what to do by the common people of the town, and so he put Agatha back in prison while he thought what to do about her. And while he was thinking, the people shouted at him through his windows:

"Kill her or let her go!" they shouted. "Kill her or let her go!"

Agatha was nearly dead by this time. She was in dreadful pain, but nothing would stop her being a Christian. But now, after a month, she began to pray to God to let her die.

"It has gone on Too Long, dear Lord," she said. "I don't think I can bear it any more at all. Do please let me die now, before the Governor comes back." And God took her to Heaven straight away.

"Thank You!" said Agatha. "I did just begin to think that perhaps You might have forgotten me, or that I wasn't Good enough, or something."

"Of course I didn't forget you," said God. "I never forget anyone. But I didn't take you away before because of the Pagans."

"I don't know what you mean," said Agatha.

"When the Governor tortured you for so long," God told her, "even the Pagans themselves were sorry for you, and they tried to make him stop. Hundreds of them are being Baptized because of your brave and faithful death."

"I didn't know," said Agatha.

"No," said God, "you didn't, and that makes you all the Braver. I am very proud of you, Agatha."

And Agatha went to find her father and mother and all her friends and was glad that God had made her stay alive so long.

Now when the Prison Warder found Agatha dead in her prison he went at once to tell the Governor. The Governor was rather frightened of the crowd outside, who were still shouting, so he let the Christians take Agatha's body to bury.

None of them were rich, and though they did their very best to afford a tombstone, they couldn't. But at her funeral they all went to pray for her. Just after they had filled in her grave a wonderful Procession of richly dressed young men rode up. They had beautiful shining horses with gold on their bridles and their clothes were all the Colors of the Rainbow. Then an even Richer-and-Nobler-looking man, who led the Procession of richly dressed young men, rode right up to the grave. He dismounted from his horse and put a Marble Notice on Agatha's grave. Then, while everyone was still Absolutely Silent with surprise, he got on his horse again and the whole Procession rode away. When they had disappeared into the distance the crowd at the funeral began to move and speak again, and they all craned forward to see what was written on the Marble Notice. It said:

Agatha, by her prayers and suffering,
has brought Peace and Deliverance
to Sicily.

Nobody knew what it meant, and they put Agatha's scarf over it to keep off the rain. They all said that the Grandest Young Man must have been Agatha's Guardian Angel with a Procession of other Angels, because not one of them was ever seen again. The Governor was furious about the whole thing, but there was nothing he could do, because every single person, whether they were Christian, Jew, or Pagan, was against him.

The next day he rode to Agatha's house up on a steep hillside to steal anything Rich and Rare that he might find there, now that the owners were all dead. When he was nearly there his horse slipped on the loose stones and stumbled and the Governor fell off and broke his neck.

Now, exactly a year after Agatha died (on February 5th it was), an Extraordinary Thing happened, and it has happened over and over again since then.

Sicily has an enormous volcano on it called Mount Etna, and on this day it Boiled Over, and melted rocks and lava poured down its sides towards the town at the bottom. Smoke and fire flew up out of its top like a giant chimney on fire, and there were Thunders and Earthquakes inside the mountain.

The people were terrified of all this red hot stuff flowing towards their town. Then suddenly somebody remembered Agatha, because of it being exactly a year since she had died. Some of them rushed to the grave and picked up her scarf, which was still there. They put it on top of a lance, like a flag, and then they all marched as near as they dared to the rolling fire. And it stopped and began to cool down! So what was written on the Marble Notice was true. Agatha had (with the help of God, of course) delivered the people of Sicily. And do you know, many times since, the same thing has happened when Mount Etna has Boiled Over.

Besides being the Patron Saint of Sicily, St. Agatha is one of the Patron Saints of Nurses, and her Special Day is, of course, February 5th. Not very many people are called after her now, but I know an Aunt Agatha and so I made this story for her.

St. Cecilia

Once upon a time there was a girl called Cecilia, and her father was a Rich and Noble Lord and her Mother was a Rich and Noble Lady, and they were all Romans and Christians, and it was Cecilia's Wedding Day.

But Cecilia didn't want to be Married at all, and so she felt very Sad and Worried when she woke up in the morning.

"Mummy," she said while she was running her Bath water, "*Please* need I be married?" I promised Our Lord that I'd spend *all* my time for Him, and I can't do that if I've got a Husband. I don't want to get Married, Mummy, and I *couldn't* eat any Breakfast!"

"Don't be Silly, Darling!" said her Mummy. "You've been saying the same thing for weeks! There are much more Important people than you to serve Our Lord. I'm sure He'd rather that you got Married like a Sensible girl! Now have your Bath and I'll bring you your Breakfast in Bed! Then you can get up quietly and put on your Wedding Veil and things and I'll help you!"

So Cecilia had her Breakfast in Bed because of being so Sad and Worried, and then she began to Dress.

She had a Golden Wedding Dress and a White Veil with Golden Stars on it and she had Golden slippers. But she was too Sad and Worried to like them very much.

"Now, darling," said her Mother, "we must be starting," and they went downstairs to where her Father was waiting, and they all drove off to the Church. And so Cecilia was Married because everyone said she ought to, and she wasn't Old enough to Argue with so many grown-ups properly.

After the Wedding and the Party Cecilia and her New Husband, called Valerian, started on their honeymoon. Now Valerian wasn't a Christian, but he was a very kind man, and Cecilia said after Supper:

"Valerian, I've got a Secret to tell you."

"What is it?" asked Valerian in an Interested Voice.

"I'll whisper it so that no one will hear," said Cecilia.

"Well, don't buzz in my ear, then," said Valerian.

So Cecilia whispered in Valerian's ear:

"I've got an angel who is always and always with me!"

"*Always?*" asked Valerian.

"Yes," said Cecilia.

"Morning, noon and night?" asked Valerian.

"Yes," said Cecilia. "It's called a Guardian Angel."

"I don't believe it!" said Valerian.

"But I *have*, Valerian," said Cecilia, "honestly I have!"

"Is he here now this minute?" asked Valerian.

"Yes," said Cecilia.

"Well, that *Proves* you're wrong!" said Valerian, "because there's no one here except you and me and perhaps some sort of god."

"And the Angel!" said Cecilia.

"I wish you wouldn't keep *on* about the Angel," said Valerian. "Such silly nonsense! Seeing's believing, and I won't believe it unless I see it with my Own Eyes. And even then I mightn't!"

"That you'll never do, my poor Valerian," said Cecilia, "unless, of course, you become a Christian."

"*That* I'll never do!" said Valerian.

Well, they went on arguing and arguing all night until it was nearly Breakfast time and they hadn't been to bed yet!

"It seems to me," said Valerian with a Big Yawn, "that I'd better be a Christian after all. I don't like thinking that there *might* be an Angel there that I can't see. How do I start?"

"Go and see the Pope," said Cecilia. "He is a friend of my father's. Give him my Kind Regards and ask him if he will be so good as to Baptize you!"

So Valerian went off to find the Pope, whose name was Urban. (What is the name of the Pope we've got now?)

Urban was very busy in the Christian Cemetery Seeing to Things. In those days there were very few Priests and Bishops and things, and so they all did a Hand's Turn when Necessary.

Urban stood up and put his Kneeling Mat into the Wheelbarrow to keep it dry and said:

"Good morning and God Bless you! What can I do for you?"

"Good morning!" said Valerian, raising his hat politely. "Cecilia sent me to ask if you would be so good as to Baptize me?"

"Are you Cecilia's New Husband?" asked the Pope.

"Yes," said Valerian, "it was our Wedding Day yesterday."

"Do you believe that there is only One God, One Faith and One Baptism?" asked Pope Urban.

"Yes, I do," said Valerian.

"Good," said the Pope, and he baptized Valerian with some water that he had been watering flowers in the Cemetery with. (Things were rather Rough and Ready in those days.)

"Goodbye and God Bless you!" said the Pope, and he took his Kneeling mat out of the Wheelbarrow and went on with what he was doing before.

"Goodbye and thank you very much!" said Valerian. And he raised his hat politely and started off home. When he got back he found Cecilia sitting Chatting to her Guardian Angel.

"So you *are* there after all!" he said. "I nearly didn't believe you would be!"

"I've been here all the time," said the Angel, "only you couldn't see me! I was laughing when you said Seeing's Believing!"

"I'm sorry I said that," said Valerian. "I must beg your pardon!"

"Granted," said the Angel kindly. "And now I've got an Interesting Present for each of you. Here are two Crowns for you that you can wear always, but they will be Invisible to everyone else. They are to show that you are going to be Martyrs one day!"

And he showed them two Crowns, one of Roses and one of Lilies.

"Which will have which?" he asked.

"Please can I have the roses unless Valerian wants them?" said Cecilia.

And:

"Please can I have the Lilies unless Cecilia wants them?" said Valerian, at exactly the same time.

"Isn't it lucky that you didn't both want the same one?" said the Angel, and he put the Invisible Crowns on their heads.

"But what will we do when the Flowers die?" asked Valerian, who was of a Practical Turn of Mind.

"They never will die," said the Angel, "unless you stop being Christians. And now, God is so pleased about Valerian being a Christian that He says He will grant you One Wish!"

"Anything in the Whole World?" asked Valerian, very pleased.

"Anything except wishing that *all* your wishes will come true," said the Angel, "because that wouldn't be Fair."

"Well," said Valerian sadly, "I *was* going to wish that. I don't think that I want anything else, thank you."

"What about Tyburtius?" asked Cecilia.

"Oh, yes," said Valerian, "I forgot all about him! Please may my brother Tyburtius be a Christian too?"

"A very Laudable Request," said the Angel, "and it will be granted."

(He meant that it was a Very Good sort of Wish.)

Well, that afternoon Tyburtius came to visit Valerian to see his New Wife. And when he had said How do you Do, he said:

"What a lovely smell of Flowers! Where are they?"

"Look for them," said Valerian, winking at Cecilia so that she wouldn't tell just yet.

Tyburtius searched all over the place!

"It's funny!" he said. "I can't find them anywhere. They can't be far or they wouldn't smell so strong. *Where* are they,

Cecilia?"

Cecilia couldn't keep quiet any longer.

"On our heads!" she said.

"Don't be silly!" said Tyburtius, looking round the room again.

"They are, though, old boy," said Valerian, chuckling at Cecilia.

"Am I mad, or are you?" he asked.

"None of us!" said Cecilia. "They are our Invisible Crowns to show we'll be Martyrs, and Oh, Tyburtius, *do* be a Christian and then perhaps you can be one too!"

So after a Bit of Talk Tyburtius was a Christian and was Baptized by Urban, the Pope.

Valerian and Tyburtius used to go out at night and do a very Useful Job. They used to collect all the Christians that had been Martyred during the day and Bury them properly in the Christian Cemetery. But no one knew that they did this.

One day the Governor found them out! (You see, it was against the Law to be a Christian or to have anything at all to do with Christians, even bury them.)

"But," said the Governor, "Valerian and Tyburtius are Noble Lords! They wouldn't do an Imprisoning thing like burying Christians!"

"Well, they do!" said one of his Minions, "because I saw them myself!"

So the Governor ordered them to be Beheaded Forthwith. And they were and they went straight to Heaven, and God said:

"I let you have a nice Quick death because you haven't been Christians very long. But I am very pleased with you both, all the same."

"What about Cecilia?" asked Valerian.

"She'll be coming soon," said God.

And sure enough someone saw Cecilia and Pope Urban burying the bodies of Valerian and Tyburtius, and Cecilia was arrested.

"Come along now, Cecilia," said the Governor. "Just offer some Incense to this Statue of Jupiter and we'll say no more about you being a Christian!"

"*Why* offer it Incense?" asked Cecilia.

"Because Jupiter is a God, of course!" said the Governor, "you know that Perfectly well!"

"No. I can't do that!" said Cecilia bravely. She was feeling very Frightened because, although she wanted to be a Martyr in Heaven, she was frightened of the Martyring part.

"Take her away to Jupiter's Temple!" ordered the Governor, "and we'll see if she'll change her mind!"

So the jailers took her away, but on the way to the Temple Cecilia explained so well about Jupiter not being a God at all, that they were all Converted and became Christians too!

The Governor was Furiously Angry and he sent for Cecilia again and shouted:

"What do you mean by it? Aren't you afraid of me? Don't you know that I am a very Important Person and that I have power over your Life and Death? Answer me!"

"Well, there you *are* wrong!" said Cecilia, although she was shivering in her shoes with fright. "I know that you have power over Death because you can Kill people. But you haven't power over Life because you can't make them alive again!"

"Now, don't be silly!" said the Governor. "You know what I meant quite well. Be a good girl, now, and offer Incense to the god."

"I never knew that you were Blind!" said Cecilia.

"What *do* you mean?" said the Governor in a Surprised Voice.

"If you weren't Blind, you could *see* that your god is made of Stone," said Cecilia, "and, anyway, if you *felt* it, you'd know it was!"

This made the Governor very Angry, and he ordered Cecilia to be killed by putting her into her own Bath filled with Boiling Water!

"But that's a Frightful way of being killed!" said poor Cecilia. "Need it be that way, *please*?"

"The Boilinger the Better!" said the Governor with a loud Laugh. "Ha! Ha! The Boilinger the Better!"

So Cecilia was taken home by two Jailers and locked in the Bathroom while the Jailers went down to the Kitchen to make up the Fire. Then the Bath was filled with Boiling Water and Cecilia said:

"Help me to be brave, Our Lady, quick; help me to be brave, or I might offer Incense so as not to have to get into the Bath!"

And Our Lady did and the Boiling Water didn't Kill her, but it was Much Too Hot!

"Well," said one of the Jailers, "would you like to offer the Incense now?"

"No!" said Cecilia. She was holding her breath because of the water being so hot and she couldn't talk much.

"Chop off her head!" roared the Governor, coming into the Bathroom.

Now, when people were beheaded, the Executioner was only allowed to have Three Chops, so as not to be Cruel and have

Nine or Ten.

But Cecilia's Executioner had a very Blunt Axe, and after his Three Chops Cecilia wasn't dead. So he left her and went home to Tea.

Cecilia's friends put her to bed and tried to make her better, but her neck hurt so dreadfully that she was glad when, after three Whole Days, Our Lady came for her and took her back to Heaven herself.

"It *was* Kind of you to come for me yourself, Our Lady," said Cecilia, whose neck didn't hurt any more.

"Well," said Our Lady, "you were so *very* brave in the Boiling Bath that God thought that you deserved a Special Treat. Valerian and Tyburtius will be glad to see you. They were wondering when you'd come."

"Did you tell them, or did you keep it for a Surprise?" asked Cecilia.

"I kept it for a Surprise," said Our Lady. "There they are, over there! Go and surprise them!"

So Cecilia did, and Valerian and Tyburtius were All Astonished because they'd no idea that she was coming so soon.

Cecilia did one thing that you mightn't know. She invented Organs (the things that play the music in Church, you know). So whenever you see pictures of her she's nearly always Playing one, with her Guardian Angel standing near and listening and with her Crown of Roses on her head.

St. Cecilia's Special Day is November 22nd, and heaps and heaps of people are called after her because all the Sheilas and Cecilys and Cicilys count too.

St. Valerie

Once upon a time there was a girl called Valerie and she lived with her mother, whose name was Suzanne, in Limoges, which is a Town in France. In those days Christianity was only Spreading, it had not actually Spread yet. So there were always Missionaries going around all the countries and preaching in the same way that the Apostles and Disciples did. Valerie and Suzanne were not Christians, but they did not mind them at all. In fact they were quite Interested.

Well, one day they heard that a Christian Missionary was coming to Limoges, where there were no Christians yet, and they thought that, as they had plenty of room and could well afford it, they would ask him if he would like to Lodge with them. Valerie went out to meet him as he came into the town, and when she told him about their spare room he was delighted with the idea.

"How very kind of your Mother to have thought of it," he said as he walked along with Valerie. "I don't know anybody at all in Limoges, and I should have had to spend the day looking for lodgings."

"It's a pleasure for us," said Valerie politely, "and my mother's a very good cook, everybody says so!"

"Good! I'm hungry," said the Christian Missionary, whose name was Martial.

So Martial lodged in Suzanne's house and went out every day to preach to the people of Limoges, but although some of the people listened to him to pass the time of day, no one was converted. But Father Martial kept on keeping on and hoping for the best.

Valerie was engaged to be married to the Duke of Guienne, whose name was Stephen. He lived a good way off and she did not see much of him, but she liked him and was looking forward to being the Duchess of Guienne.

After some weeks of talking to Martial and listening to him speaking to the crowds, Suzanne and Valerie and a few of their friends became Christians. Martial thought that at last things were beginning to move. And so they were, but not at all in the way he expected.

At about this time Stephen arrived with some horses and servants to marry Valerie and take her back to Guienne with him, to be his Duchess.

"All right, Stephen," said Valerie. "But I ought to tell you first that I am a Christian now. Father Martial has been staying with us, and some of us decided that his God and his Church were quite Wonderful and True. And so they are!"

But Stephen was furious.

"I can't have a Christian Duchess!" he said. "Whatever would my people in Guienne think? Oh no, Valerie, you'll just have to change over again, there's nothing else for it."

But Valerie wouldn't Change Over again and Stephen was more and more angry and disappointed. At last he went home and sent a letter to her by one of his soldiers, and the letter said:

> Dear Valerie,
>
> This is your last chance. If you will not change your mind and come to me with this soldier, I have told him that he must cut off your head. His name is Rollo.
>
> Yours very affectionately,
> Stephen, Duke of Guienne.

Valerie looked at Rollo.

"I can't go with you," she said. "Quite truly, I can't. Couldn't you go back to Stephen and tell him that?"

"No," said Rollo, "I have my Orders." And then and there he cut off Valerie's head.

Now that could have been the end of the story, but actually it is the beginning of the Most Unusual part of it.

As soon as Valerie got to Heaven, God said to her:

"Well done, Valerie, you were quite right. Now I want you to do one more thing for me before you come to live in Heaven for ever."

"What must I do?" said Valerie.

"You must go back to Limoges," said God, "and you must go into your body again."

"But please, dear God," said Valerie in a worried voice, "I haven't got a head on my body. Rollo cut it off."

"I know he did," said God, "I saw him. But you yourself are quite complete, aren't you?"

"Oh, yes, I am," said Valerie.

"Well," said God, "when you go into your body again you must stand up. Then you must pick up your head and take it to Martial."

"Oh, I couldn't!" said Valerie. And then she remembered where she was and said, "Of course I will, if you say that I should."

So although Valerie had been dead for a quarter of an hour she left Heaven and went back to her body, which by now had quite a crowd of people standing round it and staring. She stood up and picked up her head and carried it to Father Martial, who was preaching to a great crowd in the Market Place. Valerie put her head down beside him and left her body there too and went back to Heaven. All the crowd saw a dazzling light, and in it they saw Valerie flying up and away. They were so Astonished and Frightened and Glad all at the same time that every single one of them became a Christian that very day! There were fifteen hundred of them, and the Fame of the Christian Church grew in France after that, because of

Valerie.

Now Rollo was very frightened indeed, because he had seen Valerie get up again after he had killed her. He ran back to his master, Stephen, and told him what had happened. As he finished telling him, what with the fright and running so fast and one thing and another, he fell down dead!

Stephen was in a terrible fuss. Rollo was his best and favorite soldier, and it was all his fault that he was dead. He was afraid, too, that the people of Limoges would be angry with him for having Valerie killed instead of marrying her. So he put on his Plainest Clothes and his Saddest face and he sent to ask if Father Martial would please come to see him.

Father Martial came when he had finished his sermon, and Stephen asked him if he would pray for Rollo to come alive again.

"You don't deserve it, you know," said Father Martial (who in the end was Saint Martial), "but I will, because you wouldn't ask me to do it if you didn't think it possible. And if you think it's possible, then you must believe in God. But," said Martial, "that doesn't say that God will answer my prayer. He doesn't make Miracles for All and Sundry, you know."

"I do believe in God," said Stephen. "I couldn't help believing everything after all the things that have happened, could I?"

So Martial blessed Rollo in the Name of the Father and the Son and the Holy Ghost. Amen. And Rollo sat up. He thought perhaps he had fainted.

Stephen gave Martial a great deal of money to build Churches and Hospitals in Limoges and they were all called after St. Valerie, and some of them still are, because she is the Patron Saint of Limoges.

St. Valerie's Special Day is December 9th and her name has always been a favorite one.

St. Dorothy and Companions

Once upon a time there were Three Sisters called Christina, Celestine and Dorothy, and they were In Prison. They were there because they wouldn't say that a Stone Statue belonging to the Governor was just as good as God. The Governor's name was Fabricius and he was Very Fierce against Christians.

Every two or three days the Governor Fabricius used to send for someone in the Prison and ask them to Stop being Christians.

"If you don't," he used to say, "I'll Chop off your Head, or Pull out your Teeth One by One without any Gas, or Poke out your Eyes or Burn you to Death or something."

And sometimes the Poor Prisoners were so Frightened that they said they *would* stop. But they did not very often do that because they loved our Lord more than they did their own Lives.

Well, a week ago there had been Five girls in the Prison instead of only Three: one of them was a friend of Christina-and-Celestine-and-Dorothy's called Lucy, and the other was a girl called Marcella.

One day the Prison Keeper had put his head in at the Door and said:

"Lucy! The Governor Fabricius wants you!"

"I'm coming," said Lucy, and she said to The Others, "Pray for me, won't you, so that I won't Deny Our Lord." (Denying is when you won't have Anything to Do with someone.) And she went away with the Prison Keeper.

Soon the Prison Keeper came back without Lucy and he said:

"Well, she's another Stupid! She wouldn't Deny your Lord and so they they killed her in the Throat and she's Dead." And he slammed the Door and went away, Whistling.

"Oh! Good; now she is a Martyr in Heaven," said the Others. "I wonder when Our Turn will be."

The next day the Prison Keeper put his head in at the Door and said:

"Marcella! The Governor Fabricius wants you!"

"I'm coming," said Marcella. "Pray that I'll be Brave, won't you?" she said to the Others, and she went away with the Prison Keeper. Soon the Prison Keeper came back and said:

"Now *she* was Sensible! The Governor Fabricius gave her a lot of Money and she said that she Really did not Care Much for Jesus and she'd Rather be a Pagan." (A Pagan says there isn't such a Person as the Real God. Like Fabricius.) And the Prison Keeper slammed the Door again and went away Whistling.

"How Terrible!" said Christina-and-Celestine-and-Dorothy. "How sad Our Lord will be after He has died for Marcella and now she won't die for Him!" And they prayed for Marcella so that she would Change her Mind.

The next day the Prison Keeper put his head in at the Door

and said:

"Christina-and-Celestine! The Governor Fabricius wants you!"

"What, Both at Once?" said Dorothy. "I'll be All Alone in Prison then."

"We're coming," said Christina-and-Celestine. "Pray for us, Dorothy, so that we'll be Brave like Lucy. When we get to Heaven we'll pray for you and so will Lucy. And soon it will be Your Turn." And they went away with the Prison Keeper. Soon the Door opened and, instead of the Prison Keeper coming to tell Dorothy how the Others had Got On, there were Christina-and-Celestine!

"He said he'd Burn us Alive, Dorothy," they said, "and we were so Frightened that we said we'd Stop Being Christians. And now that we have Stopped, it doesn't feel Very Bad, and the Governor Fabricius has given us Plenty of Money. And, Dorothy, we *thought* that if we came and told you, perhaps you needn't be Killed either."

"You mean that you thought perhaps that I'd Deny Our Lord, too?" said Dorothy.

"Well, we didn't Actually Deny Him," said Christina-and-Celestine, "we just *said* we would, but we love Him Really, inside us."

"That *is* Denying Him," said Dorothy. "It's like being Too Grand to stop and talk to a Poor-and-Raggy friend of yours if a rich friend is with you, and just Walking Past them without looking at them. Or like letting some friend of yours Talk Rudely about God because you're afraid he Won't Like you any more if you tell him to Stop."

"We never thought of that," said Christina-and-Celestine.

"We'll go back and tell the Governor Fabricius. But, Dorothy, *do* pray that we'll be Brave this Time!"

"Yes I will," said Dorothy, "and it'll soon be My Turn, and, if *I* am Brave, I'll see you in Heaven. Pray for me with Lucy when you Get There."

And Christina-and-Celestine went back to the Governor Fabricius and Told him. And he was Very Angry and Burnt them Alive until they were Dead. And so they were Martyrs after all.

The next day the Prison Keeper put his head in at the Door and said:

"Dorothy! The Governor Fabricius wants you, and for Goodness' sake don't be as Stupid as the Others because you are my Very Favorite Prisoner."

"I'm coming," said Dorothy, and she went away with the Prison Keeper.

When they got to the Governor Fabricius he said:

"Well, Dorothy, I hope you are going to be Sensible and Give Up Christianity?"

"I'm going to be Sensible and Stick to Christianity," said Dorothy in a Very Decided Voice. She made her voice Very Decided because she did not want the Governor Fabricius to know that she was Feeling Rather Frightened.

"Well, how would you like to Marry me and be a Rich Governor's Wife?" said the Governor Fabricius, making a Smug Face.

"*And* stay a Christian?" asked Dorothy.

"Of course not," said the Governor Fabricius Crossly. "I wouldn't have such a thing as a Christian in my house!"

"Well, I'll stay a Christian," said Dorothy.

"Even if I Chop off your Head?" said the Governor Fabricius in a Surprised Voice.

"Yes, because I want to see Our Lord and All the Others," said Dorothy.

"How do you know that you'll see them?" asked the Governor Fabricius.

"Because Our Lord has often told me about Heaven and the beautiful Garden there is there, with Roses and Daffodils and All Sorts of Apples and Other Fruit in it. And there are all the Other Martyrs who are my friends. It's very Dull here without them," said Dorothy.

"There couldn't be Roses and Fruit at This Time of Year because it's Winter," said the Governor Fabricius Grandly.

"Yes there could," said Dorothy.

"Take her away and Chop off her Head," said the Governor Fabricius in a Tired Voice; he was Getting Sick of Christians.

"Hullo! Dorothy!" said someone just behind her as she was leaving the Governor Fabricius' house. And there was her friend Theophilus-who-didn't-like-Christians! "You and your Roses in Heaven!" he said. "Mind you send me some if you ever Get There!" And he Laughed her to Scorn. (Which is Laughing Nastily.)

"Yes, I will," said Dorothy. "Goodbye."

"Goodbye," said Theophilus.

Just as Dorothy was going to have her Head Chopped Off and the Executioner (who is the Man who does the Chopping) was all Ready with his Axe in the Air, there came a Beautiful Little Boy with Rich Purple Clothes with Stars in them and Shiny Hair and Very Blue Eyes and he was carrying a Golden Basket full of Rosy Red Apples and White and Yellow Roses!

"Here, Dorothy," he said. "Our Lord sent them to you from Heaven."

"Thank you," said Dorothy, "but I am just going there myself. Would you mind taking them to Theophilus, because I said I'd send him some."

"All right," said the Little Boy, and he went away and the Executioner Chopped Off Dorothy's Head and she went up to Heaven to see our Lord that she loved so much and Lucy and Christina-and-Celestine and all the Other Martyrs.

Theophilus was having a Tea Party when Dorothy was Killed, and Marcella was there. In the Middle of the Party he was telling his friends about Dorothy.

"She Actually Thinks that she will see God," he laughed, "and she said that she would send me some Things out of the Garden." And they all Laughed Dorothy to Scorn.

Just then Theophilus turned round and there beside him was the Little Boy with the Golden Basket!

"Dorothy sent these to you from Heaven," he said, and putting the Basket on the table, he Disappeared!

They all stared at the Basket.

Then Theophilus touched it:

"It's real," he said. "And so Heaven must be Real too! And I thought Christians were silly to Believe in Heaven."

"Some of us were Christians once!" said Marcella and all his friends.

Well, what happened was that Theophilus and his friends finished having Tea and then went to the Governor Fabricius, and the Pagan Ones said that they'd turned into Christians, and the Others said that they were sorry they'd Stopped Being Christians and that they were going to Be Them Again, and the Governor Fabricius gave them to Lions to Eat, and so they were Martyrs too! Dorothy and All the Others *were* pleased to see them when they got to Heaven!

Well, there seem to be Rather a Lot of Martyrs in this Story, don't there? And so there are Rather a Lot of Special Days, too. St. Dorothy first because the Story is really about her—February 6th—and Anyone called Dorothea or Dolly or Dora counts. Then St. Lucy: her Special Day is on December 13th and Anyone called Lucilla or Lucinda or something counts too. Then St. Christina and St. Celestine both have the Same Day because they were both Martyred on the Same Day, and they have July 23rd, and Anyone called Christine or Christian can have that day too. I don't know about Theophilus and Marcella and all his Friends, but anyway they were Early Christian Martyrs.

ST. DOROTHY AND COMPANIONS

Shall we make a bargain
If our sins allow,
All to meet in Heaven
A hundred years from now?

And we will have a picnic
In a lovely wood,
And boil our kettle properly
As here we never could.

And we'll invite Christina
And Celestine to go,
Anyone we want to have
We'd better let them know.

There's Dorothy and Lucy
And Theophilus, too,
Is there anyone at school
You think would do?

We'll find a place with bluebells
And a king-fisher's nest,
A clear stream for wading,
A green bank for rest.

And we'll remind each other
"Do you remember when
We made a bargain all to meet
A hundred years from then?

"Can it be so long ago!
It seems like yesterday.
I am glad once in Heaven
We are there to stay."

St. Barbara

Once upon a time there was a Girl called Barbara and she had a Very Bigoted Father. (Bigoted means having a Very Narrow Mind so that you can only see Straight in Front of you and Nowhere Else.) This Father was called Dioscorus, which is a Rather Funny name.

Barbara hadn't any Brothers or Sisters and she was Really Very Pretty and was the Apple of Dioscorus' Eye. So Dioscorus, who was very Proud of having such a pretty daughter, was Simply Terrified in case she Got Married and so he would Lose her.

So he thought this Thought:

"If I build a very Tall Tower with rooms at the Top and put Barbara in and then Fill Up the Front Door with a Brick

Wall, she can Never Get Out and no one can ever Get In to marry her." So he did that. And Barbara lived in her Tall Tower and let down a basket by a String for her Food and Drink and Clean Clothes and Library Books and Things, and she was quite Happy.

Now one thing that Dioscorus was very Bigoted about was Christians. He just couldn't Abide them and he was Rather Glad that Barbara was up so safe in her Tall Tower, because she couldn't Get into Mischief with Christians.

But one day, when Barbara had pulled up her new Library Books, she found that one of them was All About Christians, and it was written by a man called Origen. Barbara thought:

"I do believe Christians must be Quite Nice. Daddy seems to have Got Hold of the Wrong End of the Stick (because he is so Bigoted)."

So she wrote a letter to Origen-who-had-written-the-Book, and this is what she wrote:

> DEAR ORIGEN,
>
> My Father (who is Very Bigoted), has put me in a very Tall Tower because of not Getting Married and because of not Being a Christian. But I read your Book from the Library, and I think Christians are Quite Nice, so will you please write and teach me about them and Baptize me by Post?
>
> > With love from
> >
> > > BARBARA.

When Origen got this Letter he sent for a friend of his who was a Priest.

"Look at this Letter I have just got," he said; "it is from a girl called Barbara and she wants to learn her Catechism and be Baptized by Post! I can't go to her myself because I am Busy, but you could, couldn't you?"

"Yes," said the Priest. "I'm Rather Slack just now."

"Well, you'd better not go and say you're a Christian, because of Dioscorus being so Bigoted. You'd better pretend to be someone else. The Question is Who?"

"A plumber?" asked the Priest.

"No," said Origen, "because there's Already a Plumber who did the Pipes in the Tall Tower; besides, you aren't one."

"Well a Gardener, then," said the Priest.

"Don't be Silly," said Origen (which is a very Rude Thing to say to a Priest, but you must remember that the Priest was a friend of his as well). "Don't be Silly, if you were a Gardener you'd have to work outside and Shout Up at one of Barbara's Two Windows and everyone would hear you Baptizing her. Besides, it would be Rather Difficult to pour the water on her head from so far away."

"Well, could I be a Doctor?" asked the Priest.

"That's Quite a Good Idea, because Priests *are* Doctors of Souls," said Origen. "I'll write and tell her to Pretend to Feel Ill (because, really, her soul isn't very well), and then you Turn Up and say that you are an Eminent Physician." (Eminent is being High in the Public Estimation, which means that Other People think you're Clever.)

So Origen wrote to Barbara and when she got the letter she rang the Big Clanging Bell on top of the Tall Tower that she rang when she wanted anything.

"What is it, Barbara?" shouted Dioscorus who had been

Weeding quite nearby.

"I don't feel Very Well," said Barbara in a Rather Sad Voice, "what shall I do, Daddy?"

"I don't know, 'pon my soul I don't," said Dioscorus. "I never thought of that when I Bricked you In. Let me think."

While he was thinking, he saw a man walking Slowly Along.

"Who are you?" he said, making a Bigoted Face. "Trespassers will be Prosecuted."

"I know they will," said the man, "but I am only an Eminent Physician going for a walk."

"A Doctor?" said Dioscorus, changing his Bigoted Face into a Pleased One. "That's just what I want. Come here and help me to Knock a Hole in the Wall."

So the man (who, of course, was Origen's friend the Priest) helped Dioscorus make a Hole in the Wall.

"Why are we doing this?" he asked, Rather out of Breath with Banging the Bricks with his Walking Stick.

"Because Barbara isn't Feeling Very Well," said Dioscorus, "and you must go and see her. You'd better stay Two or Three Days so as to be sure she's Quite Well before you go. And I'll Brick the Hole up again Fairly Loosely until you're ready to come down again, because there isn't a Front Door."

"All right," said Origen's friend, and he went up the Long Curly Stairs, round and round and round. At Last he got to the Top!

"Let me have a Chair!" he said to Barbara, "I'm too Giddy to Think!"

While he was Recovering, Dioscorus Filled up the Hole in the Wall.

"Well," said Barbara, "will you teach me how to be a Christian Very Quickly, because we have only got Two or Three Days."

So the Priest Friend of Origen taught Barbara her Catechism and then Baptized her, and they laughed about her thinking that she could be Baptized by Post!

After three days Dioscorus Shouted up to one of Barbara's Two Windows:

"Hullo, Barbara, are you Better now?"

"Miles better, thank you," said Barbara.

"Well, I'll undo the Wall and let the Eminent Physician out," said Dioscorus, "or his Family will think he is Lost."

So Barbara said Goodbye and Thankyou to Origen's friend and he went away, and Dioscorus left the Wall Open for a Few Days in case Barbara felt Ill again. But she didn't.

One day, just when Dioscorus was thinking that he must start the Bricking Up, Barbara rang the Big Clanging Bell.

"Please can I have Three Windows instead of Two?" she asked.

"What on Earth for?" said Dioscorus.

"Well, because of the Three Powers in my Soul," said Barbara.

"What *are* you Talking About?" said Dioscorus in a Rather Bigoted Voice.

"You know," said Barbara, "my Memory and my Understanding and my Will, like the Father and the Son and the Holy Ghost."

"What!!!" Roared Dioscorus, and he Drew his Sword and *Rushed* up the Long Curly Stairs, round and round and round, but, when he got to the Top he was so Giddy that he had to

Recover for a Minute and by that time Barbara's Guardian Angel had taken her and hidden her in a Thick Wood.

And it happened that a Shepherd just Caught a Glimpse of her one day and he told Dioscorus, who Raced to the Wood Roaring at the Top of his Voice, he was so very Bigoted about Christians. He found Barbara and dragged her home by the hair, and the road was very hard and bumpy.

"So you are a Christian, are you?" he said, Stamping About. "Well, either you Stop it, or I'll Kill you with my Own Hand."

"I won't Stop it at all," said Barbara, tidying her Hair. "If you Kill me I'll be a Martyr, and you'll be a Murderer, and that would be a Terrible Thing for you. If you don't Kill me I'll be a Christian, and you'll have to be Less Bigoted, so you can Choose."

"You just come with me, Miss," said Dioscorus, his face red with rage, and he took Barbara to the top of a very high mountain (I can't *think* why), and Chopped off her Head!

So Barbara was a Martyr and went to Heaven, and she loved being there with God and Everyone instead of being in the Tall Tower all by herself. But as Dioscorus was going down the Very High Mountain again, after having Martyred Barbara, there was a stupendous Thunder-and-Lightning storm and the mountain fell over and squashed him.

St. Barbara's Special Day is on December 4th, and lots of People's Birthdays are on that day, and there is a Town in America called after her.

St. Beatrice

Once upon a time there was a girl called Beatrice and she lived in a big house with an enormous garden in Rome near the river Tiber. (Have you a River in the town where you live? Do you know what its name is?)

Now Beatrice and her brothers were Christians and at that time the Emperor of Rome was a very fierce Pagan who spent a lot of time hunting out Christians and killing them off in all sorts of ways because he did not want Christianity to spread so much. But as a matter of fact it wasn't any use killing them because the Christians left Rome and went to live in other places and that spread them quicker than anything.

Beatrice and her brothers kept very quiet about being Christian, but the boys used to go out at night and collect the bodies of the people who had been Martyred and bury them in a safe place. Then they would go and tell a priest and the priest would say Mass for them. And Beatrice used to keep up the fire and have hot drinks ready for the boys when they came in.

But one day they were caught and they were Martyrs themselves and their bodies were thrown into the river Tiber.

Poor Beatrice cried sadly because she was so lonely, and in the night she went out secretly to pull her brothers out of the water. She wasn't very brave in the dark because she was afraid that a Pagan might catch her and put her in prison. Besides, her brothers had never let her go with them when they went out looking for Martyrs, so she wasn't used to being out at night.

Beatrice went out at the end of the garden and across a field towards the River. It was misty, and a bird made a funny scraping noise with its voice down near the water. There was the smell of someone's bonfire smoke and the dead leaves shushed round her feet as she walked.

She started along the edge of the river looking for the two boys and she hadn't gone very far before she saw a pale patch just below her. She couldn't have a light in case someone saw her, so she knelt down and put her face near the water and touched the paleness that she saw below her. It was soft woolen stuff. She felt again, and she knew that it was her brother's coat and that she had found one of them. She tried very hard to pull him out of the water, but he was too heavy, and as she pulled she saw that her other brother was tied to him and that they were together.

It took her a long time to untie them in the dark and the string was wet and cold, and so were her fingers, but at last she managed it. Because she wasn't strong enough to lift them out, the only thing that she could do was to drag her brothers one at a time in the water until she got to the boathouse which was in the field at the end of the garden. So she started off. It took her more than an hour and she got very wet and very cold, but she carefully hid her brother in the boathouse and then went all the way back in the dark for the other one. This time it took her even longer because she was so tired, but at last it was finished and they were both safely hidden. Beatrice knelt beside them and said the Psalm which begins with: "Out of the depths, O Lord, I have cried to thee," which is a prayer

for the dead, and then she got up and went quietly back across
the field and into the garden. She went round the house and
out of the front gate and down the road to another house
where some Christian friends lived.

She crept up to their door and scratched it with a piece of
stick. She didn't want anyone outside to hear because no one
else knew that her friends were Christians. After she had
scratched again, the door opened a crack and a voice whispered:

"Two loaves. . . ."

And Beatrice whispered:

"And five fishes."

And the door opened wider and she slipped in quickly and
the door shut behind her.

("Two loaves and five fishes" was the Password and Counter-
sign that some of the Christians were using just then. Because if
you were a Christian of course you would know what it meant
and would know the answer. But if you had never heard of
Our Lord's miracle you wouldn't know what on earth anyone
was talking about.)

Their Christian neighbor took Beatrice into the sitting room
where there was a little bit of fire left and then he called his
wife. They didn't have a light in case anyone wondered what
was going on.

"What is it, my dear?" asked the neighbor's wife when she
came downstairs in her dressing gown.

"They've killed the boys," said Beatrice.

"I know," said the neighbor's wife. "We heard about it this
evening. Poor little Beatrice, I am so sorry."

"I have been out for Hours looking for them," said the
neighbor, "but I didn't find them. I will try again tomorrow

night."

"I found them and I put them in our boathouse," said Beatrice, "but they were too heavy for me to bury by myself."

"Of course you can't!" said the neighbor. "Now don't worry. I'll go and find a friend of mine and we'll do everything just the way the boys used to do for the other Martyrs. And we'll tell the priest so that he can say Mass for them in the morning."

"Oh, *thank you!*" said Beatrice, and then she cried sadly on the shoulder of the neighbor's wife because everything was so miserable. The neighbor's wife lent her a handkerchief out of her dressing gown pocket and gave her some hot milk and reminded her that the boys were Martyrs and were in Heaven with God. So Beatrice cheered up a little and the neighbor took her home when he went to find his friend.

Well, after that Beatrice lived alone with her cook and her housemaid in her lovely house with its enormous garden. She gardened a good deal and while she gardened she talked to Our Lord and told him about all the Christians that she knew and about how difficult life was for them. Although they loved being Christians and did not want to be anything else.

One day a man called Lucretius happened to be going along the road and he looked over the gate and saw Beatrice's lovely garden, and her beautiful house with the river behind it.

"I would like that house for my own," he said. "It is the nicest one that I have ever seen." And he opened the gate and went in. Instead of going up to the front door he went round the house to the garden door so that he could see more of the flowers.

There did not seem to be anyone about, so he knocked at the garden door and the housemaid came and answered it.

"I am sorry but Miss Beatrice is out," she said. She thought that Lucretius was a friend of Beatrice's because she had seen him looking at the flowers and he had not gone to the front door.

"Will you wait?" she said, "Miss Beatrice has only gone with the flowers for Sunday." And she pulled up a garden chair and Lucretius sat down to wait. Then she went away.

"Oho!" thought Lucretius. "So Miss Beatrice, whoever she may be, is a Christian, is she? And she takes flowers to the Church for Sunday, does she? Well, Well." And he hummed to himself and looked at the flowers. He was a Pagan, but he wasn't one of those who persecuted the Christians.

After a while Beatrice came round the side of the house with an empty basket, and she made a surprised face when she saw Lucretius.

"How do you do?" she said, "who are you?"

"How do you do?" said Lucretius. "I am Lucretius, and I was going past your house when I saw your lovely garden. I came in to ask you if you would sell it to me?"

"Oh, no," said Beatrice. "I am so glad that you think it is lovely, but I won't sell it. I like it too much myself."

"It is too big for you alone," said Lucretius, "that is, if you *are* alone?"

"Yes, I live alone now," said Beatrice, "but I don't want to sell my house, thank you very much. Good afternoon."

"Good afternoon," said Lucretius, and he went on down the road. But he couldn't stop thinking about the house; he wanted it very badly indeed. And every day he went back and looked over the gate. Sometimes he went in and asked Beatrice if she would sell it, but she always said that she did not want to.

At last Lucretius had an idea, and this is the idea: "If only Beatrice would go away, the house would be empty and I would buy it." Then the Devil put a really mean and wicked idea into his head, and this is the Devil's idea:

"If I told the Governor that Beatrice is a Christian, he would put her in Prison and perhaps kill her. Then I could have the house for a Reward for telling him." .

And believe it or not, that is just what he did! He went to the Governor and said:

"You know that girl Beatrice who lives alone by the river? Well she is a Christian and she teaches children their Catechism so that they will be Christian too."

"*Really?*" said the Governor. "I never knew that. She can't be allowed to go free like that. I'll have her imprisoned at once!"

"What about her house?" said Lucretius.

"What about it?" said the Governor.

"Can I have it for a Reward?" said Lucretius.

"Yes," said the Governor. "She won't need it any more, you may be sure of that!"

So Beatrice was put in prison and Lucretius moved into the house that he wanted so badly and he was delighted with it and he picked a lot of Beatrice's best flowers and put them on his dining-room table.

When the Governor sent for Beatrice he asked her the questions that nearly all the Governors asked their Christian prisoners.

"Will you stop being a Christian and worship the Pagan gods?"

"No," said Beatrice, "I couldn't do that."

"Then you will be strangled," said the Governor.

"Well," said Beatrice, "I wouldn't like that at all. Couldn't you do something quicker to me? Something like Stabbing or Chopping off my head?"

"No," said the Governor. "You will be strangled unless you deny your God."

But although Beatrice was very frightened (and so would you be, and so would I be) she wouldn't even pretend to deny Our Lord so as to save herself (Would you? Would I?), and although she asked God to save her and not to let her be strangled, she wouldn't say anything to the Governor except:

"I love God, so I wouldn't deny Him."

So in the end she was strangled, and it was even worse than she thought that it might be. When she was dead her Christian neighbor came in the night and buried her with her two brothers, whose names were Simplicius and Faustinus.

As soon as Beatrice was dead she left her body lying on the prison floor and went straight to God, who said:

"You are a very brave girl, Beatrice. I did not save you when you asked Me to because I knew how lonely you were living all alone, and now you can be with your brothers again."

"Thank you," said Beatrice. "I was really afraid because I did not think that *You* would think that I was good enough to be a Martyr."

"You are very good," said God, "and I am proud of you. Now go and see the boys."

So Beatrice did, and she forgot about her sadnesses at home because she was so happy to be near God and safely with her brothers.

But something very Odd happened in Beatrice's beautiful

house. Lucretius, who was living there, thought that he would have a Party to celebrate his new home, and he invited all his friends and relations to a Grand Dinner. He had vases with Michaelmas daisies in them in the Hall, red ones and purple ones and white ones and mauve ones and pink ones and blue ones. And on the dining-room table he had all sorts of colored chrysanthemums and dahlias, just about every color there is except blue. And he had white candles in silver candlesticks on the table to cool the people's eyes after they had looked at so many fiery scarlets and yellows and oranges and purples and crimsons and coppers and creams.

When they had all finished their Sumptuous Repast they shouted "Speech! Speech!" to Lucretius and he stood up to make a speech.

"Dear friends," he said, "I am delighted to see you all here enjoying my lovely house and flowers and dinner. I hope you will all come again soon!"

And all the people cheered and Lucretius sat down again. After a few other people had made speeches, a tiny little boy who was so young that he could not be left at home alone, stood up on his mother's lap, and everyone laughed and said "Speech!" to him for fun. Because he was too young to talk properly.

And the tiny little boy looked at Lucretius and then said very loud and clear so that everybody heard him:

"Lucretius, you are a Thief because you stole this house, and you are a Murderer because it was your fault that Beatrice was killed, and you belong to the Devil who is waiting for you this very minute!"

All the people stared because they had not known how

Lucretius had got the house. Then they stopped talking and got up from the table to go home because the fun of the Party was spoiled. And when they all stood up Lucretius stayed sitting in his chair, because he was dead and the Devil had carried him off! Now wasn't that an Extraordinary thing to have happened?

St. Beatrice's Special Day is July 29th, and anyone whose name is Bee or Beatrix or Trixie belongs to her. And her two brothers who are Saints and Martyrs too have the same day as their sister, which is nice for all three of them.

St. Agnes

Once upon a time there was a girl called Agnes, and she was thirteen years old. Do you know what Agnes means? Well, what is the Latin word for Lamb? Never mind if you don't know. What about *Agnus Dei*, is that any help? Or you might even know what the French for Lamb is. Everybody's name has a meaning, and it is most Interesting to find out about them. Lucy means Light, and my own name means God's Gift which is very nice for me. And if you don't know what my name is, look on the outside of this book and read it for yourself! So Agnes means a Lamb and that is one of the reasons that there is nearly always a lamb beside her in pictures. There is another reason for this though, and that is the story that I am going to tell you now.

At the time that Agnes lived, sixteen hundred years ago, there was a lot of persecution in Rome (you must surely know what persecution means by now) and the Pagans made every kind of Excuse to kill the Christians. They said that the Christians sold things cheaper than anyone else, that they worked against the Government, that they were spreading into so many countries that they were Spies, that if anyone's house caught on fire or their haystacks burned then it *must* be Christians who started the fires on purpose. In fact, everything wrong that happened was the Christians' fault, and they must be Got Rid Of.

One day the Governor (who was a Pagan) was talking to his Chancellors and Vice Chancellors and Minions (what is a *Vice* Chancellor?) and came to the conclusion that Something Must be Done about the Christians.

"It's all very well," said the Vice Chancellor, "but they *will* go on Spreading. We hunt them out of the country, and so they go to other countries and start spreading there and converting people and having Christian children who grow up and Spread again."

"Children!" said the Governor. "Mr. Vice Chancellor, you have got an Idea there!"

"Why? What have I said?" asked the Vice Chancellor, looking a bit anxious. One had, after all, to mind what one said these days, because the Governor was a Bit Hasty.

"Why don't you use your Brain?" said the Governor. "Surely you must know what you said! You should listen to yourself some time, you might be interested."

All the Minions laughed because they were feeling nervous. The Governor was not in a very Good Mood this morning.

"Children!" said the Governor, very Loud and Clear, and he looked round the room and at everyone to see if they saw what he meant. They didn't. The Governor suddenly stopped feeling Cross because he felt Smug instead.

"Well," he said, "one of the best ways of spreading that the Christians have, is to have Christian children in other countries who grow up and marry, and *they* have Christian children in *other* countries. See?" He looked at everyone again and they all nodded solemnly.

"All right then," said the Governor, "we will find every excuse we can to kill all the girls we can, so that they can't go abroad and neither will they be able to marry and have families here. Because there won't *be* any girls, see?" He looked round again. Everyone clapped and smiled and nodded at each other, and they all agreed that it was a Magnificent Idea.

So whatever went wrong they blamed those Naughty Little Girls for it, and put them in prison and starved them and drowned them and all that. They used to find cruel and pagan men, and say that unless the girls married them they would be killed, and they even had the old excuse of saying: "Unless you stop being a Christian, we will kill you." Though they should have known by then that that one didn't work very often.

Well, in the end of course they caught Agnes. She was so pretty that the Governor thought he would like to keep her in his own house and he said:

"Now Agnes, you have a pretty face and you would look very Decorative at the grand parties I give for my Business

Friends. If you like, I will take you home and you will escape all the horrible things that are happening to your friends, and I will give you some beautiful clothes and some Gold Earrings."

Agnes was very pleased. She had been so frightened when she was caught that she could scarcely walk properly to see the Governor.

"Thank you, Sir," she said. "How very kind you are! I always heard that you were Cruel and Crafty, but you can't be when you save me so kindly."

"Good," said the Governor, smiling a Crafty smile. "One thing of course you will understand is that I can't have a Christian in my house, and so you'll have to stop all that silly nonsense."

Agnes felt her heart go Bump and there was a horrible fluttering feeling like butterflies in her inside.

"But I couldn't!" she said. "You know I couldn't."

"Well, then, you know the answer," said the Governor. "One of the Swordsmen will kill you."

"Oh no, *please*," said poor Agnes, "it won't harm your house if I stay a Christian."

"What about my Reputation?" said the Governor. "What about that, eh?"

"I don't even know what your Reputation is," said Agnes, "but I will not stop being a Christian."

"All right, all right," said the Governor, and he rang a silver bell on his table. "Take her away," he said to the Minion who came. "Kill her off with the rest." And he picked up his pen and started writing a letter.

So Agnes was killed, and that of course means that she is a Martyr.

And now a very Interesting thing happened. After she was killed, Agnes' mother and father and friends and everybody were very sad indeed, and her mother could not stop crying for a very long time because Agnes was the only child she had. But they were very Proud of her too, because she had been so Brave although she was only Thirteen, and her father had a good idea. They buried Agnes in a place where they hoped people would come and pray that they might be Brave too, if they were so unfortunate as to be caught by the Pagans. Pagans, of course, are not *all* wicked people, but these particular ones were terribly cruel in hunting out and killing all the Christians they could find. It was a very Dangerous thing to be a Christian then. There are plenty and plenty of Pagans today who are the kindest and most generous people. We all know some of them, and it is a sad pity for them that they don't or won't find out about God, because they would be even happier. After all, there are plenty of people they could ask.

Anyway, as soon as the Pagans found that people were praying for Bravery beside Agnes' grave, they sent soldiers to guard it and to stop the people coming. They threw stones at them so fiercely that some were killed and a lot were badly hurt and the rest ran away. (And so would I, and so would you.) At last only Agnes' father and mother and a very few of their best friends were brave enough to try again.

"We *must* pray for poor little Agnes," said her Mother. "It isn't fair not to let her have our prayers just because we think she is a Martyr and was so Brave. She might be longing for people to come, for all we know." (Of course, we can pray for people anywhere at all. It doesn't *have* to be where they are buried, but sometimes it seems easier there because we are reminded of them so much more.)

"Besides," said Agnes' Father, "if we ask her, she will ask God to help us too, if *we* have to be Martyrs. They may start on the Grownups again at any time."

So on the eighth day after Agnes was killed, her Father and Mother and their few special friends went very late one night

to pray by her grave. So few people came now that the soldiers only stayed on guard during the day and went home to supper and bed. While they were praying, it got lighter and brighter and there was a light all round them, and they saw hundreds of happy girls all dressed in gold or silver and they had with them the whitest lambs anyone had ever seen.

They stood staring at this wonderful sight, and wondering what it was all about. Agnes' mother looked at all the girls' faces to try to see if Agnes was there too. While she was doing this, they all saw Agnes herself in a silver dress and carrying a Lamb. They all smiled at her because they were so very pleased to see her looking well and happy, and she said to them:

"Dear Father and Mother and all my dear friends, don't be sad because I am dead. You can see that. I am as alive as you are, and God has given us the most beautiful place to live in and we very often see Him. Now, my darling Mother, cheer up and don't cry any more. Be happy with me, please, and we'll all see each other again when the time comes."

Then the light gradually got less and less, until it was quite dark again, and no one could see Agnes and all her friends and the lambs any more. But they went home just as happily as you or I would have done if we had seen such a beautiful and surprising thing on such a sad dark night.

St. Agnes' Special Day is on January 21st and nine different people have written to ask me to write a story about her for them. So here it is and I hope your Birthday is on January 21st.

St. Lucy

Once upon a time there lived a girl called Lucy and she lived with her mother, who was a Rich Widow. All went very well until the Mother got ill. No one could find out what was the matter with her and doctors of the Utmost Fame were summoned, and they could find no cure for the Disease, whatever it was. Luckily, Lucy and her mother had plenty of money, and so they could afford to go to Hospitals and Specialists and places where there were Special Treatments for all kinds of Illnesses, but it did not seem any good at all. Lucy's mother got worse and worse, and in the end she had to be wheeled about in a chair because she couldn't walk at all and she always had a Fearful Headache. Lucy was more and more worried and she seemed to have tried simply Everything. One day she was talking to a friend and was saying how troubled she was about her poor mother.

"She has been ill for four years now and she is so good about it," Lucy said, "and she never once complains, but she is getting worse every day. If she dies, I don't know how I shall manage without her. I am not really old enough to live by myself, do you think?"

"No, you're not," said her friend, "and I *am* sorry for you both. Have you by any chance asked St. Agatha about it?"

"No, why?" asked Lucy.

"Well, because she really has done some wonderful things for Ill people. She seems to know just what to ask God, and she prays to Him so well and so kindly for the Ill person that He nearly always cures them completely."

"Why doesn't He always?" asked Lucy.

"Well, He might want them in Heaven for something else or something," said the friend. "We don't know what God has in His mind. It wouldn't do us any good if we did."

So the friend told Lucy where St. Agatha's shrine was, and as soon as they could get ready they started on their journey. Lucy's mother had to ride in a kind of hammock that was hung between two horses, because she wasn't even able to sit up in her wheel chair any more.

When they arrived they found crowds of people all bringing their Ill relations and friends, and they had to live in a sort of Camp for two days before it was their turn to get anywhere near the Shrine. But all the time they were waiting they prayed and prayed, and they asked St. Agatha if she would *please* remember them and ask God to make Lucy's mother better.

When their turn came to go to the shrine, some kind people carried the mother to the steps beside it and Lucy prayed for her again. While she was still praying she felt someone come and kneel beside her. She didn't look up, any more than we do if someone comes beside us in Church. When she finished her prayer she was just going to get up and go back to her mother when the person beside her said:

"Here I am, darling, I suddenly got better and came to thank God beside you."

Lucy was so delighted that she cried by mistake instead of laughing as she really meant to do. Soon they were both laughing and crying together, until they mopped each other's eyes and began to get their things ready to go home.

"It seems so silly to be so surprised," said Lucy. "I was sure that God *would* make you better and yet I couldn't believe it when He actually did."

"I know," said her mother, "but you know, *I* didn't expect to be better, darling. I don't understand why God should bother about an old woman like me. It is very very good of Him."

"But *I* can see why He did, my dearest patientest mother," said Lucy, "and anyway you're not old!"

When they got home, they had a great time putting away the wheel chair and the special bed and the medicine bottles and pill boxes and all that, and they were very happy indeed.

One evening when they were sitting by the fire Lucy said:

"Mother, you know all the money that Father left to me when he died? Well, couldn't we use it to help the Christians who are being persecuted in other countries? We are very lucky in not being persecuted here, and also it would be a way of thanking God for making you better."

"We couldn't use it now, darling," said her mother, "because your Father said that you could not have it for your own until after I am dead too. He wanted you to have something to live on when we were both gone. I will give it all to you just before I die."

"But, Mother," said Lucy, "you won't want it then. Much better give it now, when we want it ourselves, don't you think?"

After some thought and some talk, they gave a lot of money to help the families of people who had been martyred. Sometimes it was very hard indeed for a woman to be left with a large family to feed when she had lost her breadwinning husband.

Meanwhile Lucy was growing up and an extremely Greedy and Avaricious Man wanted to marry her. (Avaricious is being Afflicted with Stinginess.) But Lucy didn't like him, and she didn't feel old enough to get married, and she liked helping the Martyrs' families. So she said No, thank you, she would not marry anyone just yet, and stayed at home. By now they had finished nearly all their money, and they began to sell their very valuable jewelry and silver dishes and things. When the Avaricious Man saw what was going on he was Furious. After all, the reason he wanted to marry Lucy was because she would be Rich when her mother died, and now, under his very nose, all the riches were dwindling away, and to help the Christians, whom he hated, above all!

So he went to the Governor and told him what was happening.

"I always meant to marry Lucy," he said, "whether she wanted to or not, and now all the Riches are dwindling away right Under my Very Nose!"

The Governor, who did not know how greedy and cruel the Avaricious Man was, felt sorry for him. He was not a Persecutor by nature, but after all there were Limits, weren't there?

So he sent for Lucy and told her that she must stop helping the Christians at once and that she must marry the Avaricious Man, as he seemed to expect it, and that she must give him the little bit of money that was left.

To all of these three things Lucy said No.

"First," she said, "as long as I am a Christian myself, I feel I must help the ones who are not so lucky as I am. Second," said Lucy, "I wouldn't marry that man if he were the Last Man on Earth, and Third," said Lucy, "I couldn't give him any money because it doesn't belong to me but to my Mother." And she sat down on a chair near the Governor's desk and waited to see what would happen next.

"Well now," said the Governor, "you are not being very co-operative, I must say." (Co-operative means working *with* people instead of against them.) "I think the only thing is to stop being a Christian so that you won't feel as though you have to help them, and then give your new husband any little money you might have yourself."

"I have no money," said Lucy. "I have given it all to God. The only thing I have left is myself, and so I am giving myself to God, too."

"It's no good saying that sort of thing to *me!*" said the Governor. "*I* don't know what you are talking about. Keep it for your Christian friends," and because he could not think what to do with Lucy, he sent for a man who stabbed her in the neck with a sword and killed her there and then, and she went to join the other girls in Heaven, Agatha (who made her mother better) and Dorothy and Agnes and all the rest.

Now, you may have seen pictures of St. Lucy with an Eye beside her or even holding two eyes on a plate! This sounds and looks quite horrible, and some people think it was because she was blinded by the Governor or something. But it isn't, you know. This is why: In the olden days, very few people could read, but they loved looking at pictures, especially pictures of Saints and the things they did. But it wasn't any good for the artist to write the name of the Saint underneath the picture, was it? So how could the people know what the picture was about or who the Saint was? Well, they made every Saint have a Little Something that was always in his picture so that you could tell who it was. One you all know is St. Thérèse and her Roses, although of course St. Thérèse didn't live in the olden days. But if you saw a Statue of a Carmelite nun and no roses, you might think it was someone else. It was usually like a kind of riddle for people who couldn't read. Now, Lucy has an Eye or two Eyes because it is with our Eyes that we see the light and the name Lucy means light. See? What does Agnes mean? What does Joan mean? What does *your* name mean? So statues and pictures of St. Lucy have three things in them: eyes, a sword (why?) and a piece of palm leaf because the palm leaf means that the person was a Martyr. You will be able to think of lots of these for yourself, I'm sure.

St. Lucy's Special Day is December 13th and there are plenty of people all over the world called after her. Are you?

/ *St. V* ictoria

Once upon a time there was a girl called Victoria and she and her family were Pagans and they all lived happily together in a big house.

One day the Roman Emperor sent for some of his

Councillors.

"There are too many Christians around here," he said; "*far* too many. You should never have allowed them to multiply so fast. No one knows how many there are now."

"We didn't actually *allow* them to multiply, Sir," said one of the Councillors, "it just happened. They are all over the place now. But they're not really doing any harm, Sir. They spend quite a lot of money on Charity and all that."

"We don't want Christian money," said the Emperor. "It merely gives them an excuse to be Bossy if we accept it. They'll want a share in the Government next, and Then What? So," said the Emperor, "the only thing to do is to have a proper Persecution. We will forbid them to have anything at all to do with their religion and then, when they disobey, we will hunt them out and Kill them for not keeping our New Rules."

So that is what they did. A Proclamation was made saying that all Christian prayer books and Bibles and so on were to be given up to the Governors of the Towns, and that all the Churches and everything in them were to be destroyed, and that in future all Christians were to be Illegal (which means Not Allowed by Law).

Well, the Christians hid a lot of their books and they met in secret on Sundays and priests used to visit them in different houses each week so that the Pagans wouldn't notice too much Coming and Going in one place.

Now as there were so many Christians about, nearly all the Pagan children had Christian friends and the Christian children had Pagan friends. Victoria's best friends were a Christian family who lived not very far away, and she often visited them. Grown-up people were less friendly because of the Emperor who didn't like Christians.

Well, on Sunday it was Victoria's friends' turn to have the priest in their house. There were about fifty people waiting for the priest to come and say Mass and give them Holy Communion. Victoria was there too, because she was going to have lunch and tea with her friends when all the people had gone home again, but she had forgotten to tell her parents.

Suddenly the Pagan Police hammered at the door:

"Open in the Name of the Emperor!" they shouted in fierce loud voices.

Nearly everyone in the house was taken prisoner except the people it belonged to. Victoria, instead of telling the Police that she was not a Christian, climbed out of a window with her friends and hid with them in the ruins of their Church, which was quite handy. As she had been invited to lunch and tea she never thought of going home.

Her friends were rather worried about her.

"Victoria, you really ought to hurry home," said the Mother. "You mustn't get mixed up in all this when you are not a Christian. Whatever would your Father say?"

"But I'd rather stay with you," said Victoria, "and I want to be a Christian. I've wanted to for Ages, but I was rather too shy to say so."

"Well!" said her friends. "What a time to choose!" But they let her stay with them and they taught her all about being a Christian while they stayed hidden away from the Persecutors.

They hid for days in the crumbling remains of the Church, and they took it in turns to go out looking for something to eat. Generally it was the boys who went. Victoria was never allowed to go.

Victoria's family were very worried when she didn't come home for Sunday supper. They had heard the Pagan Police marching about and they knew the Christians wouldn't have time for lunch or visitors and Victoria might be anywhere.

"She must have gone for a walk, but she never stays out as late as this," said her Mother. "I'll put her supper back in the oven to keep warm. I do hope nothing has Happened." And she took Victoria's plate out to the kitchen.

"What *could* happen?" said her Father. "I expect she met some friends and hasn't noticed the time. You should teach her to be more Punctual, my dear."

But when Victoria still hadn't come home at bed-time, they sent her brother John to the Police to say that Victoria was a Missing Person, and then everybody started to look for her. They didn't think of her being with the Christians because she was a Pagan.

One night a policeman was standing near the ruins of the Church. He was just thinking about his supper when he heard a scrabbling noise. He thought it was an owl, or perhaps a cat hunting among the broken stones, and he watched to see which it would turn out to be. Then he saw a Shadow, much too big for a cat, moving slowly towards the dark wall through a little patch of moonlight. He pounced.

"Who are you?" he asked sternly. "What are you doing here at this time of night?"

The boy he had caught was one of Victoria's friends. He was carrying a bundle of blankets he had collected. He was very frightened, but he didn't lose his wits.

"Oh, I *am* sorry to have disturbed you, Officer," he said, "but I have no home. I was just passing through this Town and I thought that nobody would mind if I slept in these ruins. I haven't enough money to go to an Hotel, and it's a fine night for Sleeping Out."

"Well, I suppose that's all right" said the policeman, and the boy gave a sigh of relief. "Where exactly are you going to sleep?"

"I don't know yet," said the boy. "There are sure to be some corners in the ruins that will make a comfortable shelter for me."

"There is one very good place," said the policeman. "I saw it a week or so ago when I was looking round for Christians. I'll show you if you like."

"Oh please don't trouble yourself," said the boy in a Terrible fright. "Perhaps a ruined Church would be a bit spooky to sleep in all alone. I think I'll just walk on down the road and find somewhere else."

"It's no trouble at all," said the policeman kindly. "Just follow me and I'll show you."

He went to a gap in the broken wall and climbed through into the ruined Church. "It was just here, somewhere," he said, "but this moonlight makes everything so black and white that it's difficult to see properly." He walked about, peering into the shadows. "I remember now," he said. "It was here!" And he went to what had once been a side chapel and which still had some roof left. And there, as still as frightened mice, he saw the Christians and Victoria! Quick as a flash he blew his whistle, and before they could get away all the Christians were surrounded by police and taken prisoners.

Next day they were taken to the Governor, and somebody recognized Victoria as the Missing Person. They sent for her

Father and Mother, who were Very Relieved that she had been found but Rather Cross that she had been lost.

"But I can't imagine what she thought she was doing," said her Father. "Imagine hiding in Ruins with Christians! It might have been Raining!"

"Well, Father," said Victoria's brother John (who was trying to think of an excuse so that Victoria would be set free), "I always thought Victoria was a bit weak-minded. I should think she has been deceived by the Christians, who were going to keep her until you paid them a Ransom."

"Yes, yes, that's sure to be it," said her Father. "She was kidnaped by the Christians!"

"No, I *wasn't!*" said Victoria. "Nobody was keeping me there. I went because I wanted to be a Christian."

"Nonsense, my dear," said the Governor, who was a great friend of her Father's. "You don't want any such thing. What a thing to say!"

"But I did," said Victoria, "and I have been baptized while we were hiding. I really think I know quite a lot about Christians by now. They are good, kind people, and I am one of them."

"Now Victoria," said the Governor, "you are being a very silly, obstinate girl. Go home with your Mother at once and we'll forget the Whole Thing. Your parents have been very distressed about you these last few days. They thought that something had Happened to you."

"So have I been worried about them being worried about me," said Victoria, who loved her family, "but I couldn't leave my friends in case I was caught, and then people might have guessed where they were, and they would all be put in prison."

"Come along, dear," said her Mother, holding out her hand. "We are wasting the Governor's time."

"No, I won't go home," said Victoria, "unless all the other Christians who were caught with me are set free. I can't go home and leave them all in prison just because Daddy knows the Governor."

"What better reason?" said the Governor.

But after arguing for a long time he lost his temper and got really angry. He sent Victoria's family home and put Victoria and all the other Christians in prison. It was pitch dark in the prison. Every day the Governor went to see if Victoria had changed her mind about being a Christian. (He did this because he knew her Father.) But it was no good. Victoria wouldn't hear of changing.

Nobody gave the prisoners anything to eat or drink and they got hungrier and thirstier every day. But they prayed that God would look after them and that their Faith would be strong enough to Last Out. So they slowly starved to death (because their Faith did last out), and so they were Martyrs. It must have been a wonderful change from the dark prison when they found themselves in Heaven with all the other Christian Martyrs. The first thing they did was to say Thank You to God for letting them come to Heaven all together instead of being persecuted for years and years until they were old.

St. Victoria's Special Day is February 11th, and I made this story about her especially for two girls. One has two brothers called John Jeremy and Andrew Guy, and the other has a Mother called Susan and a brother called Nicholas.

St. Helen

Once upon a time there was a Very Rich Empress of Rome called Helen, and her son was called Constantine, and he was an Emperor, and they were both Pagans. (Pagans do not believe in God, but worship Something Else instead.)

Well, one day the Emperor Constantine was going to have a Battle with Maxentius, the Son of another Emperor, and he Rather Thought that Maxentius might Win. So when everything was all Ready on the Battle Field the Emperor Constantine said to his Army:

"I think we'd better pray to Win, or we may Lose the Battle."

So the Soldiers said "All Right," and they all knelt down.

"But who shall we pray to?" thought the Emperor Constantine. "I don't think the Roman Gods are much use in Battles." (The Roman Gods weren't Gods at all really, only the Romans thought they were.) Then he had Another Thought:

"What about the Christians' God? He seems to be a very Strong God."

So he said:

"Please, God of the Christians, if you are really a God, will you Prove it and let me Win the Battle?"

And then a Wonderful Thing happened. . . .

A Great Cross of Fire came in the blue sunny sky, and underneath it was written:

"BY THIS SIGN YOU SHALL CONQUER!"

Constantine stared and the Generals stared and the Colonels and Majors and Captains and things stared, and so did all the Private Soldiers. (To whom do the Private Soldiers belong, I wonder? Are they the General's own Special Private ones; or the King's, or whose?)

Anyway, everybody saw the Cross in the Sky, so they knew that the Christians' God must be the real one, and they were all Very Glad.

And they won a Splendid Victory over Maxentius' Army,

and the Emperor Constantine had a thing like this ☧ on his Flags for ever after to remind him of the Cross in the Sky. (And XP are the first two letters in Our Lord's Name in Greek, and X is like St. Andrew's Cross too.)

When the Emperor Constantine went home after the Battle and told the Empress Helen all about it, they decided to be Christians, and they were, and heaps of their Subjects were, too.

Well, a long time after that when Helen was a Very Old Empress of Eighty-Three Years, Our Lord told her to go to the Holy Land, which was where He used to live, and to look for the Cross that He had been Crucified on Three Hundred and Twenty-Six Years before.

So she went to Jerusalem and saw the Bishop there who gave her some Good Advice.

"If I were you, Your Majesty," he said, "I'd find Joseph of Arimathea's cave that Our Lord was buried in, because people used to bury the Crosses near where the crucified people were buried."

So the Empress Helen went round asking people and At Last she found out the Place. Earth and stones had been piled on top of it like a little hill, so that the Christians would not know where it was, and the Romans had put a big Statue of Venus on top of that so that, if any Christian *did* know the Place and prayed there, it would look as though they were praying to Venus, which was Very Mean of them.

So the Empress Helen went back to the Bishop and told him, and they got a lot of Workmen and Tools and things and they tipped over the Statue of Venus with a great crash! Then they got Spades and Pickaxes and Wheelbarrows and worked and dug and picked a very Deep Hole and, there, at

the Very Bottom, was the opening of the Cave! (Do you remember when Our Lady and her friends went very early in
the morning on Easter Sunday to the place where Our Lord
was buried, and, as they went, they said to each other: "Who
will roll us away the stone at the door of the Cave?" and when
they got there the stone was already rolled back and there was
an Angel sitting on it?) Well, that was the very cave that
Helen's workmen found. And a little way away from it, buried
even deeper, they found three crosses! (You remember Dysmas
and Gestas, the Two Thieves who were Crucified at the same
time, don't you?)

But now a very Difficult Thing happened. They didn't know
which one was Our Lord's Cross! Helen looked all round
about and she found the three Labels that had been on the
Crosses, only they had Come Off, so she didn't know which
they belonged to.

So, very carefully, they got out the Crosses and took them
to the Bishop to see if he would know which was which. But
he didn't. So they all prayed about it so that God would tell
them.

Then God gave the Bishop a Good Idea and this was it:

There was a Very Ill Lady living in Jerusalem, and everyone
thought that she was going to die very soon. So the Bishop
made three Priests carry the Three Crosses to the Ill Lady's
house and up to her Room. Then everybody asked God to
show them which was the True Cross, and then the Bishop
took one of them and touched the Ill Lady with it. Nothing
happened; except that they all stopped holding their Breaths.
Then the Bishop took another one and touched her again! Still
nothing happened! Then he took the last one and tried again.

At once the Lady got Absolutely Well!

So that was how Our Lord showed them which was His own Cross.

Now of course everybody wanted to have the True Cross in *their* Country. The French people wanted it in France, and the Italian people wanted it to stay there, and So On and So Forth, and so although they did not want to Spoil it they cut in into Three Pieces. One they left in Jerusalem where it still is, and one Helen took home with her to Constantinople (a town called after the Emperor Constantine). And the other piece she took to Rome, where it still is in a Church called the Church of the Holy Cross of Jerusalem.

Lots of Churches have what is called a Relic of the True Cross. And it is a tiny splinter of one of the Empress Helen's three pieces. Perhaps you have seen one. If not, you will one day. A Rather Sad thing is that a lot of the little pieces have been lost, and so the True Cross could never be put together again. We have only got about half of it left. So we are very very Careful with our Relics of the True Cross nowadays.

Now there are two Important Special Days belonging to this Story.

One, of course, is Helen's own Day, and that is August 18th.

The other one is the Day that the Empress Helen found Our Lord's Cross, and that was on May 3rd when she was Eighty-Three Years Old.

> St. Helen went a-journeying,
> The Holy Land to see,
> Indeed, it was a lovely thing
> To do at eighty-three.

And near the place of Calvary
She digged in the hill side,
And there she found the Holy Cross
On which our Lord had died.

And so she saw what many kings
And prophets longed to see,
Indeed, it was a lovely thing,
To do at eighty-three.

St. Monica

Once upon a time there was a little girl called Monica and
she had a very strict Nanny. The Nanny had looked after
Monica's father when he was a little boy and she ruled the
house with a Rod of Iron.

Now Monica's house was in Africa and sometimes it was
very hot and Monica and her sister used to get very thirsty.
But their Nanny never let them drink between meals.

"But *why* can't we, Nanny?" said Monica. "It isn't *wrong*
to drink some water when you are thirsty."

"No, it isn't wrong," said Nanny, "but if you drink water
whenever you feel like it, not at mealtimes, when you grow
up you will have got the Habit of drinking at Odd Times.
And then, when you are married and have your own House

and Store cupboards and Wine cellars, then you might get the habit of drinking Wine at Odd Times. People who drink too much wine get Stupid in the Head and Bad Memories and forget to wash and mend their clothes and all that."

"But *I* wouldn't drink too much wine," said poor Monica, who was feeling thirsty because of the hot weather.

"You quite likely would," said Nanny, "if you don't learn to drink only at the proper times. I've seen it happen."

So Monica and her sister were never allowed to drink except at mealtimes and they thought that Nanny was much too Fussy.

When Monica was a little older (but not grown up) her father used to send her down to the cellar to fetch up the wine for dinner in a big jug. The wine was kept in a cask with a little tap at the bottom and Monica used to go down the cellar stairs and turn on the little tap and fill the big jug. But the tap used to drip and so a cup was kept under it to catch the drips and often Monica used to taste it when she filled the jug. Sometimes the cup was nearly full so she would drink a little so that it would not overflow and make a mess on the floor. The wine had a lovely warm sweet taste and Monica was very disappointed whenever she found the cup nearly empty of drips.

Well, she became so used to her little drinks that she used to let the tap drip on purpose if it wasn't full, so that she always had a good drink.

But one day, just before dinner, when she was filling up the cup, a maid came down for something and saw her. Now Monica and the maid did not like each other much and so the Maid was pleased to find something to quarrel about.

"Ah!" said she, "I always wondered why you were so long filling the wine jug and now I see that you are a Drunkard. You should be ashamed, you with your lovely house and all!"

A Drunkard is somebody who is nearly always Stupid in the Head with drinking too much wine, and of course Monica wasn't any such thing, but she suddenly thought:

"There! Nanny was right! And I *have* got the Habit of drinking at odd times and I never even noticed. Perhaps I might drink Too Much one day and not notice that!"

Poor Monica was in such a fright about it that she never drank anything at odd times again, not even water.

When she grew up Monica married a Pagan called Patricius, which is the same name as Patrick, and she had her own store rooms and wine cellar just as Nanny had said, but she did not drink at Odd Times.

Now Patrick was a bad-tempered man, and his mother, who lived with them, couldn't Abide Monica because the servants in the house kept telling her all sorts of unkind and untrue things about her and she believed them. But after a time she saw for herself that Monica wasn't a bit like they said she was and she began to love her and they were good friends. After a while, too, Patrick wasn't so bad tempered although he was always a bit Fiery, so things were much happier.

Patrick and Monica had two sons called Augustine and Navigius and they were very Headstrong and Wild boys. Augustine wouldn't listen to any Christian talk of any kind and that made Monica sad. But every day she asked God to show Augustine that it is no good being anything except a Christian.

Augustine was a Brilliantly clever man and he taught in

Universities, and people came from miles away to hear him lecture. He earned plenty of money and he had a very good time. So Monica was very surprised one day at supper time when Augustine said:

"I'm tired of working here. I'm going to teach in Rome."

"Oh *No,* Augustine!" said Monica. "*Please* stay in Africa. Rome is Rich and Wicked and you will go from Bad to Worse."

"But Mother, you ought to be pleased," said Augustine. "The Pope lives there and there are a lot of Christian people."

"Not the people that you will be with," said Monica. "Your sort of people won't be Christians."

"Well," said Augustine, "I shall go, anyway. The students here are so noisy, and they walk in and out and round about while I am teaching. Besides, they have Rags and they burn their furniture and they paint the statues in the town and they are most Unruly. I hear the students in Rome are better mannered, so I shall go and teach there."

Monica did all that she could to stop Augustine, but when the day came he started off to the sea to find a ship that would take him to Italy. So Monica followed him and found him by the sea.

"Now Augustine," she said, "it has to be one of two things. Either you come home with me or I shall go to Rome with you."

But Augustine wanted a Gay Life in Rome and he thought that Monica had better not come and so he said:

"All right, Mother, I'll go home with you, but first I must just See Off my friend in that ship over there. I promised him that I would. You wait in that little Church for me, and when the ship has sailed I'll come and fetch you."

So Monica went to the little Church and she spent the time asking God not to let Augustine want to go to Rome because of going from Bad to Worse, but to let him be a Christian.

After a time she went to the Church door to look at the sea and there she saw the ship sailing away and in it were Augustine and his friend. Which was very mean of Augustine whichever way you look at it.

All this looks as though God wasn't listening to Monica when she prayed so hard for her son, doesn't it? But He was, because if Augustine had stayed in Africa he might never have been a Christian, and yet, after he had lived in Italy for a time he became one. Years after that he was one of the greatest saints that there has ever been.

Meanwhile Monica was so worried about Augustine gallivanting in Italy that she decided that she would go there herself after all to see what was happening to him. Patrick had died long ago so it didn't matter where she went. She packed up a few clothes, not more than she could carry in case there were no porters, and she took a basket with sandwiches and fruit and a bottle of wine. Then she set off to find a ship to take her to Italy. When she reached the sea she found a ship that was sailing to Italy that very evening and so she asked to see the Captain. When he came he looked rather surprised at a woman being all alone in his ship and he said:

"Well, Madam, what can I do for you?"

"Could you take me as a Passenger to Italy, please?" asked Monica.

"Take *you*?" said the Captain. "Are you alone?"

"Yes, I am alone," said Monica, "but I've got enough money

for my Fare."

"But I can't take a woman all alone in my ship," said the Captain. "Besides what will you do when you get there? I'd have to leave you, you know."

"My son is there," said Monica. "He'll look after me."

"Oh, will he?" said the Captain. "Then I suppose it will be all right, but it is very Unusual, I must say." And he turned away and shouted to some sailors.

Monica thought that it would be all right if she went On Board so she did, and no one seemed to take any notice of her because they were all rushing about with ropes and marline spikes and things. Soon she found a tiny little cabin with just enough room in it for one. It seemed quite clean so she put down her case and started to unpack.

"Hey!" said a loud man's voice by the door. "Who are you? Go away! That is the passenger's cabin!"

"Well," said Monica, "that is all right because I am the passenger," and she tried not to laugh at the sailor because he was so Taken Aback.

"*You* are?" he said. "Does the Captain know?"

"Yes," said Monica. "I saw him a few minutes ago."

"Well, I suppose it's all right then," said the sailor. "But a *woman!*" And he went away mumbling and muttering about how Unlucky it was to have women alone for the only passengers.

At last the ship was ready, and the Wind and the Tide were ready too and the ship sailed out to sea. Monica ate some of her sandwiches and took a sip of her wine and began to get ready for bed. While she was saying her prayers she said to God:

"I do hope, dear God, that Augustine is all right, and that I'll find him somewhere when I reach Italy. I have no idea where he is."

And God answered her very kindly because she was so tired and worried and said:

"It will be quite all right Monica, and you trust Me and I'll see that you find Augustine quite safely."

"Oh *thank You*, God," said Monica. "I was nearly at my wits' end what with one thing and another. But if You help me it is sure to be all right, isn't it?"

"Of course it is," said God, so Monica got into bed and soon fell asleep.

In the middle of the night she woke up because of the noise. People were running up and down and shouting. There were crashes and splashes and her things fell off the shelf on to the floor. Then her cabin tipped sideways and went down very fast like a lift. Suddenly it came up again and stopped with a jerk and rolled sideways again. Monica climbed out of bed and dressed. It was very difficult because the cabin never kept still at all and she staggered about. At last she opened her door and looked out.

"What *is* happening?" she asked a sailor who was running past on the wet deck.

"It's a Storm," said the sailor. "We are all going to be drowned." And he ran on.

"I wondered if it was a storm," thought Monica, "but never having been in a ship before I couldn't know for sure."

Then the Captain came along the deck holding on to anything so as to stop himself from falling.

"Come on, Madam!" he shouted, "throw everything you can

find into the sea to make the ship lighter. We'll sink anyway, but we ought to make the Effort."

Monica went out of her cabin. Sometimes the floor was full of Sea and sometimes it wasn't. It was very difficult to walk. She shouted to the sailors.

"Don't throw your things away, we are not sinking!" But nobody took any notice except to push her out of the way.

So she found the Captain.

"Listen," she said, holding his arm so that she wouldn't be Washed Away. "We are *not* sinking and we will *not* be drowned, so tell the sailors to stop throwing all those good things away. It's such a waste!"

"Don't talk nonsense, Madam," growled the Captain, "and leave go my arm, I'm busy."

"But it's true!" said Monica.

"Why?" asked the Captain.

"Because God told me this very night that I was going to see my son in Italy, and I couldn't if we were drowned, now could I?"

"*Did* He?" said the Captain. "Oh well, then of course it's all right." And he shouted to the sailors to stop throwing Valuable things away and to pull themselves together, and they did.

By the time it was after breakfast the sun came out and the sea was blue and they all spent the day tidying up and they soon got to Italy.

It would take too long if I told you about all the people that Monica met in Italy, but she did find Augustine quite safely and she kept house for him and a friend of his. At last, after years and years he was a Christian and he couldn't think why he hadn't been one before.

"I am so Late in loving God," he said. "All the time that I was looking for Him He was there. I never saw how beautiful He is; I only saw the beautiful things that He made. I never thought that they would never have been there at all if He hadn't made them."

And Monica didn't say "But I told you long ago and you wouldn't believe me," because it wouldn't have done any good. But she smiled to herself and she said to God that Augustine always had been a Stubborn and Headstrong boy.

St. Monica's Special Day is on May 4th and people all over the world are called after her and everybody likes her because she used to get Bothered over the same things that we do now.

St. Sylvia

Once upon a time there was a girl called Sylvia, and she lived in France and she was a very Rich Orphan (what is an Orphan?), and she went to a Convent School by the sea. She was a greedy girl and she loved Silks and Satins and Scent and Furs and Jewelry and Staying in Bed late in the mornings and doing exactly as she pleased. Of course, everybody likes these things, but not Too Much and All the Time, the way Sylvia did.

(*Well*, you will say, what a beginning for a Saint! But you just wait!) The nuns in the school taught her reading and writing and History and Geography and Catechism and Arithmetic and all that, but mostly they tried to teach her not to set such store by Luxury. (Luxury is Extravagant Indulgence in the Pleasures of the Senses.)

"You don't have to be too Austere," they told her. (Austerity is the opposite of Luxury.) "Just stay in the middle and enjoy the ordinary things of life." But Sylvia took a long time before she even began to understand what they meant. After all, if you have every single thing of the very, very Best, then you can have nothing to look forward to. You can never say, "Wouldn't it be fun if we could do this?—or have that?" because you would have it or have done it, and you would be So Bored.

Well, as time went on Sylvia *was* bored. She couldn't think of anything else she wanted or even that she might like to have. She had it all. So, for something to do, she began trying to see what she could do without. She soon found that it was a sort of Game that she could play with herself, like the one people play when they try to get thinner. You must have seen people doing that, haven't you? They *could* have anything there might be on the table—but no, they just eat an apple or a tomato or something, and they stand on the scales again and see how much weight they have lost.

Well, Sylvia played this game of seeing what she could do without, and the nuns began to be quite pleased with her progress. But Sylvia, once she had started, did not seem to be able to stop. She had less and less of more and more until she even stopped eating much of her school dinner. Then she began to say that she wouldn't wash because of wasting water and she wouldn't have a clean handkerchief because it would be a waste of soap to wash the dirty one. The nuns were quite worried.

"You are going much too far the other way, Sylvia," they said. "Even the poorest of nuns must be clean. And you must eat your good dinner, too. God gave you your body, and it is your duty to look after it properly."

"I never thought about God coming into it at all," said Sylvia. "I was just playing a game *for* myself *with* myself. Nothing to do with God."

Well, she must have been very self-centered indeed to have lived in a Convent for years and still think like that, but there it is.

So now Sylvia began to think about God and the beautiful body that God had given her.

She ate more and washed more, but she would only swim in the cold sea, and would not use hot water, even in winter when the sea was *too* cold. But now she began to do these things as a kind of prayer.

"Our Lord was very poor," she said, "so I will be poor too. But He was well and strong and He walked for miles and miles, so I won't be silly and starve myself and get weak."

All the money that she used to use for Luxuries she gave away to buy Necessities for people who had very little money, or none at all. She stayed with the nuns until she was twenty-five, because she wanted to learn more and more. She was so clever and good with her books that the nuns wanted her to stay with them and be on their Teaching Staff, but she did not want to do that.

"Perhaps I shall do it later," she said. "But first I want to travel and see God's world before I leave it. First, I want to go on a Pilgrimage to the Holy Land. (Everybody wants to do that, and quite right too.) "When I come back we'll see."

So Sylvia set off with a walking Pilgrimage so as to be as poor as possible, and they walked for months and months. When they left Palestine to go back to France she visited all the shrines and Cathedrals in the countries they passed through. Then she went to Rome, and then Constantinople and Marseilles, and everywhere she went, she walked. And she always helped other Pilgrims who were not so used to roughing it as she was. She showed them how to camp and keep their fires from going out, and which were the best Inns and how to live on next to nothing if the occasion arose. She found out, and learned a lot about medicine, and she could deal with blisters and sunstroke and temperatures and chills and all kinds of other things. By the time she was getting old, Pilgrims all over the world had heard about her and she was quite Famous. But she had no idea of this at all.

Once, when she was on the way back from Jerusalem once more, there was a Bishop in the Pilgrimage, and they were all very hot and tired and thirsty. Towards the end of the day they came to a stream and some shady trees, and the Bishop heaved a great sigh of relief and he took off his shoes and sat in the shade. He bathed his feet in the cold water and washed his face and hands, and then he leaned back and fanned himself with his hat.

"I am surprised, my Lord Bishop," said Sylvia, "to see you pampering yourself in this way. If I may say so, shouldn't you be setting an example of Austerity?"

"No," said the Bishop, "I don't agree with you. There is a

good deal of austerity in this Pilgrimage as it is, and if I am
to keep well enough to lead it and to teach about the things
we see as we go along, then I must see to it that I don't go
Lame or get Sunstroke."

"You must be very Soft, my Lord Bishop," said Sylvia. "You
are younger than I am. I am sixty and I have never touched

warm water since I was a child and I have never touched cold
water for the luxury of it as you are doing now, but only to
wash in at the end of a long day. But of course, I am used to it,
I have done that kind of thing all my life."

"Well, mind that you don't get too Pleased with yourself

about it," said the Bishop. "We can't all be as Austere as you are. I use hot water when I'm cold and cold water when I'm hot." (And so do I, and so, I expect, do you.)

On that last stay in Jerusalem and on the journey back to France Sylvia kept a long and very interesting Diary which we still have. From it we know many and many a thing about Pilgrimages in those days. Who traveled in them, what the pilgrims wore and ate and talked about. We know the kind of medicines they used and how people got their horses and camels and tents (if they were that kind of Pilgrimage) and where the best Inns and watersprings were. She wrote a lot about Jerusalem itself and the people who went there and the people who lived there and the places that the Pilgrims liked best. And all through her writings we can see her great love of God and His Pilgrims. She was a very Great woman, but it never even entered her head that this was so.

St. Sylvia's Special Day is December 15th, and people all over the world are called by her name and they should be very Proud of it. She lived at about the same time as St. Francis and St. Dominic and St. Clare, but we do not know if she ever met them. She doesn't say anything about them in her Diary.

St. Constance

Once upon a time there was a girl called Constance. Her father was a very well-known Emperor called Constantine, and she had the most fearful Spots on her face and she was a Pagan.

Physicians of the Utmost Fame came to see her from all over the world. They gave her medicines and exercises and poultices and diets. Some of them made her stay in bed and Rest and some of them said that she ought to Get About more and that she should go for a long Walking holiday. But not one of their treatments did any good at all, and when they had done everything that they could think of they all murmured the same thing to her Father while he was paying them their fees.

"There is no Cure for this Disease," they said, and they went home.

Constance cried and cried, she was so disappointed, and that, of course, made her face look Worse than Ever. Her father (who was the Emperor Constantine) despaired of her ever getting Married.

"No one could live with you, my Poor Dear," he said, looking out of the window so as not to see Constance's Spots; "it would be too gloomy for words for him to see you every day."

Constance sniffed sadly and said that she'd given up hope and that if things got any worse she'd have to wear a Mask.

"Don't be ridiculous!" said her father, but actually he rather agreed.

Well, one day a friend of Constance's called Martina came to see how she was getting on and they talked about all the doctors and things and about how Hopeless it all was.

"Do you know what?" said Martina.

"No, what?" said Constance.

"Well," said Martina, "my cousin told me that a friend of hers had Spots and she was Cured. I've just remembered about it. Mind you, she was a Christian."

"What happened?" asked Constance. "I don't suppose it would Cure *me,* whatever it is."

"Come on, cheer up!" said Martina, "and listen to me. This friend who had Spots went to Rome where there are a lot of Christian Martyrs buried. There is one called Agnes, and she was only a Girl herself, quite young. It seems that if you pray by the place where she was buried and ask her to help you, sometimes she does. At least she did for my cousin's friend."

"But you said that she was a Christian," said Constance; "it won't be any good for me. Why should it?"

"Why *shouldn't* it?" said Martina. "Why not at least Try? You can't be any worse off even if it doesn't work. Do buck up, Constance, and remember that the Gods help those who help themselves. They don't expect to do all the Work while you just sit back and Wait." (You remember that they were Pagans?)

Now at that time a great friend of the Emperor's, who was a Roman General, had a very Sad Thing happen to him. His Wife died. He was very upset, of course, and his house became untidy, and he brought his Armor into the sitting room to hammer the Battle dents out of it, and he used to leave oily rags about on the Chairs because nothing seemed to matter any more. His meals were Late and Badly Cooked and he was *much* too Lonely. The Emperor was terribly sorry for him, and one day, when they were chatting, he said:

"My dear chap, why don't you Marry again? I know that it won't be the same as your first Wife, but why should it be? It will be just as nice only Quite Different."

"Well—" said the General, "it might be a good idea, but I can't think of anyone that I like enough to Marry."

"What about Constance? I'd be very pleased if you'd have her, and she is very Fond of you. She's a good girl and I'd like to see her settled."

"It's really very kind of you, Sir," said the General. But to himself he thought, "I know she's a very nice girl and all that, but I couldn't bear to have to see those Awful Spots every day." Then, because he did not want to hurt the Emperor's feelings, he said:

"I'll tell you what, Sir. As you know, I am just off to Oppose an Inroad of Barbarians who are coming into Thrace. I'll think it over while I am away. Perhaps I should tell you, Sir, that I have promised to become a Christian if the Campaign is Successful. I don't suppose that Constance would care for that, would she?"

"I really don't know, old boy," said the Emperor. "The Empress and I are by no means Anti, you know."

(Do you remember that the Emperor was the son of Helen and that she was British and was born in Colchester, which is where I do my Shopping because I live near there? She was St. Helen afterwards, and you will find her Story in this book.)

So the General went off to Oppose the Inroads of the Barbarians and he put off having to decide about Marrying Constance and her Spots.

A few days after all this Constance set off for Rome with Martina to see if St. Agnes would be so very kind as to help a Pagan. The journey was long but not really very Difficult because of being an Emperor's daughter. They had plenty of Servants and Horses to carry the luggage, and they themselves rode in a kind of Bed which rested on poles laid across the backs of horses. Every now and then the horses were changed so that they all had a turn and so did not get Too Tired. These

beds were called Palanquins or Litters, and they had little Silk Roofs and Curtains all round. They were like Tents. Constance kept her curtains drawn round because she did not want all the people to Stare at her Spots, but Martina kept hers drawn back so that she could see everything that went on. She only drew hers round at Bedtime when the Palanquins were lifted off the horses and set down on the ground for the night.

At last they arrived in Rome and asked their way to St.

Agnes' Tomb. Once there, they found a great Crowd of people all waiting for their turn to be Cured of something. Sometimes the people were Ill in their Bodies with things like broken Backs or Blindness. And sometimes the people were Ill in their Minds with things like Sadness or Fear or Loneliness. But no one seemed to have such awful Spots as Constance had.

While they were waiting for their turn to go near to St. Agnes' Tomb, Constance and Martina talked quietly about what they were supposed to do when they got there. They watched the other Pilgrims and saw that they went up to the Tomb, knelt down and touched it. After a few minutes they got up again and made room for someone else. Sometimes they were so Ill that their friends carried them.

"Do you think that that is all we do?" asked Constance.

"Perhaps we whisper to Agnes to ask her to Cure you," said Martina.

A Christian Woman who was waiting beside them heard what they were saying, and she said:

"May I explain to you Ladies? Perhaps you are not Christians and you do not understand."

Constance and Martina were a little Worried because they thought that the Christians might not like Pagans to come to visit St. Agnes, but the woman looked so kind that they said that they *were* Pagans.

"You see," says Martina, "poor Constance has such dreadful Spots that we hoped that perhaps your Agnes would Cure her even though she isn't a Christian."

"Well it isn't actually *St. Agnes* who sometimes Cures people," said the woman.

"*Isn't* it?" said Constance and Martina both together. They were so surprised that they quite forgot to Shake Little Fingers and Wish.

"But why do we come here, then?" asked Constance.

"You see," said the woman, "it is *always* God who does the Cures, no one else can. But when Especially Good people go to Heaven we sometimes ask them to take Messages to God, or to ask Him, *for us*, for whatever it is. It is something like choosing the nicest one of the Family to go to your Father for something Special. Then sometimes he might say 'Yes,' when if *you* asked he would have said 'No.' (Perhaps because you had been rather Disagreeable at Breakfast.) Do you see?"

"Yes," said Martina, "we didn't know that. What do we say to Agnes?"

"Well," said the woman, "you ask her if she will pray to God *for* you and *with* you for whatever it is that you need. You must have Faith and Hope and you mustn't be Cross if nothing happens. Often it doesn't—why should it?"

Before they could go on talking any more about it, it was time for Constance and Martina to go to the Tomb. Constance wrapped a Scarf round her face and head so that people would not Stare at her. They knelt beside the Tomb and put their hands on it.

"Please," said Martina very quietly to St. Agnes, "please *would* you ask God to make poor Constance better? It really is Horrible for her. She has very few friends and she is so very Shy about meeting people. We are not Christians, but perhaps you wouldn't mind that because of poor Constance."

But Constance was too Shy to say anything at all. She just held on to the Tomb and Wished and Hoped that St. Agnes wouldn't mind her Spots too much and that she would ask

God to help her.

Then they both got up to make room for other people and went slowly back to their Palanquins and Horses. They sat down to talk it all over.

Suddenly Martina looked at Constance.

"Constance!" she said, "you've still got your Scarf on! Take it off quickly and let's see if anything has happened."

"I daren't," said Constance. "I didn't really say any Proper Prayers, I was too Shy. So I don't suppose that Agnes bothered. It's my own fault, of course."

"Oh *Constance!*" said Martina. "Come on, let me see!" and she took the Scarf away.

"It *has* happened!" she said. "Oh, Constance, you look Lovely, you really do! How marvelous! Come on, let's go home quickly and tell your Father." And she settled herself in her Palanquin and told the men to start off with the Horses. But Constance turned back to the Crowd and went slowly back towards the Tomb.

"Where are you going? You are going the wrong way!" Martina called after her.

"I'm going to say Thankyou," said Constance, "and then I'm going to be a Christian."

And so she did, and so she was.

Meanwhile, the Roman General had won his Battle with the Barbarians and so *he* was a Christian too, as he had said he would be. So can you imagine how pleased everybody was when everyone arrived home again and told their Adventures? The general and Constance did not get Married after all, because the General had found somebody that he wanted to have for a Wife while he had been away. Constance did not mind at all, because she had been thinking of going to live near St. Agnes' Tomb so that she could help other Pagans who might not know what to do when they arrived there. And that is what she did.

The Emperor Constantine was so impressed by all that had been Going on that he never forgot the God of the Christians. And one day, in another Battle, he became a Christian, too, and you can Read all About it in St. Helen's story.

St. Constance's Special Day is January 28th, and she, in her turn, is Kind to people who have Spots and things.

St. Pauline

Once upon a time there was a very nice wife of a rich Roman Senator and her name was Pauline, and they were both Christians.

Pauline's husband went to work in the Government every day while she kept house and brought up the children and looked after her household and fed the dogs and told the gardeners what plants she wanted them to plant in the garden. They were all very happy until the children were just about grown up, and then the Roman Senator died.

When everything had settled down again Pauline collected her children together after dinner one day and she said:

"You are all nearly grown up now, my dears. Some of you are really *quite* grown up, so you don't really *need* me any more. Now that your father is dead, I am free to do what I have always wanted to do. I shall go on a Pilgrimage to Palestine and see all the Holy Places. I have heard and read about them so often. I shall start as soon as I can get ready!"

"But Mother!" said a son called Luke, "we *do* need you! You can't go right away from us like that!"

"I expect I'll come back some time, darling," said Pauline.

"But who will look after everything?" said a daughter called Aurea. "We don't know where things are kept."

"Who will bring us hot drinks in the night when we have colds?" said someone else.

"And who will send our clothes to the laundry?"

"And who will listen to our Tales of Woe?"

"And what about all the Housekeeping?"

"Mother, you can't go!" they all said at once, and they all shook little fingers. (Which, in case you don't know, is the proper thing to do when two or more people say the same thing at the same time—shake your little fingers together, and make a Wish.) While they were all quiet, thinking of what to wish for, Pauline said:

"Now listen. The house will not fall down just because I am not in it. Aurea and Lucilla are quite old enough to run the house. All the servants are good and helpful and after a few days you won't even notice I'm away. So let's hear no more about it."

And no matter what they said she was quite determined.

"I have made up my mind," she said.

So Pauline sailed away and had a nice sea voyage to Palestine.

She enjoyed it very much because she really needed a rest, what with her big household and sitting up at night with the Senator before he died.

She loved the Holy Places and she saw them all. The Garden of Gethsemane, the Lake where the disciples did their fishing and Our Lord walked on the water. She saw the house where they had the Last Supper and the balcony where Pontius Pilate washed his hands. She saved Bethlehem for the last. All the time she was there she prayed and talked to God about how she had looked forward to being there and how now she really felt that she was at the Beginning of Things.

A day or so before her Pilgrimage was due to go back to Rome Pauline had a most wonderful long dream. It must have been a dream that God had sent specially for her, because I don't think she could have had it all by herself. She dreamed that she was walking behind St. Joseph and Our Lady when they were looking for somewhere to stay the night. She followed them from inn to inn and she felt more and more worried because it was getting so late and cold and there wasn't any room for them anywhere.

"Oh, whatever will they do?" she said to herself in her dream.

She smiled with happiness when at last an Innkeeper's wife said that if they liked they could spend the night in the stable. It really *was* a relief, she thought. It had seemed as if they would have had to walk about all night.

She followed them into the stable (it was still a dream), and she saw the Ox and the Donkey. She heard the angels singing "Glory to God in the Highest" and she saw the shy shepherds peeping in at the door. She saw Our Lady putting her Baby into a manger of hay and St. Joseph going across the yard to the

Inn to get food and bring it back for them. She saw the Three Kings and their Camels and Horses and Servants and Gifts.

It was the most wonderful dream, and when she woke up and heard a donkey braying outside her window she could hardly believe at first that it was Only a Dream, and that she hadn't really walked behind Our Lady's donkey looking for an Inn, but had spent all night asleep in her bed.

When she went out after breakfast and saw the places again they seemed so much more real because of her dream, and she felt that she could never leave Bethlehem again. She thought and she prayed and she asked God to tell her what to do.

On her way back to lunch she found out that there was very little in the way of doctors and nothing in the way of hospitals in Bethlehem, and no schools for the children—who, of course, were mostly not Christians.

"It seems extraordinary," she thought to herself, "with all the Pilgrimages and things that keep crowding the town, that the people have made nearly no arrangements for Ill Pilgrims or for Mothers with little babies, or even for the people who live here to get their children Educated." So she decided she would stay there and see what she could do to help. Two or three of the women who had come on the same Pilgrimage with her said that they would stay, too. And one or two girls who lived in Bethlehem joined them. They all lived together, rather like nuns, but of course they weren't nuns really, to begin with.

But after a few years the Bishop of Jerusalem said that he thought Pauline ought to be a nun and so ought her friends, because he thought it "would make things easier." So then they were, and Pauline was the Abbess.

There were a good many of them by this time, and Pauline

divided them into Three Lots. One Lot was to work in the fields and grow their own vegetables and fruit and look after the goats and chickens. Another Lot was to teach in the School they had started (because a school to teach the local children seemed to be the thing that was Needed Most and cheaper than building hospitals and things, which could come later). The third Lot were to look after the household and to clean and sweep and to do the washing and the cooking. But all three Lots had their meals together and went to Chapel together and slept together in the big dormitories.

Pauline said that they must all live as poorly as they possibly could, so that they would have more money for their work. She wouldn't let her nuns have sheets or tablecloths or anything made of linen except Hand Towels. After so many hundreds of years I still wonder why that was the only thing she let them have. There must have been some good reason that we have forgotten about after all this time. Perhaps people's hands got chapped in Bethlehem more than in other places.

Some of her nuns were very young and they didn't like being so poor and uncomfortable. They said so, and they were Cross and Sulky.

"Never mind," said Pauline. "I would rather have you Good and Uncomfortable than have you Rich and Willful." If they were really naughty she made them have their meals in a little room by themselves until they said they were sorry. But if any of her nuns were Ill, Pauline was *very* kind to them. She let them have pillows on their beds and hot water to wash in and let them choose what they would like to eat until they were well again.

Because of her Roman Education and Very Good Head,

Pauline was much cleverer than the rest of her nuns. She could read and write in Latin and Greek and Hebrew and French, which must have been very useful to her when she was training her nuns to teach.

So Pauline never went back to her family and they only saw her when she had to go to Rome now and then to see the Pope on business matters. Of course they were delighted to see her when she came, but they had soon learned to manage for themselves. And it was good for them to stand on their own feet instead of someone else's, and not to be able to expect their mother to do every little thing for them.

Pauline lived and worked in her convent until she was very old. When at Last she went to Heaven to see God and find her Roman Senator again all the people of Palestine, Jews and Arabs and Christians, said that they had lost a very good Mother to them All.

St. Pauline's Special Day is January 29th, and people everywhere are called after her. Especially one I know who has a sister called Glenys, which is a Welsh name. And of course Paulas and Paulettes can have her for their saint, too.

St. Gladys

Once upon a time there was a Rich Pagan and his beautiful wife, and they had a daughter called Gladys, and they lived at Brecknock, in Wales, a very long time ago. All the people in those days were very Fierce and Warlike. Not the sort of War that we have nowadays, but Villages fought Battles against Villages and Towns against Towns, and even Families against Families!

Supposing that your father didn't like Mr. Prodgrub, who lives down the road, and Mr. Prodgrub couldn't bear your father. And supposing one day that your father said:

"Come on, chaps! I'm going to have a crack at that old Prodgrub. I can't stand the sight of him any longer. And Supposing that your father took his Gardening Fork and your mother took her Umbrella and all you children took pokers and trowels and tins of water and things, and the cook and the gardener and the Village people who liked your father best all brought things to Poke and Hit Mr. Prodgrub, and you all went down the road and Attacked Mr. Prodgrub's house! And supposing all the Prodgrubs and their friends fought back. It would be like a proper Battle, and people might get Killed, and most certainly some of them would get Hurt. And supposing that your father Won, and you all went into Mr. Prodgrub's house and took away all the things that you had always wanted and

137

you put them in your own house to make it look nicer! Well, that is the sort of thing that was always happening when Gladys was a girl. And the next week probably the Prodgrubs would come and take back their things and some of yours, too. And so it would go on.

One day a Swashbuckling man called Gundleus saw Gladys, and he thought that she was so beautiful in her Rich Silk Dress that he went to her Rich Pagan Father and said:

"Good morning, Sir; I have come to ask you if I can have your daughter's Hand in Marriage."

"Well, you can't have it, see?" said the Rich Pagan Father rudely.

"I *do* want her for my Wife," said the swashbuckling Gundleus sadly.

"You heard what I said," said the Rich Pagan Father. "Now go away!" And he slammed the door in Gundleus' face!

Poor Gundleus felt Sad, and then he felt Angry. The more he thought about it the Angrier he got, until at last he Muttered to himself:

"Of all the Rude, Unmannerly, Discourteous Abominations I ever saw, that man is the Worst!" And he got all Red and Swashbuckling, and he went home and collected Three Hundred friends and relations, and they all marched back to Gladys's house and Attacked it. Gladys's Rich Pagan Father was taken by surprise, and when Gundleus had got into the house he found Gladys gossiping with her sisters in the Garden.

"Come on, quick!" he said to Gladys, pulling her hand.

"Why!" said Gladys, and she dropped her knitting because she was so Fussed.

"I want to Marry you," said Gundleus.

"Oh, all right," said Gladys.

And she jumped up onto the horse that Gundleus had brought for her and they galloped away with all the Three Hundred friends and relations, and a fine Clatter they made.

As soon as he had Pulled himself Together the Rich Pagan Father collected *his* friends and relations to chase after the others. When he saw that there was going to be a Battle, Gundleus put Gladys to ride beside him in the most Dangerous Place, so that her father wouldn't Attack them in case Gladys was Killed.

At last they got to Vochriw, which was where Gundleus lived. And there, sitting on the very Top of the Hill, there happened to be King Arthur and two of his Knights of the Round Table, who were playing Dice. When King Arthur looked down to the bottom of the Hill and saw Gladys riding by he was quite Overcome.

"I have never seen such a Beautiful Girl in all my life!" he said to his two Knights. "I want her for my own!"

"But she belongs to Gundleus," said one of the Knights. "Look at him riding with her!"

"Then let us go down to the bottom of the Hill and take her away from Gundleus," said King Arthur, who was feeling a bit Possessive.

The Knights didn't think that this was a very Good Idea, because Gundleus still had his Three Hundred people with him, you remember, and there were only two of them! But everyone has to do what the King says, and they didn't know how to get out of it. At last one of them had a Plan.

"Well, Your Majesty," he said, "we could easily take her away if we were in your country. But this is Gundleus's country and, actually, we are Trespassers. I should *think*," said the Knight, rattling the Dice Box gently, "that we might be Prosecuted if we took her away from Gundleus in his own country."

But King Arthur was still Entranced as he stared at Gladys, and he was just going down the Hill himself when the other Knight said:

"Just a minute, Your Majesty! You know that everybody, especially Foreigners, thinks that you and your Knights are the very Acme of Chivalry, and that you always help the Needy?"

"Yes, of course I do!" said King Arthur with a Pleased Smile.

"*Well*," said the Knight, "I just thought that it would make a Better Impression if we helped Gundleus and his friends against the people who are chasing them."

"So it would!" said King Arthur, and he peered at the Rich Pagan Father. "What a very Unpleasant-looking gentleman that is in the Front!"

And King Arthur and his two Knights hurried down the Hill so fast that the Rich Pagan Father thought that there must be lots more Knights behind the Hill. So he and his followers rode home as fast as they could, and King Arthur and Gundleus shook hands at the bottom of the Hill and said Good Afternoon to each other, and King Arthur had a good look at Gladys because of her being so beautiful.

So Gladys and Gundleus got married (in a Pagan church) and they lived very happily in Gundleus's castle, and they did a lot of Fighting and some of Gundleus' ships went Pirating, and they got very Rich. Then they had a son called Cadoc.

Now Cadoc wasn't the Swashbuckling sort at all, and he never wanted to Pirate or to Raid or to Loot or to Wreak Havoc in the country round about the way Gladys and Gundleus loved doing, and when he went away to finish his Education he became a Christian.

Gladys and Gundleus were terribly Disappointed! Such a thing had never happened in the Family before! They thought for some peculiar reason that Christians were Meek and Mild (which is a milk-and-watery sort of thing to be and not Christian at all). "However," said Gundleus, "what's done's done and we must just put up with it I suppose!"

One day when they were sitting round the fire after tea, Gladys was refooting some stockings for Cadoc, and Gundleus was rubbing his dog's ears, and Cadoc was sorting Trout Flies, Gundleus said:

"It's very Dull just now, isn't it? We haven't had a Good Fight for weeks!"

"Yes," said Gladys, "what about Attacking the house along the River; they've got some good horses that I should like. Just pick up my wool for me, will you, dear?"

Gundleus picked it up, and Cadoc said:

"Why Attack them?"

And Gladys said:

"Well, we always do Attack someone don't we, dear?"

And Cadoc said:

"Yes, and they Attack you."

"Ah," said Gundleus, "but that is because they don't like us, not because they are Swashbuckling Freebooters like we are."

"If you didn't Attack them they'd like you," said Cadoc; "you are very nice people, really."

"But we *must* fight *something*," said Gladys; "we always do."

"Couldn't you perhaps fight the Devil and all God's enemies?" said Cadoc, taking out some March Browns and putting them aside for tomorrow.

"Who is God?" said Gladys. (Did you remember that she was a Pagan?)

And Cadoc told them about God and Lucifer and the Battle in Heaven and all that. You know the story, don't you?

"So," he said, "you could easily fight *and* be Christians if you fight the people who are not on God's side. Only, of course, you must be sure first, which *is* God's side. The Church can always tell you that if you are not Quite Sure."

Gundleus said that nothing would Induce him to be a Christian, and he went on about it so much that Gladys said:

"Well, dear, I feel inclined to trust our Son, so that when we get to Heaven he will be a Father to us because he knows so much more about it than we do."

So they went to a priest that Cadoc knew, and were Baptized, and were Christians. And they got to know God very well, and were terribly sad that they hadn't known Him before.

They became so good at fighting Battles with the Devil that everybody loved them, and they each built a Church so that would help in making up for all their years of Swashbuckling. Gladys built one at Pencarn, in Monmouthshire, and Gundleus built one at Newport.

After a very long time Gundleus died when he was an old man, and Gladys was a Widow. So she went to live in a little house by herself on a cliff just above the bridge over the river Ebbw. There is a spring of very cold water near her house, and she bathed in it every day, Summer and Winter, and everyone was Astonished because she was an Old Lady and yet she never caught a Cold.

St. Gladys's Special Day is on March 29th, and there are lots of people called Gladys in Wales and out of Wales, too.

St. Julia

Once upon a time there was a girl called Julia, and she was Engaged to be Married to the Provost. (Which is a sort of Head Man of the Town.)

Now Julia and all her family were Pagans who didn't believe in God, but just before her Wedding Julia turned into a Christian all Secretly.

When her father found it out he was Furious with Julia.

"What do you mean by it?" he shouted. "How do you expect the Provost to marry a Christian?"

"I don't really mind if he doesn't," said Julia, "and I can't change from being a Christian now."

"Why not?" said her father. "You'll *have* to!"

"But I *can't*!" said Julia, "any more than you can change your name. Whatever you like to call yourself your name will still be the same, won't it?"

"You'd better go and see what the Provost says about it," said Julia's father. And Julia went.

When she got there the Provost said:

"My dear Julia, why are you Making a Mock of me like this?"

"I'm not Making a Mock of you at all!" said Julia.

"But you are!" said the Provost; "everyone will Roar with Laughter at me if I marry a Christian. Pagans can't marry Christians!"

"And Christians can't marry Pagans!" said Julia.

"Oh, indeed! So what?" said the Provost.

"Well, you be a Christian, too," said Julia, "and then it will be quite all right!"

"But the Emperor will have me Executed if I do!" said the Provost crossly. "You know perfectly well that Provosts can't be Christians!"

"Well, if you are afraid to disobey *your* Emperor," said Julia, "*I* am afraid to disobey *mine*!"

"Who is *your* Emperor?" asked the Provost, all Astonished.

"Christ the King," said Julia. "I can't disobey *Him*!"

Then the Provost got Angry.

"I was nice to you at first," he said, "because we were going to get Married. But as being nice doesn't seem to Work, you shall be Tortured until you obey *me* and not your Christ the King!" And getting out of his chair with a Grunt (he was very Fat), he summoned his Minions. (Minions are people who run about and do what they are told.)

Now Julia always had her hair in Two Plaits, and the Provost told the Minions to tie the plaits together and hang Julia up on a hook by them until Bedtime.

"Now we'll soon see her a Pagan again!" he said to himself as he went away rubbing his hands and chuckling.

When he came back at Bedtime he said:

"Now, my dear Julia, are you going to be Sensible?"

"Yes," said Julia. Her head hurt very much because her Plaits were nearly pulled out by the Roots.

"Good! I thought that that would do the trick!" said the Provost, and he told the Minions to unhook her.

"Well," he said, "now that you are a Pagan again, we can be Married!"

"But I'm *not* a Pagan!" said Julia, rubbing the Roots of her Plaits.

"You said that you would be!" said the Provost. "You can't play Unfair Tricks like that!"

"I *didn't* say so," said poor Julia. "I said I'd be Sensible, and I wouldn't be if I stopped being a Christian, I'd be Silly!"

The Provost was so Angry that he Roared to his Minions:

"Chain her up in the Deepest Darkest Dungeon that we've got and leave her there until tomorrow morning!"

So Julia was taken away and chained up with Clanking Chains and left in the Dark.

After a little while she began to cry. Poor Julia! She had a terrible Headache because of her Plaits being pulled so hard. And there was nowhere to sit except the damp Stone Floor, where there might be Spiders and things. And the Chains hurt her, and she was Cold and Hungry and Frightened.

Suddenly she looked up. There was an Angel standing in the Dungeon, making it all lovely and light.

"Never mind, Julia," said the Angel Kindly, "God has sent me to say that you'd better stop being a Christian and be a Pagan again, because the Provost will certainly Kill you if you don't."

Julia was Very Surprised indeed!

"Did God really say that?" she asked. "I thought that that was one of the Worst Things to do!"

"Well, it is, generally," said the Angel, "but God is so sorry for your poor Headache and things, and He doesn't want you to be killed!"

Then Julia said very quietly to God:

"Please, God, do You *really* want me to Deny You? I don't quite understand this Angel."

And God said very quietly to Julia:

"Ask. him, in My Name, who he is."

So Julia said:

"In the Name of God, who are you?"

And the Angel said:

"*Bother!* Now I'll have to tell you, I suppose. I'm the Devil pretending to be an Angel. I thought that while you were all Miserable and Tired that you would be glad to believe me, and then I could have your Soul instead of God."

"Well," said Julia, "it was a Very Mean Trick! You ought to have known that God would look after me! Go away at *once!*"

And the Devil-who-had-been-pretending-to-be-an-Angel went away, muttering to himself and slipping on the Damp Stone Floor.

For the rest of the night Our Lady came and stayed with Julia and made her head feel better, and told her that if only she would be Brave she would soon be in Heaven.

"You see," said Our Lady, "God wants to make an Example of you if you are Brave enough."

"How?" asked Julia.

"Well," said Our Lady, "every time you are Nearly Killed He will make you better again. And so lots of people will become

Christians because of it."

"Oh," said Julia, "I see!"

"I know you'll be very hurt," said Our Lady, "but it's Worth it, every time." And Julia was very happy with Our Lady, and she said she'd do her best to be an Example.

The next morning the Minions came and took Julia to the Provost again, but when he saw her he said:

"What *has* happened? I thought that you'd be looking very Miserable and Frightened, and here you are looking Happier than I have ever seen you!"

"Our Lady came and stayed with me," said Julia, "and so I wasn't Frightened."

"Rubbish!" said the Provost. "Now are you going to be a good girl and stop being a Christian?"

"No," said Julia, "I'm not." She began to wish that she needn't be an Example, but she remembered what Our Lady had said and felt a little Braver, but still Rather Frightened.

Then the Provost told the Minions to tie Julia on to a wheel with Knives sticking out all over it. (Like St. Catherine's Wheel, but not the same St. Catherine that is in this book.)

When the wheel was spun round, Julia was all cut up, and it hurt frightfully, and she cried and was Nearly Dead. Then an Angel came and made her better and Broke up the wheel and went away. And all the people Cheered and a hundred and thirty of them became Christians. The Provost was so angry about it that he ordered his Minions to Behead them then and there! So all those very Lucky people were Martyrs before they had time to do any sins, and they all went happily to Heaven together.

"Well, Julia," said the Provost, "have you had enough Torture?"

"Yes, thank you," said poor Julia, "but I won't stop being a Christian though."

Then the Minion's lighted an Enormous Bonfire and then put on it a Huge Saucepan full of lead. When it was Boiling they put Julia in and clapped on the lid!

Julia screamed because it was so hot, and then, suddenly, the lead got quite cool and her Burns got better. And she waited to see what could happen next.

After a little while the Provost came along.

"There you are!" he said to all the people who were watching. "You see, I *always* get the best of it! Julia thought that *she* would win, but she's been Boiled Alive and now she's Quite Dead!"

And he lifted off the Huge Saucepan lid to show the people.

And Julia stood up and looked at him!

All the people cheered again, and some more of them became Christians and had their heads chopped off.

The Provost was Livid with Rage! He stamped about and shouted and roared, because, of course, all the people had laughed at him when he was wrong about Julia being dead.

"I *won't* be made a Mock of!" he yelled, his face getting quite purple. "Cut off her head! There'll be no Jiggery Pokery this time!" Now Julia was getting very frightened because, although she got better each time, all the Tortures hurt horribly while they were being done to her. And so she said to God:

"*Please* may this be the Last Time? But, of course, if You want me to go on being an Example I will. But please, dear Lord, will You make me Braver? I screamed last time, and I'm frightened this time."

"You have been Extraordinarily brave," said God to Julia.
"I am very proud of you, and you'll soon be here now!"

"Thank You so very much," said Julia, and the Executioner
cut off her head.

Julia went straight to Heaven, and there she found God
waiting for her and Our Lady smiling at her.

"You were a wonderful Example, Julia," said God. "Just look
at all these people who were Martyrs because of your being
so Brave."

And Julia looked round and there she saw all the hundreds
of people who had had their heads cut off while she was being
Tortured!

"Hullo!" she said, feeling Rather Shy as she walked up to
them.

"Thank you, Julia!" said All the People.

"Why?" asked Julia in a Surprised Voice.

"Well," said All the People, "if it hadn't been for your being so Brave we wouldn't have been Christians or Martyrs. And then we wouldn't have been able to come to this lovely Heaven."

"Oh, I see!" said Julia, and she was very Glad.

St. Julia's Special Day is May 22nd, and a Good Few people are called after her. Especially one who has Mary for her Other Name.

St. Jennifer

Once upon a time there was a little girl called Jennifer, and she lived near Paris with her Mother and her Father, who was a shepherd, and she was seven years old.

One day the Pope said to his Secretary:

"You know, those Pelagian people in Britain are becoming a Perfect Nuisance." (Do you remember the Pelagians that St. David argued with? They were the people who said: Everything you *can't* do you *needn't* do!)

The Pope's Secretary waited to see what the Pope was Getting At.

"We must send one of our Bishops over to Britain," said the

Pope, "and we will see if he can get some Sense into their heads. I thought Bishop Germain would be a good man."

So the Secretary wrote to Germain, and he started the very next week, and on his way to Britain he had to go through Paris and stay the night there. (Now you know why I am telling you all this!)

When the people in Paris heard that the Bishop was coming and that he would say Mass in the morning, they all got up early and went to Church to hear what he had to say. But instead of a Sermon he said:

"I want you all to come to me one at a time and I will Bless you all." And they did, and when it was Jennifer's turn the Bishop blessed her and then he said:

"Whose little girl is this?" and the people said:

"She belongs to the shepherd, and her name is Jennifer."

"Well, Jennifer," said the Bishop, "so you are going to live for God, are you?"

"Yes, Father," whispered Jennifer. She was very Shy, because the Bishop was talking to her with all the other people Staring.

"Good," said the Bishop, and then he bent down and picked up a little piece of money with a cross on it (somebody must have dropped their Collection), and he gave it to Jennifer and he said:

"Keep this to remind you to live for God, and never miss Mass on Sundays or Holy Days. Ask someone to make a little hole in it and wear it round your neck like a Medal." Then Jennifer went away to make room for the next person.

After that Jennifer always wore her little bit of money, even when she was grown up.

One day it was Ascension Day, and her mother was getting ready to go to Mass, but she didn't say anything about Jennifer going.

"Please may I go and get ready, too?" asked Jennifer.

"You aren't going," said her Mother, and she began looking for her coat.

"*Please,* Mummy," said Jennifer. "The Bishop did say that I must, and I do want to, because of living for God."

Jennifer's mother was Angry.

"Do as you are told!" she said. "Holy Days of Obligation are for grown-ups and *not* for children. Now, that's enough!"

"But . . ." Jennifer began to say, and her mother came and slapped her on both cheeks very hard and said:

"Be quiet! And now, to serve you right, I won't let you go to Mass on Sundays either!"

Now nearly always people's mothers are Absolutely Right. But this time Jennifer's mother was Absolutely Wrong, which is a Most Unusual Thing. God didn't like the way she was behaving, and He didn't want Jennifer to miss Mass on Sundays. Besides, He wanted Jennifer to be one of His Special People when she grew up. So to serve her mother right He made her Blind in both Eyes!

"Oh dear, oh dear, Jennifer," she said. "I can't see! You must have drawn the curtains, you naughty girl! Draw them back at once!"

"But the room is all sunny!" said Jennifer; "it isn't dark at all!"

Her mother stayed blind for more than a year, and all the time she wouldn't let Jennifer go to Mass at all. At last she said to herself:

"I must be Blind because I never let Jennifer go to Mass. God must have done it to show me." And she began to pray, and to tell God how sorry she was that she had been so Stupid. Just then Jennifer came in with a jug of water to fill the kettle.

"Come here, Jennifer," said her mother, "dip your finger in the water and make the Sign of the Cross on my eyelids."

And Jennifer did, and her mother could see a little, and in three days she was quite well again, and after that she always took Jennifer to Church with her.

When she grew up Jennifer was a Nun, and she lived in Paris. She was very good at Massage (which is Rubbing a thing Better), and she used to carry a little bottle of Oil in her pocket so that she could Rub anyone who needed it.

"God must have blessed my Hands," she used to say, "because He so often uses them to make people better."

One Sunday a man with a Lame Hand came to her. He couldn't move it at all.

"How did it get like that?" said Jennifer.

"It came like that when I was a little boy," said the man.

Jennifer felt in her pocket for her little bottle of oil, but when she got it out it was empty!

"Oh, *dear!*" she said, "the oil is finished! I am afraid that I will hurt you if I do it with nothing. Could you come tomorrow and I'll buy some more oil. I can't today because it is Sunday."

But the man couldn't see her the next day (I don't know why), so Jennifer said to God:

"Please what shall I do, because there is no oil? The poor man has a very bad Lame Hand, dear Lord, please help me to make it better."

Then she picked up her bottle to put it back in her pocket, and she saw that it was full of oil! It had a lovely Sweet Smell, and it lasted her for years.

So Jennifer took hold of the man's hand, and she moved it and she rubbed it with the oil, and she bent his fingers and she pulled them, and all that, and when she had finished it was Quite Cured, and he was so pleased that he sent her six Eggs and some Lettuces for a present.

Once Attila, the King of the Huns, was fighting in France, and he got nearer and nearer to Paris because he wanted to Capture it. The people in Paris were in a Great Way. The men all got their weapons and their helmets out and put food and things in their pockets, and went out to fight him, and all the women began Packing their Things.

"Why are you all Packing your Things?" asked Jennifer in a surprised voice.

"Because Attila is coming, and we want to save our Goods and Chattels," said the women.

"Are you going to be Refugees, all along the roads?" asked Jennifer.

"Yes," said the women. "There's nothing else to do."

"Well," said Jennifer, "it would be much more Sensible not to Clutter up the roads for the soldiers. Why don't you all come with me to the Church and pray that Attila won't come? With God on our side it will be much better staying here than being Refugees."

Some of the women said that she was quite right, but some of them said that she was a wicked Spy on Attila's side. In the end they nearly all went to the Church, and Jennifer prayed, and they all prayed, and when they came out of the Church they met all the soldiers coming home.

"But what about Attila?" asked all the women.

"Well," said one of the soldiers, "it is a very Funny Thing, but a little while ago Attila and all his Huns turned round and marched away!" And so Paris was saved; and Jennifer's idea about the women was a good one, wasn't it?

Jennifer's favorite Saint was St. Denis, and she very much wanted to have a Church in Paris called after him. So she asked some priests if it could be built. But they said that no one could ever build anything ever again because the people had forgotten how to make the lime for the mortar to stick the bricks together.

"The Romans used to make it when they were here," said the priests, "but that was ages ago, and we haven't any lime Kilns." (Kilns are places where lime is made.)

"Well, you go and stand on the bridge in the middle of Paris," said Jennifer, "and you shall hear what you shall hear."

So the priests went and stood on the bridge, and felt a bit Awkward just standing there and doing nothing.

Soon two Swineherds (which are people who look after Pigs as Shepherds look after Sheep) came walking along, and as they passed the priests one Swineherd said to the other:

"Yesterday one of my Pigs ran into the Forest, and when I found it, it was by an Enormous Lime Kiln full of Lime. It must have been left there by the Romans."

"What a funny thing!" said the other Swineherd. "Because I saw a blown-down tree the other day in the Forest, and at its roots there was a big Lime Kiln full of Lime! Isn't that an Extraordinary Coincidence!" (A Coincidence is when two things happen at the same time.)

The priests were Delighted. They ràn after the swineherds and found out where the lime kilns were, and there was plenty of lime for the Church of St. Denis, and it was built at once.

One of these days you must read a book about St. Jennifer because so many things happened to her that I have only had time to tell you one or two of them.

St. Jennifer's Special Day is on January 3rd, and she is the Special Saint for Paris. Anyone called Geneviève can have her for their Saint, because Geneviève is the French for Jennifer.

ᴶ *St. Brigid of Ireland*

Now *this* story can be for Scotch *or* Irish people, and there is only one difference—if you are Scotch you pretend that there isn't a G in the middle and call her Bride, and if you are Irish you pretend that the D at the end is a T and call her Bridget.

Well, one day Brigid, who was living in Ireland, thought she would like to go across to Iona and see how her friend Columba was getting on. (Columba was telling all the Scotch People about being Christians and Brigid was telling the Irish People.)

So she went down to the Sea and she asked a Fisherman could she Borrow his Boat so that she could go across to see Columcille. (Columba was often called Columcille, which means "Columba of the Church," because he was born in a little house which was close up against a Church.)

"Well," said the Fisherman, "I would like to lend you my Boat but I am afraid I am So Busy that I can't Spare the Time to come and sail it for you."

"I can sail it myself, then," said Brigid.

"But a lady can't go All Across the Sea in a Boat Alone!" said the Fisherman. "You must have a Gillie, Brigid, you really *must*. What would we all do, at all, if you were drowned or lost on the way?"

(A Gillie is a Boy, or sometimes a servant or sometimes a son.)

"I have some Gillies of my own who know the way," said Brigid, "and thank you very much for lending me your Boat."

So the Fisherman put up the sail and Brigid got in, and the Fisherman pushed the Boat out. And as he pushed he thought to himself:

"Well, *I* can't see any Gillies!"

Just then Brigid said:

"Come, Gillies! I am ready now!"

And there came flying round Hundreds of little Birds called Oyster-catchers with red legs and black and white feathers. And some of them flew behind the Boat to make a Wind for the Sail, and some flew in front of it to show the way, and away sailed Brigid to see how her friend Columba was getting along in Iona!

When she got there, after she and Columcille had been chatting for a bit, she said:

"What shall we do for all my little Gillies that brought me here so safely?"

"Let's ask St. Michael," said Columba, "because he looks after all the Sea and Islands."

So they did, and St. Michael rather wanted to make them All White instead of Black and White, but Brigid said:

Oh! *please* no! I *love* them being black and white with their dear little red legs. Do let them stay like they are, only let the white part be like a Cross, so that when they fly, people will remember Our Lord."

So that now, if you look at an Oyster-catcher, when he is flying over your head, you will see that his White Part is shaped like a Cross. And in Scotland they are still called Bride's Gillies.

St. Brigid's Special Day is on February 1st, and I know that Hundreds of People are called after her because she was so Nice.

St. Gwen

Once upon a time there was a girl called Gwen, and she lived with her family in Brittany in the North of France.

They lived there quite happily until suddenly there began to be a lot of bother in the towns round about, but nothing to do with Gwen's family. Well, people were fighting and burning each other's shops and barns, and soldiers came to stop them, and that made the fighting worse.

One day after dinner Gwen's father said to her mother:

"You know, my dear, this fighting is getting to be a nuisance,

I never know who I'm going to meet round the next haystack. And when I do meet him I never know if he is on anybody's side or not. I think we'll leave."

"Leave here to go somewhere else?" said Gwen's mother. "Where shall we go? What with the children and all perhaps it *would* be better if we weren't here."

"We'll go to England," said Gwen's father. (That is what everyone says when it's Time to Leave.)

"It's rather a long way, isn't it?" said Gwen's mother, who wasn't a Good Sailor.

"Oh! no, there's only a little bit of sea between us and England," said Gwen's father. "I'll get a boat tomorrow that will take us and the family and all our Goods and Chattels." (Chattels are all the things that will move, *not* the house and garden.)

So they all sailed away just as soon as everything was packed, and Gwen was very excited because she'd never been in a Ship before, only a Boat.

When they were in the middle of the bit of sea between France and England they saw another ship sailing towards them.

"Look!" shouted Gwen to the others, "it's coming towards us!" And they all crowded to the side of their ship to watch the other one.

"What can they want?" said Gwen's father. "They wouldn't come so close in all this sea unless they specially wanted to see us."

Suddenly the Captain shouted:

"Pirates!" and all the sailors went rushing about with swords and cutlasses and things, and Gwen and her family, who were only passengers, were bundled down inside the ship to be out of the way.

Gwen stared out of the little round window in her cabin to see what she could see, until the Pirate Ship came so close that it blocked up the window. So she sat in the dark and listened to the shouts and crashes that the Pirates and Sailors made in their Battle.

Soon she heard people running about inside the ship, opening and banging doors and shouting.

"Good," she thought, "we've won the battle and the sailors are telling everyone they can come out."

She was just going to open the door when it banged open, and there stood not a Sailor but a Pirate! He had blue breeches and bare feet, and a raggy shirt and a red spotted handkerchief round his head, and huge golden earrings, and a very brown face, and round his waist was a yellow sash with a cutlass stuck in it. So he couldn't possibly be anything but a Pirate, could he?

"Ho!" he shouted when he saw Gwen; "and what have we here, my pretty poppet?" And before Gwen could even *think* Jack Robinson he picked her up and popped her into a bag, put her over his shoulder and hurried up to the deck. Then he climbed over the railings onto his own ship, and Gwen bumped about on his back and hoped that the bag wouldn't burst while he was between the two ships. The Pirate, whose name was Percy, dumped his bag (with Gwen in it) down on the deck beside a lot of other bags and began singing with the Pirates that were already there. Soon they had all come back with their bags from Gwen's father's ship and as they sailed away and left it they gathered round and took it in turns to empty their bags on the floor to show what prizes they had

Looted. (Looting is the sort of stealing that soldiers and sailors do.)

"Nobody's got the same as me!" said Gwen's pirate when it was his turn. "Out you tumble, my poppet!" And he shook out his bag and Gwen fell out onto a pile of all sorts of Goods and Chattels.

All the Pirates burst out laughing when they saw Gwen.

"What on earth do you want with that?" they said.

Percy hadn't expected them to laugh at his Prize and he said:

"I shall sell her in London for a Huge Sum and then see if you'll laugh!"

Poor Gwen was very frightened when she heard that Percy

was going to sell her, and she began to cry. But all the Pirates shouted at her to stop it, so she did. Soon Percy came and gave her a plate of fish stew which looked very Odd, but tasted quite good. Gwen felt better when her tummy was full, and she sat on the pile of Goods and Chattels, where the Pirates said she must stay, and looked at them. There was her sister's best coat and her Mother's workbox with her jewelry in it, and a bag of dog biscuits and some books and three red blankets and her Father's fishing rod and her own silver thimble! Carefully she reached out and picked up the thimble. She put it on and then shut her hand so that no one could see it. Then she went to sleep.

When she woke up the ship was sailing up a river with green fields and cows and things on each side. While she was staring at them she heard one of the pirates say it was the River Thames. Now Gwen had learned in her geography lessons that the River Thames runs through the middle of London and out the other side, and so she began to get frightened because they were nearly in London.

"I *won't* be sold," she said to herself, and she began to look round her to see it she could get off the ship and swim to the river bank. But whenever she moved away from the pile of Goods and Chattels a Pirate would shout:

"Get back there!" so she did because they all had cutlasses.

At last they came to London, and the Pirates got ready to tie the ship up to the side. They were all so busy that they didn't see Gwen quickly climb over the rails. She was hanging by her hands and she was just going to drop onto the ground as the ship touched the side, when Percy the Pirate saw her.

"Hey! You!" he shouted, and he drew his cutlass and raced

towards her. Gwen let go the rail, but she was just too Late, and just too Early. Late because Percy just got to her in time to cut off two of her fingers as she hung on the rail, and she was just too early to land on the ground, but she fell between the ship and the side into the water! Percy was very angry to have lost her, but he couldn't be bothered to get soaking wet trying to rescue her, so he left her and walked off the ship into London.

Gwen swam away as fast as she could. She didn't know about her fingers yet, because the water was so cold that her hands were Numb. She swam and swam down the river and when she got tired she turned on her back and floated—all the time she was getting nearer and nearer to the sea.

Soon she got so tired that she forgot to keep her back straight when she was floating and she kept dropping off to sleep, and then the water would flow over her face as she sank, and wake her up again.

"One of these times," she thought, "I will go to sleep just too long and get drowned." So, although it was nearly dark, she looked out for a log or a plank or something to hold onto. After a while she saw on the bank, just out of the water, something that looked like the side of an old chicken house, and she tiredly swam towards it. It was stuck in the mud, and she almost couldn't push it into the water. While she was pushing and pulling and dragging, her fingers hurt her, and when she looked at them she was Horrified to find that she had lost two of them.

"And I *would* lose the one with the thimble on it," she sobbed. "I did want my thimble."

At last the side of the chicken house, or whatever it was, floated on the water and Gwen lay on it and floated down the river. She was so tired that although she was sopping wet and very cold she went to sleep at once.

Now while Gwen was floating down the river, All her family were in a great Way because of the Pirates.

"The only thing to do," said Gwen's father, "it's too late now, so tomorrow morning we'll count all our things and find out what we've lost and what we've still got." So they did, and he was very annoyed about his fishing rod. Soon he heard Gwen's mother crying.

"What's the matter my dear?" he asked kindly.

"My workbox!" wailed Gwen's mother.

"We can buy another in England I expect," said Gwen's father.

"But all my jewelry was underneath the darning!" said Gwen's mother.

"Well, upon my soul!" said Gwen's father. "Of all the idiotic places to put your jewelry. You must be mad, woman!"

"Well, it's gone now," said Gwen's mother.

Just then some of Gwen's brothers and sisters came to say what they'd lost.

"I've lost my best coat," said her sister.

"What has Gwen lost?" said her brother.

"I haven't seen her," said everybody, and then everybody at once said:

"WHERE'S GWEN?" And then they all shook little fingers and wished.

Well, they were all in a terrible way and searched the whole of the ship for her, but there was not a sign of her anywhere. (But you know where she was.) And Gwen's mother settled down to pray and pray until God should tell her where Gwen was.

At last, in the evening, one of the sailors shouted that he could see something in the sea.

"What is it?" shouted the Captain; "is it valuable?"

"I don't know what it is," said the sailor; "it looks like a lump on a flat thing. I shouldn't think it was very Valuable."

"We'll leave it, then," said the Captain; "we're late as it is, what with those Pirates and all."

But as they sailed nearer to the thing floating on the sea, they saw that it was a person floating on a sort of raft!

The Captain sent a sailor in a little boat to pick up the person and bring whoever it was to the ship, and when he got there it was Who? Yes, of course, it was Gwen!

Well there *was* an Excitement. People came with blankets and dry clothes and a hot water bottle and a hot drink and everyone came to look at where Gwen's two fingers weren't while her mother fetched some bandages.

So Gwen was the Heroine of the whole Journey and told everyone all her adventures until at last they sailed into Poole Harbour and up the River Frome to Wareham in Dorset.

Anyone who lives there now will, I am sure, have seen St. Gwen's stones, even if they haven't found one yet for themselves. When Gwen grew up in Wareham she was Famous for Kindness and Good Cooking, and there is a Shrine at Whitchurch Canonicorum in Dorset, but I haven't been there myself, have you?

St. Gwen's Special Day is October 3rd and more people are called after her in Cornwall and Wales than anywhere else. Gwen means White, so anyone called Candida or Blanche or Alba can have St. Gwen for their Special Saint.

St. Winefride

Once upon a time there was a little girl called Winefride and she was Welsh.

Well, one Sunday, at Breakfast, her Mother said:

"Winefride, dear, why aren't you eating your Porridge?"

"Because I've got a Sore Throat," said Winefride, and she Swallowed, to see how Sore it was.

"Well," said her Mother, "I don't think you'd better go to Church this morning, because you might be Sickening for Something."

"But what about Not Missing Mass on Sundays?" said Winefride.

"If you're Sickening for Something it doesn't matter not going," said her Mother, "because God wouldn't want you to get Much Iller by going, and besides, what about All the Other People and your Germs?"

"All right," said Winefride, "I'll stay and Look After the House."

So the Others all went off to Church and Winefride was Left Alone.

Just as she was in the middle of putting some more coal on the fire, there came a knock at the door!

Rat Tat Tat!

"Who's there?" said Winefride.

"Me," said a Voice.

"Who's me?" asked Winefride.

"Open the Door and See," said the Voice.

"Perhaps you are a Robber, though," said Winefride.

"Perhaps I am," said the Voice.

Winefride Very Quietly went upstairs and Peered out of the Window, and there was a man called Caradoc, who lived not very far away.

"What do you want, Caradoc?" she asked.

"As a Matter of Fact, I want to Ask you Something," said Caradoc.

"All right," said Winefride, and she went downstairs and opened the door. Caradoc came in and hung up his hat and put his umbrella in the stand.

"Where does your Father keep his Money?" he said in a Growling Voice.

"Why?" asked Winefride, in a Frightened one.

"Because I am going to Steal it," said Caradoc, "so be quick and tell me!"

So Winefride said to Our Lady:

"Please, Our Lady, will you help me to be Brave, Quickly?" And then she said to Caradoc:

"I shan't tell you, thank you" (because she was always Polite).

"You'd Better," said Caradoc, "because I've got a Sword," and he Drew it.

Winefride saw the Sword and she suddenly ran past Caradoc and out into the Garden and along the Church Path. "I won't tell you," she said as she ran towards the Church.

Caradoc ran after her and Cut Off her Head with his Sword! When Winefride's head fell on the path, a very funny thing happened. A hole full of water came in the path, and it got deeper and deeper and fuller and fuller until it turned into a Well! And *still* it got Fuller and the Water flowed over the edge and down the path towards the Church!

Caradoc was so Surprised that he just stood there with his mouth open! Then he tried to Run Away and he found that his feet were Stuck to the Ground and he couldn't move One Inch!

Soon all the Others came out of Church.

"What *is* all this Water?" said Winefride's Mother. "It looks as if it's coming from the House. Winefride must have left one of the Taps running, Tiresome Child!"

When they came to the Path in the Garden they saw Winefride's head on the ground, *and* the Well, *and* Caradoc, standing Stuck there with his Sword!

"Good gracious me!" said Winefride's Father, "What *has* been happening?"

Just then the Priest, who was coming to Lunch, came up the Path. He had been putting things away after Mass, and so was a Little Late.

When he saw Winefride, he picked up her head and put it on her neck where it was Cut Off, and he said:

"If everyone kneels down and prays very hard while I bless Winefride, perhaps God will help."

So they did. And when the Priest had Blessed Winefride they all stood up again and Winefride stood up, too! God had made her head stick on again, and there was only a Thin Red

Line, like a piece of red thread, round her neck where the Join´
was! Everyone Cheered!

Then they noticed Caradoc, still Stuck to the ground and
Very Frightened.

"Well," said the Priest, "I hope that whatever you Deserve,
will happen to you!"

And as he said it, Caradoc Suddenly Fell Down Dead and
the Devil came and carried him off!

So Winefride lived Happy Ever After and the Well is still
there, and you can go and see it if you like. And the Funny
Thing about it is that heaps of Ill People who drink the Water
and Pray Very Hard get Completely Better!

St. Winefride's Special Day is on November 3rd, and
Winefride is a Very Favorite Name in Wales.

ST. WINEFRIDE'S WELL

This well was made by Winefride's
Completely chopped off head,
Which grew again to show that God
Can even mend the dead.

And if you drink here you may cure
A sick soul or a cough,
But it's well to go before your head
Has Actually Come Off.

SSG–L

√ St. Audrey

Once upon a time there was a Princess called Audrey. (Her Grand Name was Etheldreda but her English one is Audrey.)

Well, when Audrey grew up she married King Egfrid of Northumbria who lived near Carlisle. Now Audrey didn't like King Egfrid much, and she certainly didn't want to marry him. But Those in Authority said she must and she daren't say she wouldn't. So she put up with him for Years (Twelve years, it was). Until at last she said that she couldn't possibly live with him any Longer.

"I always wanted to be a Nun," she said. "I'll go to Coldingham Abbey and be one."

"But you're Married to Me!" said King Egfrid. "You can't be a Nun. Who would do all my Housekeeping?"

"Someone else would, I dare say," said Audrey.

"Well, I won't have it!" said King Egfrid. "You must go to the Bishop and he'll soon tell you what's what!"

"All right," said Audrey, and she went to the Bishop of York, whose name was Wilfrid.

As soon as she had started off, King Egfrid sent a Messenger by a Short Cut to York with a letter for the Bishop and this was the letter.

From King Egfrid to Wilfrid Bishop of York:
My Lord,
Queen Audrey is on her way to see you about being
a Nun. Now if you can Persuade her that she is talking a lot of Nonsense I will give you a Sum of
Money to help you to mend your Minster, which I
hear is Falling Down.

Wilfrid, Bishop of York, sent the Messenger back with an
answer. And this was the answer:

From Wilfrid Bishop of York to King Egfrid of
Northumbria:
You mustn't Bribe Bishops.

When Audrey got to York she told the Bishop all about it.
"But," said the Bishop, "you are *married* to King Egfrid.
Once you are married you have to go *on* being married!"
"But I'm not *really* married," said Audrey, "because I was
made to marry him. We don't like each other, and he doesn't
want me, he only wants a Housekeeper. Sometimes I don't
even see him for weeks."
"Oh," said the Bishop, "I see. Well, if you've got a real
Vocation to be a Nun they'll soon find it out at the Abbey. Go
and try it out and I'll see King Egfrid for you."
So Audrey went to Coldingham Abbey, in Berwick, and
Wilfrid Bishop of York went to see King Egfrid.
"What's all this about you and Queen Audrey?" he asked.
"She says she was *made* to marry you when she didn't want to."

"I know," said King Egfrid, "but she did marry me, all the same."

"But," said the Bishop, "the Church says that if people are *made* to marry someone, then it doesn't count. So I think, your Majesty," he said, "that as you are *not* properly married the best thing would be to let her Majesty go to some Convent like Coldingham or somewhere, to see if she *has* got a Vocation."

"All right," said King Egfrid. "As a matter of fact she is a very Trying Woman and I shall be glad to get rid of her."

Audrey got on very well at Coldingham Abbey, and there was a very nice Abbess there called Ebba. (An Abbess is the Head Nun of an Abbey, as an Abbot is the Head Monk.)

Some time went on and Audrey *did* have a Vocation and so she was a Nun.

Now King Egfrid tried lots of other people, but no one was such a good Housekeeper as Audrey. So he thought to himself:

"I'll go and get Audrey out of the Convent. After all, she did marry me, more or less, and even if I *did* promise to let her be a Nun, I can easily break my Promise."

So he started out with a Retinue to get Audrey.

Now one of the Nuns at Coldingham Abbey happened to be on the Roof seeing to Downspouts or something when, far away, she saw King Egfrid and his Retinue riding Grandly along the road. She hurried to the Abbess.

"Oh, Mother Abbess!" she said, "there's a Retinue coming, and I do believe it's King Egfrid!"

"Thank you, Sister," said the Abbess politely (her name was Ebba, in case you forgot). "Will you please go and find Sister Audrey and ask her to come to me at once?"

When Audrey came Ebba the Abbess said:

"Now, Sister, I think King Egfrid is coming to fetch you with a Retinue. Do you want to go?"

"No, thank you, Mother Abbess," said Sister Audrey. "I'd much rather stay here."

"Very well," said the Abbess whose name was Ebba. "I know a Secret Place where you can hide until he has gone. When he comes I'll just say you're not here. None of the other Sisters will know where you are."

Ebba's Secret Place was a rocky Point sticking out into the Sea about three or four miles away from the Abbey. No one lived anywhere near it.

Audrey hurried across the moor, but when she was Nearly There she looked back. There was King Egfrid and the Retinue hurrying after her! Someone must have seen her and Told him. Audrey ran as fast as she could and got to the Rocky Point. The tide was coming up fast, and some of the nearest part was already covered with water. But there was a Tall Bit at the other end. Audrey climbed down the cliff and out onto the Rocks. She looked at the water. It wasn't so very Deep. She got down into it and waded across to the Tall Bit. Then she climbed up to the very Top and stood up to see if she could see King Egfrid. She couldn't because the Cliff was in the way, so she sat down and began to dry her feet.

In a very few minutes she heard a Terrific Shout:

"Audrey! Come back at once!" There was King Egfrid, with the Retinue, standing on top of the Cliff. The Sea had come up quite a lot, and Audrey's Tall rock was a proper Island by now.

"I can't!" shouted Audrey. "It's too deep!"

"Well, swim then!" shouted King Egfrid.

"No!" shouted Audrey.

"Well, I'll come and fetch you!" shouted King Egfrid and he started climbing down the Cliff.

"I don't think you can!" said Audrey, when he had got a little nearer. "Anyway, I hope you can't!"

And King Egfrid found that he couldn't, because the Tide was getting higher and higher all the time, and what with Rocks and Waves and Currents it would have been Highly Dangerous to have Attempted it.

He called to his Retinue, who were all Peering down from the top of the Cliff:

"How long will it be before the Tide is Down again?"

"About ten hours, I should think, Your Majesty," said one of them.

"Oh, I can't wait all that time, *Possibly*!" said King Egfrid, crossly. "Let's go home!" So they did, and King Egfrid married another wife called Ermenburga, who was very Stiff and Proud. But King Egfrid liked her.

And for ever afterwards, the Rocky Point that was the Abbess's Secret Place has been called St. Ebb's Head. (Ebb is short for Ebba, which was the Abbess's name. Sometimes it is called St. Abb's Head. I don't know why, unless perhaps someone couldn't spell.) There is a Lighthouse there now, and I expect the people who live round about there have often seen it.

Now Audrey had a brother called King Adulph, and he had a great deal of money. One day he wanted to do something for God in return for something that God had done for him. So he went to Coldingham Abbey and asked to see Sister Audrey.

When she came, he said:

"Look now, Audrey, I'm not very Good at knowing what to

do for God. I thought you might know. Here you are!" And putting a Great Bag of Money on the table, he hurried away before Audrey had time to say anything at all!

When she had Pulled herself Together she took the Bag of Money to Ebba.

"Look, Mother Abbess!" she said. "What *shall* I do with it?"

"Better ask the Bishop, Sister," said the Abbess. "The money was given to you and you must Take the Responsibility."

So Audrey went to York, and there she found Wilfrid the Bishop and told him about King Adulph's money.

"Well, Sister," said the Bishop, "what about a new Cathedral and Monastery? There are not many Churches in some parts of the country. In some places it is very difficult to get to Church on Sundays, they are so Few and Far."

"Where is the Farthest?" asked Audrey.

"I think the Fens are about the Worst," said the Bishop.

So Audrey went down to Cambridgeshire to the Fen Country. Now in case some people don't know about the Fens, this is what they are.

In Cambridgeshire and round about it, the ground is very marshy and wet. And in wet weather it always got Flooded and was Under Water. But here and there in the marshes are Hard Bits, and there the people built houses and things. They called the Hard Bits "Islands." They weren't real Islands, of course, but in Flood Time they were.

Nowadays we have made Dykes and Canals and Locks and things and drained the Marshes, and most of the water gets away properly. But even now sometimes there is too much Rain, and the poor people in the Fens are all Flooded Out except the ones on the Hard Bits.

Now one of the biggest Hard Bits is called the Island of Ely, and in those days it belonged to Audrey, because of her being a Princess as well as a Nun. And so here she came to build a beautiful new Cathedral and Abbey for the People living in the Fen Country.

When it was built she went back to the Bishop.

"Ely Cathedral and Abbey are finished, my Lord," she said. "Shall I go back to Coldingham now?"

"No, Mother Abbess," said the Bishop.

"*I'm* not an Abbess!" said Audrey in a Surprised Voice. "You must be mixing me up with Ebba."

"Oh, no," said the Bishop. "*You* are going to be the first Abbess of Ely!"

Audrey was delighted and she was an Abbess there for a long time. And the Fen People were Delighted too, because she was their Princess as well as their Abbess.

I expect lots of people have seen Ely Cathedral. And those who haven't will one day, and I hope that they like it as much as I do.

St. Audrey's Special Day is June 23rd. Lots of people who aren't called Audrey have their birthdays on that day, and when they do, this can be *their* Special Story as well as the Audreys'.

St. Hilda

Once upon a time there was a little girl called Hilda, and thirteen hundred years ago she lived with her Father in Yorkshire, which is the Biggest County in England. Hilda's Father's name was Hereric, which is a Very Funny name, but no one is ever called it now, so it doesn't matter, we just say "Eric" for short.

Hereric wasn't a Christian, and so of course Hilda wasn't either, but she was a very happy little girl, and used to play by herself in and around Robin Hood's Bay (only it wasn't called that then, because Robin Hood hadn't been born yet). And she used to collect a Special Kind of Stone off the beach, and they are called St. Hilda's Stones to this Very Day. One of her Favorite things to do was to be allowed to stay up late enough to see the Lighthouse shining at Whitby (because there was a Lighthouse there even Thirteen Hundred Years ago, and Whitby used to be called The Bay of the Lighthouse).

One day Hereric went to the top of the Cliff and called Hilda:

"Hilda! Come up here a minute!"

"Just a minute, Daddy!" shouted Hilda. "I want to put my shoes on, the path is so Prickly!" And Hilda sat on a stone and tried to rub the wet sand off her feet. Well, you all know how difficult that is! So Hilda dragged her shoes on to her sandy feet and Stumped up the Steep Path to her Father.

"What is it, Daddy? Am I late for Tea?" she asked, Puffing and Panting and pulling the neck of her Jersey.

"Oh no, I want you to come and see a friend of mine, called Paulinus. I left him in the Garden," said Hereric. "He wants to tell you something."

"What?" said Hilda.

"He'll tell you that himself," said Hereric. "He's a nice man, Hilda, you'll like him; he comes from York." And they went in through the Garden Gate.

Walking about and smelling the Roses, Hilda saw an Old Man dressed all in Black.

"Good afternoon, Hilda," he said. "Come and sit over here and I'll tell you a Story."

Hilda thought that perhaps she was getting Rather Big for Stories (she was nearly fourteen!), but she went politely and sat on the Garden Seat beside Paulinus.

Then Hereric said:

"I'll be back soon, Father!" and went off into the house.

Hilda stared at Paulinus.

"I never knew I had a Grandfather!" she said in a Surprised Voice. "You don't look much like Daddy, do you?"

Paulinus laughed:

"But I'm not your Grandfather!" he said.

"Well, why did Daddy call you Father, then?" asked Hilda in a *very* Surprised Voice.

"That's just what I was going to tell you," said Paulinus. "You see, your father is a Christian now, and Christians call their Priests Father."

"But what about me?" said poor Hilda. She thought of being Pagan all by herself. "Why *did* Daddy go and do that?"

"He thought that you might be one too, you see," explained Paulinus; "he didn't think you'd mind, Hilda."

"But I *do* mind, I *do,*" sobbed Hilda. "Now I'll be All by Myself!"

"Well, I'll tell you the Story while you pull . yourself together," said Paulinus, who was the Archbishop of York, "and then we'll see."

So he told Hilda the Story that you know very well. About Our Lord at Bethlehem and at Calvary and in the Blessed Sacrament.

Hilda listened and sniffed and Generally Mopped Up. She

had never heard all this before, being a Pagan, and she could scarcely believe it.

"It's too Good to be True," she said at last. And many and many people have said that same thing.

But after Paulinus had stayed with them for a few weeks Hilda was Baptized and Confirmed, and she was happier than ever because now she was never All by Herself any more because of her Guardian Angel. (And that is a Good Sort of Thing for *you* to remember, my Little Funny One, if ever you get Frightened in the Night. Wherever you are, even if you are too Far away to call anybody, you needn't bother to shout very Loud. And Why? Well, because Our Lord is always there and your own Special Guardian Angel is always there too. And they are *never* too busy or asleep or something, to Smooth you down. In fact your Angel has Nothing else in the World to do except Look After *you*! And it would be frightfully Un-interesting for Anybody's Angel to be forgotten when Any-body got Frightened or Imagined Things. Angels are Specially good at making People Unfrightened again, and they do it as soon as you ask them to, always.)

Well, when Hilda was a little older she went to a Convent School in France. Then, when she grew up, she was a Nun in Hartlepool, and then she went to Whitby, and then, in time, she got to be the Abbess there. In case you don't know, an Abbess is a Head Nun. The abbey, or place Hilda was Head of, was a Simply Enormous Place, and had heaps and heaps of Nuns living in it. They all grew their own Vegetables and Flowers and Fruit. And they had their own Fields and Farms and Horses and Fishing Boats and Chickens and Pigs and Sheep. And because they had all these things and they couldn't do all the work themselves, there being so much, they had to have More than a Hundred Workmen and Farm men and Gardeners and Stablemen and Cowherds and Fishermen and Dairymaids and Swineherds and Shepherds and Hen Wives and things. And most of the Workmen and Farm men and Gardeners and Stablemen and Cowherds and Fishermen and Swineherds and Shepherds had their Wives and Families. Some of the Wives and Families were the Henwives and Dairy Maids and things. So you can see that Whitby was quite a Good Sized Town by the time they had all got their own Cottages and Tool Sheds.

And Hilda was the Head of the Whole Lot, and she ruled her Abbey very wisely and well. But she sometimes wished she hadn't so many Accounts to do, and so much Housekeeping to see to, because it didn't leave her much time for talking with God and Our Lady, which was the thing that she wanted to be a Nun for. Hilda got so Wise that Kings used to go and visit her to learn how she managed to keep Peace in her Land, and how she kept the people well and happy.

Well, one day on Midsummer's Eve, Hilda said to her Nuns: "Let's give a Party, a Huge Party, to all our People, because it's St. John the Baptist's Feast Day tomorrow!"

And the Nuns said:

"Yes, let's!"

And so all the Nuns Bustled about and Cooked and Washed and Ironed and laid Enormous Tables and invited Everybody with all their Wives and Children to the Party.

They had to have the Party out-of-doors in the Garden where there was Plenty of Room, and Hilda and all the Other Nuns waited at table and saw that everyone had all they wanted.

After the Feast they had Community Singing and Dancing and everyone made up songs (there weren't many written down in those days because Paper was Terribly Expensive and Scarce), and they sang their Made-up Songs and played their own Accompaniments. Everybody was very happy except one young Cowherd. He sat solemnly all through the Banquet, and when they had all finished eating and started singing he got up and slipped away quickly. But some of his friends saw him:

"Hi! Caedmon!" they shouted; "where are you off to?"

Caedmon stopped. He wished they hadn't seen him.

"I'm going home!" he said in a Gruff Voice.

"But the Fun is just beginning!" shouted the others.

All the same, Caedmon turned away from them and ran home!

Now Hilda had seen that Caedmon was looking unhappy, but she hadn't asked him why just then because she didn't want to make him feel Shy.

So when they all started singing she said to herself:

"I'll just pop round the Big Table and see why my poor Caedmon is looking so miserable." But Caedmon was gone!

"Where's Caedmon?" Hilda asked some of his friends.

"Oh, he's gone home, Mother Abbess," said they. "He sings like a duck Quacking and he hates us laughing at him."

"*Poor* Caedmon!" said Hilda, "and how Heartless of you to laugh at him." And on her way back to her place she thought:

"I'll say a prayer for Caedmon so that he won't be so Unhappy and so that Others won't laugh at him." And she did, and then she went on Seeing to Things.

When Caedmon went away from the Party, he went to his own house, sat on a Three-Legged Stool and Burst into Tears!

How he cried! *Poor* Caedmon!

And can you guess why? Of course you can, but in *case* you can't I'd better Just Mention it.

Caedmon couldn't sing!

Now we know that lots of people can't Sing in Tune, and nobody minds that so long as they don't try. But everyone else in Whitby except Caedmon *could* sing and make up songs. Anyone who didn't was generally Sulky and *wouldn't* (not *couldn't*). So you see why poor Caedmon was sad? If he hadn't minded about it and had laughed at himself, he would have felt better. But he was too Miserable.

He thought he'd go and see how his Cows were getting on, and he went down to their Stable. He loved his Cows because they never Laughed at him, and they were Slow and Quiet.

Caedmon stroked them all and fed them, and when it got Dark in the evening he thought:

"I don't want to go to bed! No one has come back from the Party yet, it will be Dull in the House. I'll stay here for the Night where there's plenty of Company."

So he went to the Stall of his Favorite Cow, who was Red and White in Patches and whose name was Tidy.

"Now, Tidy!" said Caedmon, "move over a bit and give me some Room!"

Tidy moved over and lay down. Caedmon sat in the Straw and leaned against Tidy's side: her breathing felt like a Rocking-Chair, and Caedmon soon fell asleep.

Suddenly he began to Dream. He dreamed he heard a voice say:

"Get up, Caedmon, and sing!"

Caedmon was very Surprised and Rather Cross.

"You *know* I can't sing!" he said. "Why does everybody try to *make* me, and then laugh at me? I *can't* sing!"

But the voice said:

"Sing, Caedmon! Sing for me!"

The voice was so Kind that Caedmon stood up.

"After all," he thought in his Dream, "no one can hear me down in the Cowshed even if I do make a Mess of it!"

So he took a Deep Breath and opened his Mouth and Sang!

And what a Lovely Song! Caedmon was so happy that he forgot everything but his Song. It was a Wonderful Song! When he had sung it he dreamed that he lay down again beside Tidy and went to sleep.

Early in the morning Caedmon woke up, patted Tidy, and went out on the Cliffs by himself.

"I wonder if I really sang that Song?" he thought. "I can remember every word of it, and all the Tune! But I daren't try in case I make the Noise like a Duck!"

But soon he began very quietly to Hum his glorious Song. It didn't sound like a Duck! Soon Caedmon was singing Loudly and Beautifully, and the Wind and the Waves made an accompaniment for him.

Caedmon went home singing at the Top of his Voice! Everyone came out to see.

"Caedmon!" they cried. "It's *Caedmon!* Caedmon is singing a Glorious Song!"

Well, one person spoke to another, and that person spoke to somebody else, until at last someone told Hilda.

She smiled as if she knew all about it, and said:

"Send him to me and let me hear him!"

When Caedmon came she asked him about his Dream, and

then she asked him to sing.

Caedmon sang, and as he sang he made up the Words and the Tune, and everybody was Astonished!

"We must thank God," said Hilda, "because He has given such a lovely Present to Caedmon." And they did.

Then Hilda taught Caedmon to write so that he could write his songs down, and she kept the first Glorious Song that he sang in the Night and put it Carefully away. Anyone can read it and sing it now, if they trouble to learn it, and very beautiful it is.

Later on, Caedmon became a Monk and taught the Choir to sing so well that people came from Miles Around to hear them.

Saint Hilda's Special Day is November 17th, and there are lots and lots of girls called after her, especially in Yorkshire. But if it happens to be Anybody's Birthday they can have St. Hilda for their Special Saint as well as their Namesake.

✓ St. Grace

Once upon a time there was a man called Probus and he lived in a village called Tresillian in Cornwall. Probus had had a very lucky life. He had made enough money (not Too Much, but Enough), he had never been ill or very sad or anything. He was a Happy and a Comfortable man and he lived in his own small house.

One sunny day while he was clipping the hedge in front of his house he looked at the blue sky and the flowers and he thought:

"God has been good to me, He really has! I wonder what extra thing I could do for Him in return?" Then far, far away he heard the church bells of Truro striking five.

"Ha!" he thought, "tea time! It is lucky," he thought, "that the wind was blowing my way. Sometimes I can't hear the church bells at all."

Then he thought, "Ha!" again because he had just had a good idea. "I know," he thought, "I will build a church in *our* Village and then God will be loved and honored here and I will be able to hear the Bells whichever way the wind is blowing."

So that is just what he did, and as he hadn't Too Much money he found a cheapish builder to do it for him instead of an expensive man from Truro. The new Church was Plain but Good. Probus wanted it to be very beautiful, but he wasn't rich enough. All the same he and the Builder did the best that they could afford. When the Church was nearly finished Probus said to the Builder:

"I am longing to start the Tower! I wonder how many Bells we will be able to afford. I know that bells are very dear, but they make All the Difference."

"*Tower?*" said the Builder. "*Bells?*" he said. "But we can't have those! We have only just enough money to finish off the inside, and even then the door will have to have a very Plain handle."

"What, no Tower?" cried Probus. "But we must! You

shouldn't have spent so much on the rest of it!"

"You know very well," said the Builder, "that we were as Economical as we could possibly be." (Economical's careful and watchful of Expenditure, or Scraping and Saving.) "So," said the Builder, "I can't help it if you're not rich enough, now, can I?" and he sat down on the step in the Church porch and stared up at Probus. Then he tipped his hat over his eyes to keep out the sun.

"No, I suppose you can't," said Probus. "What shall we do?"

"Do without," said the Builder.

"No," said Probus.

"All right," said the Builder, and he leaned his back against the wall and sunned himself.

Probus thought very hard and then, without saying anything more to the Builder, he walked away down the road and out of the village of Tresillian. Soon he came to the next village and there in the middle was a big Front Gate. He went in and walked along a path through a big garden until he came to a beautiful house with a carved wooden door knob. He knocked at the door and a maid answered it.

"Is the lady who lives in the house In?" asked Probus.

"Yes," said the maid. "What name shall I say?"

"Probus, from Tresillian," said Probus.

"Step inside," said the maid, "and come this way."

So Probus stepped inside and followed the maid down a long wide passage, and as he went he looked at all the Rich and Sumptuous things they passed. (Sumptuous, in case you don't know, means Indicating Expenditure on a Lavish Scale.)

Then the maid stopped at a door on the right and opened it.

"Probus of Tresillian to see you, Madam," she said, and

Probus went in and the maid shut the door behind him.

"Good afternoon," said a tall lady, and she shook hands with Probus. "Won't you sit down?"

"Good afternoon," said Probus, and he and the lady sat down near the window.

"What can I do for you?" asked the Tall Lady, whose name was Grace.

Probus told her all about his Plain Church that he was building to thank God for his Happy Life.

"What a good idea! I wish I had thought of it myself," said Grace, "but why did you come and tell me about it?"

"Well," said Probus, "I know that you are a very Happy Person, and, as well as that, you are a very Rich person, and I thought that perhaps you would like to Join In."

"With the building, did you mean?" asked Grace.

"Yes," said Probus.

"I hoped that you meant that," said Grace, "but I was afraid that perhaps you wanted to keep the Church all to yourself."

"But the Church isn't for *me*," said Probus, "it is for God. And He always likes people to Join In."

"So He does," said Grace; "we Join In in Church and in Games and in Families and in Parties and in Schools and in all sorts of other things. So you and I will join in with the Builder to make a better Church than you could have made all by yourself. Let us go now so that I can see how far you have got and then we can think what else we would like to buy."

So they went out at once down the path through the garden and out of the front gate and along the road back to Tresillian. There they found the Builder still leaning against the wall with his hat tipped over his eyes.

"Hello!" said he, when Grace and Probus came up.

"Hello!" said Grace and Probus.

They all three went all over the Church and they made a List and they chose all the most beautiful and expensive things that they could think of.

"Of course," said Probus, "I don't suppose that we could do *all* the things on the List, but isn't it grand to be able to think of them All and to afford to have even a Few?"

"We will have them All," said Grace.

"But you won't have any money left at all, if we do," said Probus.

"That doesn't matter," said Grace; "you haven't either if it comes to that."

So they bought Marble for the walls, and Gold for the Altar things, and Crystal for the flowers, and some lovely Silver Lamps. They had Silks and Velvets and Embroidery for the curtains and the vestments and the very finest Linen and Lace for the Altar linen.

Carvers came to carve the wood and Artists came to paint the ceiling. The most famous of all the Goldsmiths and Silversmiths came, and Coppersmiths and Blacksmiths too. (What do Blacksmiths work with, if Coppersmiths work with Copper?)

At last Probus looked at the lovely Church and said:

"I *am* longing to start the Tower. I wonder how many Bells we can afford. I know that bells are very dear but they do make All the Difference!"

Then, both at the same moment, Grace and Probus looked at each other.

"The Tower!" they said. "We've nearly finished all the

money and we haven't begun the Tower!" They had been so interested and excited over all the other part that they had Actually Forgotten the tower until that moment.

"But that is the reason that I first went to you!" said Probus, "because I couldn't afford a Tower. How silly!" and he went home to think.

But Grace went to her Sumptuous house and packed a few things and moved into a tiny little Empty Cottage. Then she sold her lovely house and all the priceless things that were in it and then she went to Probus.

"Look!" she said, and she opened a big sack that she had brought with her in a wheelbarrow. Probus looked. It was full of Golden money. Hundreds and hundreds of pounds of it!

"Grace!" he said, "how clever you are! Now we can build the Tower."

He was so delighted that he forgot to ask her where she had got the money. And at once they both started to make a List for the Tower and they found that they both wanted a Whole Peal of Bells!

When it was getting dark and it was time to go home Grace said:

"Probus, what do I give my Chickens before they go to bed? Hard food or Soft food?"

"Why?" said Probus, "doesn't your Chicken man do them for you?"

"I haven't got a Chicken man any more," said Grace; "I stopped having him so as to leave more money for the Tower."

"He must have been a very Expensive Chicken man," said Probus.

"Oh, well," said Grace, "I didn't only stop having a Chicken man, there were some other things as well."

So Probus told her how to look after the chickens and they both went home. Probus went to his little house and Grace went to her tiny little cottage that only had one room in it. She didn't make herself a very nice supper because she had never cooked anything before and she did not much like the burnt cabbage that she did make. So she went to sleep on a rug on the floor because she had sold her Valuable bed.

After a while it got round to Probus that Grace had sold her house and he went to see where she was living. When he saw the tumbledown cottage he couldn't think whether to Point with Pride or to View with Alarm.

"Why didn't you *tell* me?" he said.

"You never asked me," said Grace, and she laughed.

"You could have lived in my house and I could easily have lived here," said Probus.

"But I'd rather live here," said Grace. "I'm getting used to it now and I love Our Lord having all my Possessions. Now everybody can Join In and use them in the Church for God's glory."

So Grace lived alone in her tiny cottage for the rest of her life and Probus helped her with the Chickens because he knew all about them.

When the Church and the Tower were perfectly finished it was the most Beautiful Church that had ever been seen in the West Country and Probus smiled happily to himself whenever he heard the Church Bells.

St. Grace's Special Day is on July 5th. (Some people say it is on September 28th.) People all over the world are called after her, especially in England and America.

And I will tell you another thing. The Church in Tresillian in Cornwall is dedicated to St. Grace and St. Probus and I think that it is the only Church in the world that belongs to them. And one more thing is that the village of Tresillian isn't called Tresillian any more but is called Probus after St. Probus who started to build the first church there.

St. Belinda ✓

Once upon a time there was a girl whose name was Belinda and she lived in Belgium and her father was a Rich and Noble farmer. She was very tall and beautiful, and her father was proud of his lovely daughter who looked after him and kept house for him so well. Belinda looked after the farm laborers and their families too, and did every other kind of work that came her way. Her mother had died when she was a baby and she had no brothers or sisters.

Belinda was very happy in her busy life until a sad thing happened. Her father got Leprosy, which used to be thought a very catching illness, but isn't now. So he had to stay at home all the time in case anyone caught it from him. None of his friends came to see him because of Infection (which means Transmission or Acquirement of a disease), so he was very lonely and miserable. Belinda did everything for him. She cleaned his room and did his washing and ironing and made his bed and cooked every kind of delicious thing she could think of. Then she made a special garden for him outside his window so that he could see something in flower all the year round. She planted aconites and snowdrops and yellow jasmine to flower in the Winter. And she planted daffodils and primroses and apple trees to flower in the Spring. For the Summer there were roses and lupins and lilies and in the Autumn there were Michaelmas daisies and red apples and sunflowers. She found and dug up some flowering trees and put them round the Special Garden. These were cherries and pears and peaches and pussywillows. She was a very good gardener.

As well as all this extra work she still looked after the farm. Whenever anyone was ill or any of the animals were sick or hurt it was always Belinda who was sent for, and she nursed them and made Special Medicines and Special Food for them. People said she was the best person for miles around for sick cows.

But in spite of all Belinda's work her father got very Cross and Spoiled because of all the attention he had. He thought that she should give him *all* her time and that his friends should come and sit with him and play Chess. But of course they couldn't, because of catching the leprosy. One day he called Belinda in from the garden where she was staking up some plants and said:

"I am too hot."

"So am I," said Belinda. "What would you like? Shall I get you some cold spring water?"

"Yes, please," said her father, "that would be very nice indeed."

So Belinda went away to the spring and brought back a jug of water and a silver cup. The water was so cold that the outside of the jug was all misty. Her father had a long drink and put down the cup.

"I think I'll have some, too," said Belinda. "It is very hot working in the sun." And she picked up the cup and rinsed it out and filled it for herself. At once her father went into one of his Rages.

"I suppose I am not fit to use the same cup as you!" he shouted. "You're too grand to use my things. All this farm managing and being the Mistress of the place has gone to your head. Kindly remember that it is still all mine and that I am your Father!" He threw off the rug that had been round his knees and flung his spectacles on the floor.

"I'm sorry," said poor Belinda as she picked them up again. "I only rinsed the cup because of leprosy being so catching." She tucked the rug round his knees. "If I get it too, there will be nobody to look after you!"

"Oh no," said her father. "That wasn't it at all, and you know it. Well, I'll take you down a peg or two. When I die I shall not leave you anything at all, and from now, this is no longer your home, my fine Madam! You can go away this very day and be grand all by yourself!" And Belinda had to pack up at once and go.

She went and stayed in a Convent where she had friends among the nuns, and there she helped them in the Infirmary and the garden and the farm, and she prayed every day for her father, who was really very ill, even if he was very bad tempered too.

One night she had a very Unusual Dream. She dreamed that

she was looking out at the dark blue sky and it was full of stars. While she was looking she heard people singing, and dark shapes flew across the sky, blotting out the stars as they passed. She stared in surprise, and suddenly she knew that they were Angels, carrying away her father's soul.

In the morning she went to the Reverend Mother and told her about the Dream.

"It does make me worried about my father, even if he hasn't really died," she said. "He may need me now and wish he hadn't sent me away. Do you think I should go home?"

"Yes, I think you should," said the Reverend Mother. "It may mean nothing, but it may, as you say, mean that your father needs you. If he does, you ought to go and see what you can do for him."

So Belinda hurried home and found that her father had died in the night, and that everyone was wishing she would come back and see to things. So she did.

After her father's funeral, the Farm People would not let Belinda go back to the convent.

"We need you here," they said. "Nobody is as clever as you are with the sick animals. Besides, you belong here, where you were born. Please do stay, Belinda."

So Belinda stayed and worked in her own home until she grew old and died, as we all do when we have finished with our bodies for the time being and need to go away to God. The Farm People hollowed out the trunk of an Oak tree to bury her in because Oaks are strong and beautiful and so was Belinda.

The people in Belgium still ask St. Belinda to help when their cattle are sick, and they say that if a tree is transplanted on her

Feast Day, it will be sure to grow well. It does too, I've tried it myself. (Do you remember the trees she dug up and transplanted to make the garden for her Father?)

St. Belinda's Special Day is on February 3rd and a great many people are called after her. One I know has two brothers called John and Andrew and a sister called Penelope.

St. Patricia ✓

Once upon a time there was a girl called Patricia and she was twenty-two and she lived in Italy. Now Patricia's father was quite a rich man and he had a lot of land. Next to his land were some very good fields that led right down to the sea and a very good little harbor. He very much wanted those fields, because then he would be able to send his corn and sheep and olive oil straight to Naples, where the market was, by ship, instead of carrying everything over hill and dale to the next harbor.

The man who owned the fields was an Ugly Man with an Ugly Temper. He was a good farmer for his corn and hay and olive trees but a wicked one for his cows and his donkey and his dogs. Everybody knew this, but it did not stop Patricia's father from having this Idea:

"If I can get him to marry Patricia," he thought, "then his land and my land will belong to us both and between us we ought to be able to make a good deal of money." So he went to see his ugly neighbor, whose name was Mario.

"Good morning, Mario," he said. "I was just thinking that you could do with a bit more land."

"So I could," said Mario, and he kicked a dog who had come up to look at Patricia's father. "So I could, but the only land I want is yours, and you won't sell it."

"No, I won't," said Patricia's father. "*But* if you married my daughter Patricia, all the land would belong to both of us, and we might be able to make a good deal of money."

"So that's your idea, is it?" said Mario. "I'm not a marrying man, you know, but for the sake of the land I wouldn't mind trying."

"Good," said Patricia's father, and they Sealed the Bargain by shaking hands and he went home.

"Patricia," he said at dinner time, "you must marry Mario next month."

"No!" said Patricia. "Of course not! He's a horrid man with an Ugly Temper. Why must I?"

"So that we'll both have all the land between us, and then we ought to be able to make a good deal of money."

"But what about me?" said Patricia. "I won't make any money, and I'll have to live with Mario! No, I won't do it." And she got up from the table and took the dishes to the kitchen, where their maid Emilia cooked and washed up for them.

Well, Patricia's father (I don't know his name), kept on and on about it, arguing and shouting, until it was time to go to bed.

"All right, my girl," he said as he clumped upstairs. "We'll

see it all settled in the morning. I'll have no more nonsense!"
And he slammed his door.

Patricia went through to the Kitchen to see Emilia and tell
her all about it. Of course Emilia had heard a great deal, what
with the shouting and all.

"What *can* I do?" said poor Patricia. "I really couldn't marry
Mario, he is such a cruel man."

"The only thing I can think of is to run away *now*," said
Emilia.

"Now?" said Patricia. "Do you mean Now this very Minute?"

"Yes, I do," said Emilia. "My Aunt Magda lives in Naples. I
will take you there myself. You can stay with her until you
think of what to do next. She would love to have you, I know.
Of course you would have to pay something. She is rather poor."

So they packed a few things and made up a Picnic Basket
and damped down the kitchen fire and quietly went out of the
back door.

They had a long way to go over hill and dale. They walked
all night, and by breakfast time they were too tired to go any
further.

"Do let's find somewhere to rest and have our picnic," said
Patricia. "I can't walk another step!"

"I shouldn't think your father would find us now," said
Emilia, and she sat down by the road and began to unpack the
basket. "He doesn't know that I've got an Aunt in Naples."
She pulled some cooked sausages out of the basket. "Here, you
divide these, and I'll butter the bread."

After their breakfast they rested for a time in the shade, and
then they packed up the picnic basket and started off again.
They walked all day, and late in the evening they came to

Naples. Luckily Emilia's Aunt's house was one of the first they came to. She was delighted to see them both.

"But fancy your walking all that way!" she said. "You must be Exhausted!" And she hurried away to get their beds ready. They only just had time to tumble in before they were asleep. They didn't even have time for supper.

The next day, after a huge breakfast, they told Emilia's Aunt Magda all about Mario and the fields and everything, and she said that they had been perfectly right to run away.

"The very idea!" she said, "to marry you off to that Mario just because of a few fields!"

So Patricia and Emilia both stayed with Emilia's Aunt Magda, because Emilia dared not go back after having run away with Patricia.

There was a lot to do in Naples while they were waiting to see what they would do next. The town was full of Sailors' children with no one to look after them. Their fathers were at sea and their mothers were either out working or else they had gone away altogether. They had left quite little children and babies all over the place.

Patricia and Emilia thought they ought to do something about them. They found a good shed down by the harbor that no one seemed to want for anything. So they cleaned it up and put a long plank table down one side, and they polished up an old stove that was already there. Then they collected the Left Over Children and fed them and washed them and mended them, and if their mothers did not come to fetch them they let them sleep there, too. Quite soon they had a flourishing Day Nursery, and that, in time, grew into a kind of Home for Foundling Children. Patricia and Emilia were

so interested in what they were doing that they decided to stay in Naples. Other girls joined them and a bigger house was found and still more Left Over Children were looked after.

"You know," said Patricia one day to Emilia (who was now Housekeeper and Cook), "we will have to do something about Teaching the older children. They can't just grow up knowing nothing."

"Couldn't some of the Girl-Helpers do it?" said Emilia. "After all, some of them haven't left school very long. They could learn to teach."

"Who would teach them to teach, though?" said Patricia. "I don't think I could."

"Could the Parish Priest teach us to teach?" asked Emilia, who was always full of ideas.

So off they went, then and there, to the Parish Priest, who said he really hadn't time to teach as well as all the other things he had to do.

"But go and see the Pope, that's what I should do," he said. "He's very interested in Child Welfare and he might even send you somebody who could teach you to teach."

So Patricia went to Rome and Emilia went back to the Children's Home. When Patricia got to the Vatican the Pope very kindly saw her that very same day, and she asked him what to do about teaching.

"What, exactly, have you been doing?" the Holy Father asked.

"Well, Your Holiness," said Patricia, "we really started by collecting a few Left Over children round the docks and feeding them. Just Emilia and me. Then we got more and more children and other people came to help us. Some of our children really ought to be at School now, but no one will take our orphans."

"How many children have you got now?" asked the Pope.

"Three hundred and five," said Patricia.

"And how many people to look after them?"

"Thirty-one counting Emilia and me, Holy Father," said Patricia.

"Three hundred and five is a *lot* of children," said the Pope. "It seems to me that you are doing a very good work, Patricia, but it must be difficult for you to manage it all by yourself. I think you had better run it more like a Convent, you know, and then your helpers will be better organized. I will send a Teaching Nun back with you to help you get started, and then in a year or so, if you would like, I think you should be a Teaching Order of Nuns yourselves. Or perhaps just nuns who make a Home for Children and they can Go Out to School. I can arrange that."

"Thank you very much, Holy Father," said Patricia. "I like that last idea better than teaching them ourselves. It would be more like a real Home. There is just one thing more—

"Emilia and I would very much like to visit the Holy Land before we settle down for good. We always meant to, but we have never had time so far."

"No," said the Pope. "Your work is far too Important to leave. Going to the Holy Land will take quite a year, perhaps more. You can't leave all your Children for such a long time."

"*Please,* Holy Father," said Patricia. "Some of my helpers are very good indeed. I am sure they could manage. Do let us go!"

"No Patricia," said the Pope. "You are doing God's work in Naples, and you mustn't leave it just to please yourselves. Now, I will send you a Teaching Nun tomorrow and she will travel home with you. Go in peace, and God bless you."

So Patricia went home to Naples with a very kind nun called Sister Mary Cleophas who knew all about teaching people to be teachers.

When she had got Sister Mary Cleophas's room ready for her and had shown her the house and the children, Patricia went to find Emilia in the kitchen and told her what the Pope had said.

"What a shame!" said Emilia. "I do think he might have let us go." And she stirred the soup in the big iron pot very fast and then banged the lid on again.

"But he *is* the Pope," said Patricia, "and I suppose he must know best what we ought to do."

"I'm sure they could manage without us for a year," said Emilia. "Especially now that Sister What's-her-name has come. *She'll* see to things. Come on, let's just catch the next boat and go. It can't really matter."

Patricia wanted to go so badly that in the end she agreed to go with Emilia to the Harbor, and there they went on board a ship which was just about to sail for the Holy Land. The Captain wasn't best pleased at having two women passengers. He said they brought Bad Luck. But Patricia offered to give him extra money, and he agreed to take them. They had a little cabin to themselves, and they unpacked their few things and settled down. After they had been at sea for three days and were beginning to enjoy their voyage there came a great Storm of Wind. The ship rocked and tossed and pitched.

The sails split and ropes flew through the air and a sailor fell overboard and was drowned. Patricia and Emilia couldn't stay on their feet, so they lay on their bunks and held on tight. Even then they sometimes fell right out onto the floor.

For three whole days the wind roared and screamed, and the Captain was sure it was the Bad Luck brought by his women passengers. After they had pitched and tossed in their cabin for three days and three nights, Patricia half woke up from being half asleep and noticed that things were quieter. She called to Emilia:

"Emilia! Wake up! The wind is stopping." They both sat up and listened. They could hear clumping footsteps and men shouting. Then they heard steps outside the ship.

"I do believe we're there!" said Patricia, and she stood up on her bunk to look out of the porthole at the Holy Land. But do you know what she saw? Naples Harbor! The wind had blown them right back to where they had started from. So that is what Patricia got for disobeying Orders.

After that Patricia stayed in Naples for the rest of her life looking after her Orphans and Foundlings, and she was loved by everyone in the city. When at last she died an interesting thing happened.

All the Parishes in Naples wanted to bury her in their own Churchyards, and no one could agree on which Parish should have the honor. So at last the people put her coffin on a cart and harnessed two Bulls to it that had never pulled a cart before. Instead of galloping madly about, as you would expect, the Bulls walked quietly to the Church of St. Marcian, and so Patricia was buried in St. Marcian's Churchyard and everyone

St. Patricia's Special Day is August 25th, and girls in every country are called after her and she is the Patron Saint of Naples.

St. Mildred

Once upon a time there was a little Girl called Mildred and she lived with her Father and Mother and Sisters at Wenlock, in Shropshire.

Now Mildred was a Princess, and her father was King Merwald and her mother was Queen Ermenburga.

One day, Mildred's Cousin Egbert (who was a King who lived near Canterbury) did a Horrible Thing. He let a wicked friend of his, called Thunor, murder Queen Ermenburga's two little brothers who would be Kings themselves when they grew up.

King Egbert was terribly sorry when it had been done because he hadn't really *meant* Thunor to do it, and so he went to the Archbishop of Canterbury and told him about it in Confession.

"Well," said the Archbishop of Canterbury, "it was a Perfectly Frightful Thing to do. It was all your Fault because it was *your* friend and you could easily have stopped him; you knew he was going to do it."

"I know I did," said King Egbert, "but I didn't think he *really* would."

"That's neither Here nor There," said the Archbishop of Canterbury. "For your Penance you ought to go round all your Kingdom barefooted, telling all the people that you are Sorry. But because you are so very Sorry, I'll tell you what you must do. Send for the Little Boys' sister, Queen Ermenburga. Tell her what you have done; and take whatever Punishment she gives you."

So messengers were sent to Shropshire, and King Egbert settled down to wait for his Cousin, Queen Ermenburga, to come. He was very worried about having to tell her about her Brothers, and he wondered how Angry she would be.

But one of the Messengers couldn't keep the News to himself and he Told about the boys being Murdered when he gave the Queen the Letter asking her to go to Canterbury.

She was very sad, and she read King Egbert's letter.

"I don't mind so *much* about the Boys," she said to her husband the King, "because they are with God now, but poor Egbert has got a Horrible Mark of Murder on his Soul. What *can* he do to try and make it better?"

"Couldn't he build an Abbey?" said the King, "where Monks or Nuns could pray for him?"

"Yes," said the Queen, "and I'll go there with Mildred. The Others can stay with their Aunt. That will leave you free to Fight your Battles without thinking about whether we are Safe or not."

"That's a Good Idea," said the King.

So Queen Ermenburga and Mildred went to Canterbury, in Kent, which had been the Queen's home before she was married and went to live at Wenlock, in Shropshire, with King Merwald.

King Egbert and the Archbishop of Canterbury went out to meet them.

"Now," said the Archbishop of Canterbury, "go on!"

"What *will* she say?" said poor King Egbert. (He didn't know that the Messenger had already Broken the News.)

"Never mind what she will say," said the Archbishop of Canterbury. "*Whatever* it is will be your Penance."

So King Egbert went and knelt in front of Queen Ermenburga, his Cousin, and Told her about her two little brothers, and asked her to Forgive him.

"Yes, Cousin Egbert," said the Queen, "I will forgive you. But I am very Worried about your Soul. Never mind about the Boys, because though their Bodies are Dead their Souls are Alive and with God. But *your* Body is Alive and your Soul was Dead. It is a lot Better now that you have been to Confession, but it won't be quite well again until you have done your Penance."

"What is my Penance?" asked King Egbert, who was very Anxious to know.

"Didn't you have one when you went to Confession?" asked Queen Ermenburga, all Surprised.

"No," said King Egbert. "The Archbishop of Canterbury said that whatever *you* told me to do would be my Penance."

"All right," said Queen Ermenburga. "You must build an Abbey on some of your own land, where Nuns can pray for you."

"Of course I will," said King Egbert; "which part of my Kingdom would you like it to be built on?"

"The Isle of Thanet," said the Queen.

"The *Whole Island?*" said the King.

"No," said Queen Ermenburga. "Only as much as my tame Deer will run round in one Morning. And because you have been so sorry about the Boys, and have given such a Grand gift to God to try and make up for it, I will give you Mildred to be a Nun in the Abbey, and to be its Abbess, and she shall pray for you all her life!"

Mildred was very Surprised. She had had no Idea that this was going to happen to her. But she was very sorry for poor Cousin Egbert, and so she smiled at him and said she would do her best for him.

King Egbert was Delighted.

"Thank you, Cousin Mildred," he said; "you may go to School in France until the Abbey is ready for you and you are Old Enough, and *I* will pay the Expenses!"

Then they all went to King Egbert's Palace at Eastry, where they were going to stay for the next few days.

Now in those days the Isle of Thanet was really an Island, and Westgate and Ramsgate and Minster were all on it, and when people wanted to go to these places they had to go by Boat instead of walking or going in a bus as we do now.

The next morning they went to the Stable nice and early and got out the tame Deer and put it in the King's Boat, and the Queen and the King (with his friend Thunor, who wasn't in Prison, but I *can't* think why) and Mildred and some Retainers all got in too, and they sailed from Sandwich to a place near Minster where Horses were waiting for them. And they all rode along the Cliffs through Birchington to Westgate where the Starting Place was. Queen Ermenburga leaned down and patted her tame Deer.

"Now!" she said to it, "we are going for a nice Exercise. You run in front of me like a good Deer and I will Pretend to Hunt for you!"

The Deer had played that game before, and he was very pleased. It was a lovely day, and he had been in the Stable for some time. He thought it would be grand to go for a long Exercise. So he started off, trotting across the Downs towards Minster.

Now anyone who lives near Minster will know the old Chalk Pit called Thunor's Leap. But did you know *why* it is called that? Well, King Egbert did not want to frighten the Deer, so he and Thunor rode up to the hill that is now called Mount Pleasant so that they could watch where it went. But when they saw that the Deer was going to go right round the town of Minster, Thunor could not Bear it!

"You'll be giving her your Whole Kingdom if you're not careful," he said. "I'll go and Head Off the Deer." And before King Egbert could stop him he galloped down the hill, jumping the bushes and not bothering about the Paths. Suddenly, much too Late, he saw the Chalk Pit! Down they crashed and Thunor and the Horse were Killed. And more than a Thousand Years afterwards we still call it Thunor's Leap. Well, the Deer went trotting round Minster, along Chipman's Way until it got to Sheriff's Court, and there it Stopped.

King Egbert went to meet the Queen.

"You've got a Good Big Piece of Land," he said; "it's more than I thought."

The Queen laughed. "But I like having plenty of land for my Abbey!" she said, "and remember it's all for your own

Good!"

"*I* know!" said King Egbert.

Now we'd better get on with Mildred. After all, it is her Story, and we've only Mentioned her once or twice so far. While the Abbey was being built Mildred went to School at a Convent near Paris. It was the same School that St. Hilda had gone to when she was little, and Mildred liked being there very much. So she stayed there until she was Grown Up. People didn't Come Home for the Holidays in those days, because traveling was so difficult, and so she was Years and Years in France. Then the Reverend Mother thought she was Old enough to leave School, and, instead of writing to her Mother, who was Queen Ermenburga, to say she was coming, and could she please send her some Money to Travel with, Mildred just Started Off with her maid. She wanted to arrive at home suddenly and give everyone a Surprise. The Maid's name was Dorothy.

They wanted to go to Belgium, where they could get a Boat and sail to England. But, as I said, they hadn't waited for any Money. So there was nothing for it but to Walk. They walked and walked and walked! They had more than two Hundred Miles to go, and the roads were hard and wet and Stony. Sometimes they had nothing to Eat, and sometimes they had nowhere to Sleep, and they got Thinner and Mingier, and *still* they walked! At last, after nearly Three Weeks, they came to Belgium, and soon they saw the Sea.

"Now," said Mildred, "we'll soon have a Boat and all our Troubles will be Over!" And they went about asking when the next Boat would be Sailing to Richborough. (That was the nearest Boating place to the new Abbey.)

"Richborough?" said all the people she asked. "There'll be no more Boats for England until the Spring! It's nearly Winter now, and the Channel is *much* too Rough!"

Poor Mildred and Dorothy were terribly Disappointed. Mildred went down to the Sea and tried to look across to England. (The same way you can see France from Margate.) But it was too Cloudy and too Far. She sat on the Cliffs and stared and stared until at last Dorothy came and found her.

"Now there!" said Dorothy. "Look at you sitting there in this Bitter Wind! Looking won't get you any nearer England! You'll catch your Death of Cold!"

And she was Quite Right. Mildred caught a dreadful Cold, and she was ill for weeks and weeks.

At last it was Spring and Mildred and Dorothy sailed across the Channel and then sailed to the Isle of Thanet. Queen Ermenburga was Tremendously Surprised when she heard from some of the Sailors down on the Quay that Mildred was Coming Home. She went down to Ebbsfleet to meet her, and see the Boat come in. Mildred was so excited when she saw her Mother waiting that she did not wait for the Ship to land in the proper place, but jumped off on to a Rock and ran along the shore to kiss her. (The Rock that she jumped on is still called St. Mildred's Rock.)

Queen Ermenburga was just as pleased as Mildred.

"Darling, why have you come so Suddenly?" she said.

"Because it got Rather Awkward at School," said Mildred, "so Reverend Mother thought that I had better come this year instead of next. Besides, I wanted to give you a Surprise."

"Well, you did," said Queen Ermenburga. "What are you going to do, now you are here?"

"Can I start being a Nun at once?" asked Mildred.

"Of course!" said Queen Ermenburga. And so Mildred did, and soon, when she was Old Enough, she was the Abbess, and the Queen was the Infirmarian. That is rather a Long Name to be called, but it means the Nun who looks after Infirm People, who are weak or ill and not very Firm on their Legs.

Well, Mildred turned into quite a Famous Abbess, and one day she had to go to a Meeting. And this is what the Meeting was about:

All the Kings and Princes and Nobles and things had given so much land to build Abbeys and Monasteries and all that (the way King Egbert did), that there was scarcely any Ordinary Land left. And so there were almost no soldiers. So, when the Enemy (who were the Danes) came they always Won, and, because they were Pagans, the Christians got Fewer and Fewer and the Pagans got More and More. Which was a very Bad Thing.

So a King called King Whitred made a great Meeting to Talk things Over, and all sorts of Bishops and Abbots and Abbesses and things went to it, and so did Mildred. (Because she was an Abbess.)

The Meeting was at Bapchild, near Sittingbourne, and, because it was the easiest way, Mildred went in a Boat. After the Meeting she got into the Boat and began to sail Home. She sailed past Whitstable and Herne Bay and tried to turn up the river at Reculver. But the Wind was so strong that, try as she would, she *could* not turn, and went sailing on to Birchington. There she tried to turn again, but the Sea got Rougher and the Wind got Worse, and there was nothing for it but to go on again to Westgate! But when she was nearly up to the big beach she saw Rocks in the way. She tried to steer Between them or Round them, but it was no good. Her Boat banged into the Rocks in a little Bay and broke in Two and Sank. Mildred fell in the Sea and swam to the Beach, where some people took her into their House and dried her. That little bay in Westgate is always called St. Mildred's Bay, and most of the people who live there don't know why. But you do!

Quite a lot of interesting things happened to St. Mildred, and if you ever go to Margate or Ramsgate or Westgate or Broadstairs for your holiday you will be able to see some of her places and find out more Stories.

St. Mildred's Special Day is July 13th, and Hundreds of People are called after her. Are you?

Sts. Judith and Salome

Once upon a time there was a King in England and he had a niece called Salome and he was very fond of her because he hadn't got a daughter of his own. And anyway, she was nice. Salome lived in the Palace, and the King said that although she couldn't actually be Queen when he died, he would leave her a lot of money and some land in his Will.

Well, one day Salome went to see her Uncle, the King.

"Good morning, Uncle King," she said. "I would very much

like to go to Jerusalem to see the Holy Places if you wouldn't mind. Would you allow me to go, do you think?"

"Well, my dear," said the King, "it certainly is a thing that anybody might want to do, but are you sure you would be all right? After all, a Young Girl traveling alone—"

"Not so young as all that, Uncle King," said Salome. "I am twenty-four, and I wouldn't be quite alone, I would take my maid Penelope with me."

"Two maids," said the King, "at *least* two."

"But I've only got one," said Salome.

"Then I'll give you another," said the King. "You'd better take Belinda."

"Well, I could," said Salome. "Perhaps she would be good company for Penelope. After all, they are sisters."

"Be careful, my dear," said the King. "I don't want to lose you. I should think you'll be gone about a year."

"Not more than eighteen months anyway, Uncle King," said Salome. "Expect me for the Christmas after next."

And so it was arranged, and Salome set off with her two maids, Penelope and Belinda. After some months the King had a letter from her which another Pilgrim brought back, and after a year he had another letter to say that Penelope had married a Pilgrim she had met in Nazareth but that Salome and Belinda were starting back. They were coming over land, not by sea, and she would certainly be home for Christmas, and she sent her love to her Uncle the King.

Just before Christmas everyone in the Palace got things ready for Salome and Belinda. They dusted their rooms and made their beds and lit fires to air their things. But Christmas came and went with never a word from them.

"Perhaps they have been held up by bad weather somewhere," said the King to his sister Judith who kept house for him and who was getting his tea ready.

"I expect we will hear from her soon," said Judith, and she went on cutting bread and butter as any well-conducted person should in a crisis.

But April came and June came, and yet no news from Salome. She had been gone two whole years.

"I must say, she might have let us know," said the King. "I am beginning to be a bit anxious." And he sent messengers to Palestine to find out what they could.

Traveling was very slow in those days, and (if they didn't go by sea) people went on horseback or on foot, and it was just over a year before the messengers got back. They had found out that Salome and Belinda had at least *started* for home. But nobody seemed to know what had happened after that, or even whether they had actually left Palestine.

"I'd better go and look for them myself," said Salome's Aunt Judith, who was a Princess and the King's sister.

"I think, my dear," said the King, "that it *would* be the most sensible thing to do."

So Judith set off and went all through the Holy Land, looking and searching and asking. But although some of the people she met remembered Salome and her maids, no one knew anything about where they were now. Judith went to every one of the Holy Places, and in every one she asked God to help her find her niece. God did not answer her, but she kept on looking and searching.

At last, after years, she started back towards home and searched all the villages and towns in the countries on the way back, just in case anyone knew anything. It took ages and ages. Some times she came across people who remembered Salome and Belinda but who couldn't remember where they had been going to next. Sometimes she went for months without hearing a thing. Every now and then a Pilgrim would take a letter from her to her brother the King, telling him how she was getting on.

One day as she was traveling slowly through Bavaria in Germany she came to the town of Passau. She didn't know anybody there, so she went to the Benedictine Monastery to ask the monks if they knew of a place where she could spend the night.

"Well, now," said the Brother Porter, "I don't know of anywhere in the town. But there is a woman who lives in a little cell joined on to the Monastery Church. She came here, very ill, years ago. She had been robbed and wounded, and she was quite alone. We were afraid she would die. We looked after her, and she got better. But she had lost her memory and couldn't remember who she was or where she came from or where she was going. She is a very nice woman and we made her a little window in her cell, in the Church wall, so that she can see the Altar. Go and ask her if she will let you stay overnight with her. But there isn't much room, let me tell you."

So Judith went round to the South Side of the Church and saw the little room built out from the wall. It was very small indeed. She knocked at the door and a thin, oldish-looking woman with gray hair opened it. And it was Salome, and she was nearly blind.

Salome did not remember Judith at first, until she said who she was, and reminded her of her Uncle the King in England.

Then she laughed and she cried and she bustled about and made up a bed for Judith and then got them some supper to eat.

"How long have I been here?" she asked her Aunt Judith.

"Quite twelve years," said Judith, "so you must be about thirty-six or -seven by now. You don't look very well, my dear."

"I never am well," said Salome, "but it doesn't matter. It *is* lovely to see you again, Aunt Judith!"

Then she told Judith some of her adventures, for seeing Judith had brought all of her memory back again. One of her adventures happened on a wet night when she was all by herself. (I don't know where Belinda had got to. Perhaps the robbers killed her when they robbed Salome.) Well, Salome was all by herself, as I was saying, and she was looking for somewhere to sleep, out of the rain. She found a sort of shed-thing and opened the door. It was warm inside and she heard some rustling noises in the dark. She took a step forward and tripped over something that made the most fearful clatter. It was an enormous dogs' feeding dish! She had got into a Kennel of Mastiffs, which are nearly as big as donkeys, and even heavier. The dogs were very kind to her, she said, and instead of driving her out, they moved up a bit and made room for her in their warm straw bed. When the Kennel Man saw her there in the morning, he was Horrified!

"These are the fiercest guard dogs we have," he said, "I am surprised they didn't kill you!"

"They were good to me," said Salome. "No one else was."

Well, Judith thought Salome seemed so delicate and ill, and had such a terrible cough, that she decided to stay with her and nurse her. She knew all about nursing, of course, being a King's Sister. The good Benedictines made her another little cell next to Salome's, and Judith wrote to her brother the King telling him all about it.

"Salome will never be really well enough to travel," she wrote, "so I had better stay here with her and look after her."

Salome did not live very long after this, but Judith looked after her until she died, and she was buried in the Monastery Churchyard. By this time Judith had settled into her little cell and the Benedictines said she could stay if she liked and they would be grateful if she would help them to teach the town children. Judith *did* like, and so that is what they decided.

She prayed a lot and she taught the children their Catechism so as to make more time for the monks to do other things. She looked after ill people and made medicines for them out of herbs. But at last she too began to go blind. (It must have been in the family, I suppose.) As she could see less and less, the children she taught used to come and help her. They would go out and gather herbs for her, and one boy called Albert, who was specially friendly, looked after her little garden and brought her fresh vegetables from it. But Albert was a mischievous boy (though kind hearted), and one day he played a horrid trick on Judith.

He perched a tame owl on his head and covered all the rest of himself in a black cloak and crept into her cell and hooted. Judith, nearly blind, screamed. She thought this fearful-looking Person was the devil himself. But she bravely grabbed at his head—and it came off! (It was the owl, you remember?) Horrified, Judith threw it in the fire. Luckily for the owl, it flew out of the fire again so fast that it was not really hurt, but there was a horrible smell of Burnt Feathers! Albert burst out laughing, but Judith was quite sure it must have been the devil.

"Nothing else could have made such a Horrible Smell," she said.

Albert had quite a job to get her to believe that it had all been meant for a joke. He was very sorry he had frightened a nearly-blind old lady so badly, and he was always specially good to her after that.

Judith lived in her little cell, working and praying, until she was too old to go on any more. Then the Benedictines took care of her until she died, still in her little cell that was so nice and near to the Altar of God.

St. Judith's Special Day is June 29th. Her name is getting more and more popular, and there are thousands of Judiths and Judys now. Salome is a saint, too, and she shares the same day with Judith, but hardly anyone is called after her.

St. Maude

Once upon a time there was a girl called Maude and she married a Duke called Henry. Henry was very good at catching birds and was often called Henry the Fowler. (What are fowls? Well, they are not *only* the Chickens, but are any kind of Bird. Don't you remember All the Fowls of the Air fell a-Sighing and a-Sobbing?)

Maude and Henry had a very splendid wedding with Crowds and Bands and Processions and Henry gave Maude a Whole Town for a wedding present.

After a time, more people than was expected died, and so Henry became the King of Germany and so of course Maude was the Queen of Germany.

"Well," she said to King Henry, "I must say I never thought that I'd be a Queen. What shall we do with our Kingdom?"

"I should think," said King Henry, "that it might be a good idea to be the Good kind of King and Queen so that our subjects will like us. So many Kings lately have been terribly Tyrannical."

So that is what they did, and one of the first things they did was to make the Taxes less.

Maude had two sons all in due time, Otto the Elder, and Henry (called after his father), who was so trying that he was always called Henry the Quarrelsome, even after he was grown up.

King Henry (the Fowler) had a very weak chest and every winter he had to stay in bed and have it rubbed with Camphorated Oil or something, and Queen Maude always looked after him herself, and she kept the steam kettle going Night and Day. Well, one winter he was so ill that Queen Maude went out to the Church to pray for him. She prayed and she prayed that he wouldn't die because she loved him very much and she couldn't think what she would do without him. While she was still in the Church someone came in quietly and touched her shoulder. She looked up and saw that it was King Henry's servant whose name was Fritz.

"What is it, Fritz?" she whispered. "You should not have left the King until I came back."

"I am sorry to have to tell Your Majesty that the King has died," said Fritz in a sad voice, "and they want you back at the Palace."

"I see," said Queen Maude; "thank you, Fritz. But first, since I am already here, I must see the priest and·ask him to say his tomorrow's Mass for King Henry."

You do know about Mass for people who have died, don't you? In case you don't, perhaps I had better just tell you. When ordinary people die they are not clean and good enough to go and live beside God in Heaven straightaway, are they? But they are certainly not bad enough to go and live in Hell, perhaps no one ever is. So they go to Purgatory. (Purgatory is a word which means A Place to get Clean in.) So of course, it all depends on how grubby you have made your soul, as to how long it takes to make it clean again, which is very sensible. But the Miserable part is that when you have just died, the very first Person that you see is God, and usually He says, "I am afraid that you are not clean enough yet to live with Me, so you must go to Purgatory for a while." And so you have to leave Him just when you have found out that He is the Person you love Best of All. And all the time that you are in Purgatory (the Cleaning Place) you wish and *wish* that you were back with God again and you can't think of anything else at all because you are so sad. So the people that you leave behind when you die ask God to let your Cleaning Time be as short as it can possibly be so that you can go back and be happy with God again.

Well, what is the very best Prayer of all prayers? Yes, Mass, of course, because Our Lord Himself is there. So we ask a priest to say a Mass for someone who is dead and to pray that whoever it is may see God soon.

So the first thing that Queen Maude thought of when King Henry died was to ask for a Mass for him, so that he wouldn't be too long in Purgatory. She went to the Sacristy and found the Priest.

"Please, Father," she said, "would you say your next Mass for my husband King Henry? He has just this minute died."

"Of course I will, Your Majesty," said the Priest. "How dreadful for you to lose him, I hope you won't be *too* lonely."

"Yes, I think that I will be," said poor Queen Maude. "Will you say the next Mass for him and the next and the next and the next, for weeks and months and years?"

"Well," said the Priest, "I'm afraid that I couldn't do that because there are all sorts of other people and other things to pray for in this Parish."

"But what about King Henry?" asked Queen Maude, and

she began to cry because everything was so sad for her.

"Now don't you cry, Your Majesty," said the priest kindly; "come into the Presbytery and my housekeeper will get you a nice hot Cup of Something before you go back to the Palace. It will do you good and we will see if something can be Arranged."

So the Queen sat in a rather Stiff red velvet chair in the Priest's sitting room and while she drank her hot Cup of Something they had a short Discussion.

"Could there perhaps be a Special Priest *only* to pray for the King?" asked Queen Maude.

"If there were, he'd have to have a Special Chapel so that the ordinary Church Services wouldn't be interrupted or anything," said the Priest.

"Oh dear," said sad Queen Maude, "I am so worried that I can't think properly, but I believe that I haven't enough money to build a Chapel. King Henry wouldn't like me to spend so much on him when there are so many Poor People to look after."

"Well, I don't know what to suggest, I'm sure," said the Priest. He was very sorry for the poor Queen but he really couldn't do what she wanted.

Queen Maude sobbed, and that shook her cup and some Hot Drink splashed onto the front of her queenly robe. She sniffed and took out her handkerchief and began to rub the Wet Marks and to dry the Golden Buttons. They were beautiful buttons and there were seven of them. Each one had a big Jewel in it and each jewel was different. The top one had a white Diamond and the next a green Emerald, and then a purple Amethyst, then a red Ruby, and another green Emerald.

Then came a blue Sapphire and the last of all was a yellow Topaz, and if you started at the top and read downwards they spelled the word Dearest, like this:

Diamond
Emerald
Amethyst
Ruby
Emerald
Sapphire
Topaz

and King Henry had once given them to her for a Christmas present.

"There!" said Queen Maude, cheering up a bit. "I will cut off my Dearest buttons, and if you will sell them for me, Father, they will pay for a new Chapel"; and she took the Priest's penknife off his desk and cut off the buttons and set them in a row on his red tablecloth.

"Thank you for my lovely hot drink, Father," she said, and she went quickly out and up the road to the Palace.

Now as soon as King Henry saw God after he had died, God told him what Queen Maude had done.

"Well," said Henry, "she was always a good wife to me, but this is the kindest and quickest thing she has ever done for me. She set great store by those buttons, and I call it very unselfish of her. Please, dear God, will You look after her specially well while I am in Purgatory?"

And God said that He would.

Queen Maude's son Otto was King after his father, and he

and his brother Henry the Quarrelsome never stopped quarrelling and arguing. The only thing that they agreed about was that neither of them wanted Queen Maude to stay in the Palace, and they told her so.

"You spend all the money on Poor People who can quite well do without," said Henry.

"And anyway, even if they *can't* do without, it makes less for me," said Otto.

At last Queen Maude tidied up the Palace and paid all the bills and went to live in the little country town that she had had for a wedding present all those years ago.

"Really," she thought, "it is much better like this because I shall have plenty of time to work for God."

So Queen Maude started to make her own little town the most comfortable town in Germany, and these were some of the things that she did.

Her town was in a very cold part of Germany, and in the winter the snow was very hard and thick and a lot of the people who couldn't afford Fires nearly froze. So Queen Maude had big Bonfires all the winter in all the Squares and Spaces in the town, and because there was no street lighting she had lanterns everywhere about so that the people would not slip on the ice and hurt themselves.

Another thing that she did was to have an Enormous Stove in her kitchen so that anybody who liked could have a Good Hot Bath to warm them up.

Saint Maude's Special Day is on March 14th, and if anyone happens to be called Matilda, then that will count because Maude and Matilda are one and the same name.

St. Edith

Once upon a time there was a Royal Princess called Edith, and her great-grandfather was Alfred the Great (who burnt the cakes).

Little Princess Edith went to school at a Convent in Wilton, near Salisbury. She was very soon Top of her class at Cooking and Sewing, and the Reverend Mother said that for a reward she could go to the Gate with the Door Sister in the Morning and Look After the Poor-and-Raggies there.

So the next morning, directly after Breakfast, instead of lessons Edith went with the Door Sister to the Kitchen. The first thing that happened was that Sister Cook put an Enormous white apron of her own on Edith. Now Sister Cook was a Comfortable Body and so the apron was miles too big for Edith. But they Managed, by pinning it up round the hem and tying the strings round Twice. Then they collected plates and spoons and forks and cups and things and Edith helped Door Sister to carry them outside.

"Are we going to have a Picnic, Sister?" asked Edith.

"Wait and see!" said Door Sister, making a Secret Face, and they went back to the Kitchen. There Sister Cook had got ready an Enormous Saucepan full of Soup and a Huge Jug of milk and Twenty loaves of bread and a Black Tin Bandage Box.

Edith helped Door Sister to carry these out as well, but she couldn't help wondering why they had a Bandage Box.

Then the Door Sister opened the Big Gates, and there were Crowds of Poor-and-Raggies all waiting to be Looked After!

"Now don't Push!" said the Door Sister to the Poor-and-Raggies. "There's no Hurry!"

And they all came in and they each took a Basin and a Plate and a Cup and then stood in a long row.

Then they walked past Edith and Door Sister, and while the Sister was filling the Basins with Soup and the Plates with Bread, Edith filled all the Cups with Milk. She loved doing that, and she felt very Proud and Important in her Enormous white apron!

When everyone had finished his or her Meal, Door Sister said:

"Will everyone who is Quite Well please go away until to-morrow? And will everyone who is Rather Ill or something come to me?"

Nearly everybody went away, but several stayed behind and Door Sister said to Edith:

"Now, Edith, you'll find some scissors in the Bandage Box. Keep them ready, and when I say 'Snip,' Snip!"

The first Invalid had fallen down and cut his Knee. Sister washed it and put some Pink Gauze on it and bandaged it up. When she wanted the Bandage to be cut she said to Edith:

"Snip!"

And Edith cut it off, and Sister fastened it up with a Safety Pin.

Then there was a Girl with a Cough, and she had some Red Lozenges out of a Box.

Then there was a Boy with a Pain in his Middle, and he had a White Pill out of a Bottle.

Then there was a Lady with a Bad Cut on her hand. Sister washed it and put some Pink Gauze on it and Bandaged it up.

"Snip!" she said.

And Edith cut it off, and Sister fastened it with a Safety Pin.

Well, it would take too long to tell you what was the matter with *all* the Poor-and-Raggies, but Edith loved this part of the work even better than the Bread and Soup and Milk part. And when they had finished she asked Reverend Mother if she could *always* help Door Sister in the mornings.

"No," said Reverend Mother, "because what about your lessons?"

"Can't I *ever* again?" said Edith in a Sad Voice.

"Not in Lesson Time," said Reverend Mother.

"May I in Recreation?" said Edith, "and on holidays and Sundays?" (In case there are people who don't go to Convent Schools reading this Story, Recreation is Playtime, or Break, or Recess or whatever else you call it at your School.)

"You may try," said Reverend Mother, "but you mustn't do it *all* those times or you won't get Sufficient Exercise."

So Edith, whenever she was allowed to, helped Door Sister with the Poor-and-Raggies, and she got so good at it that Sister used to let her do some of the Bandaging herself when she was Older. Edith always chose the Raggiest and Grubbiest people to look after, because nobody liked them so much as the Clean ones.

"I'd Rather they weren't so Grubby," she said, "but Our Lord never Minded who He looked after, He even touched Lepers. So why should *I* mind?"

Well, one day when Edith had given up her Spare Time for years and years and she was Quite Old, about Sixteen, an Interesting Thing happened.

On this special day that we are talking about there was another Helper as well as Edith, because there were more Invalids than usual. They were all working as hard as they could when the Other Helper said to Edith:

"Look at that *Awful* little boy!"

"Where?" said Edith, looking round about.

"Over there, near the end of the row," said the Other Helper. "I do hope Sister gets to him before I do, I'd be afraid of Catching something!"

"He does look rather Chicken-Poxy," said Edith, "but he

can't help that. I expect he feels Horrible!"

"He *looks* Horrible!" said the Other Helper; "look at his Spots, and his hair, and his nails, and his feet!"

Edith looked. She hoped that Sister would get to him first! She couldn't *bear* people with Spots, but the people never knew that, because she was always Specially Nice to them in *case* they guessed that they made her feel Sick.

"I wouldn't like to be that boy!" she said to herself. "He really is Horrible!" Then she thought, "But if I *were* that boy would *I* be Horrible?" Then she thought, "If people wouldn't touch me because I was Horrible when I was Ill, I should cry and cry, it would be so sad for me!"

She looked at the boy out of the corner of her Left Eye.

"He does look Rather Sad," she thought. "I wonder if he feels as awful as I would?"

She snipped off the Bandage that she was putting round an old man's arm and said:

"There now! I do hope that will soon feel better!" And she smiled at the old man.

"Who shall I look after next?" she thought, when the old man had gone off. "*Not* the Horrible boy!"

Suddenly she thought:

"I *will* do the Horrible boy because he must *know* that we are all trying not to be the one to do him! It must be Dreadful for him. But I wish he didn't make me feel sick. I wonder if Our Lord felt like that about the Lepers He touched? Because although I hate the boy being so Horrible, I can't help loving him because he *is* so Horrible." Edith sighed and picked up her Bandages and things. She went quickly to the Horrible boy.

"Good morning!" she said, smiling at him. "What would

you like me to do first?"

"*Would* you put some cold cream or something on my Spots?" said the boy. "But if you think you'd Rather Not, never mind, because I know I look Horrible."

"Of course I will!" said Edith. "And you don't look Horrible at all. In fact, in some lights they'd scarcely show. You must be very Uncomfy, I *am* so sorry!" She got out the cold cream. "*Poor* you!" she said kindly, as she put it on. "Does that feel better now?"

"Thank you, Edith!" said the boy, and he Disappeared! Edith stared at the place where the boy had been sitting, then, without saying a word, she went and told the Reverend Mother what had happened.

"Wasn't it Extraordinary, Reverend Mother?" she said.

"No, Edith," said the Reverend Mother; "it wasn't, when you come to think it over. You see, you've given up *all* your free time for the Love of Our Lord for years and years, even when you would Rather have been doing something else. So Our Lord thought He'd come and see if you'd do a really Difficult thing for Him. And it *was* a Difficult thing to decide that you'd look after that boy when you could easily have left him for Door Sister to do."

"Yes, it was rather, at the time," said Edith, "but I *am* glad I did. I never could have guessed that it was Our Lord Himself pretending to be Horrible to see what I'd do."

"Our Lord said that anything Kind that we do for Other People we really do for Him," said Reverend Mother, "and then sometimes He comes Himself to give us a Lovely Surprise."

"Like He did for me," said Edith.

"Yes," said Reverend Mother, "like He did for you."

When she grew up Edith was a Nun in that convent in Wilton, and she built a beautiful new Church there with the money that she had because of being a Princess.

St. Edith's Special Day is September 16th, and anyone called Ada or Ida or Edna can count because all those names are all different ways of saying Edith, which is Rather Funny but Quite True.

St. Olga

Once upon a time there was a girl called Olga, and she lived in Russia nearly a thousand years ago. One day, she was standing by the river near her home, watching the geese flying in great *V*-shapes to the place where they were going to build their nests. Have you ever seen geese or swans or ducks flying with one in front and two behind it, so that when there are a lot of them they look like an arrow-head pointing the way they are going? Or a capital *A* without the cross-piece or (if they are going the other way) like a *V*. Have you seen airplanes flying in *V*-formation? Well, we got the idea from the birds, who have done it for thousands of years. Anyway, Olga was watching the geese and she did not hear a horse stop near her. Suddenly she heard a voice beside her saying, "It's a lovely evening, isn't it?"

She turned round, and there was the Duke who lived in a wonderful castle a few miles away and whose name was Igor.

"Yes, lovely," said Olga. "I was watching the geese."

"Oh yes," said the Duke. "It's a nice evening for a little stroll, don't you think?"

"Well, that's as may be, your Grace," said Olga, "but I must be getting home to supper. Good evening." And she turned away toward her home.

"Don't go!" said the Duke. "I want to talk to you. You are very pretty, did you know?"

"Thank you kindly, your Grace," said Olga, and went on walking up the path.

"Come back!" said the Duke, and Olga thought perhaps she had better do what the Duke told her because all the land round about and her father's house belonged to him.

"What is your name?" said the Duke.

"Olga."

"Oh, Olga," said the Duke, "you *are* so pretty! Come with me and be my love!"

"Oh no!" said Olga, "now I really must be getting home," and she turned away again and walked up the path.

Igor looked after her. "She *is* pretty," he thought, "pretty as a picture! Pretty as a little Duchess! Oh goodness!" he said, jumping on his horse. "Oh, *what* an idea!" and he trotted along the path until he caught up with Olga.

"Olga!" he said, "Olga, do stop a minute, please!"

Olga slowed down and stopped, and Igor got off his horse.

"Olga!" he said, "will you come with me and be my Duchess?"

"Thank you, your Grace," said Olga, "I should like to do that very much. I always did think you were such a very Handsome young man."

So they went on to Olga's home and told her parents, who were delighted, and in next to no time they were married and Olga went to be the Duchess of Kiev and to live in the wonderful castle that looked as though it came out of a fairy tale.

Now the Duke and Duchess of Kiev (Igor and Olga) were not Christians because there were not many in Russia at that time and they were very Warlike with their neighbors, but no more, really, than the neighbors were with one another and with Kiev. Their chief enemy for the moment were the Drevlians who lived some fifty miles away. Igor had been winning a lot lately and he was always sending raiding parties to loot the Drevlians' towns. (Looting is taking people's Goods and Chattels and horses and what-have-you away and using them in your own Town, rather like Land Pirates.) So Kiev got Richer and Richer and the Drevlians, who had not many good soldiers at the time, became so poor that at last they decided that they really must *do* something about it.

So they watched and they waited to see if they couldn't Capture the Duke of Kiev himself and get rid of him. Several raiding parties came without the Duke, and the Drevlians very craftily let them come and go and pretended they were not able to fight at all.

"It's too easy, your Grace," said one of Igor's generals, "the Drevlians *can't* be as feeble as that! You mark my words, your Grace, there's something Brewing!" (What is a brewer?)

"I'll go with you next time," said Igor, "and we will find out."

So off they rode one night to find out why the Drevlians

wouldn't fight back. No sooner had they got into the first town when hundreds of Drevlians ran out of the houses, and in less than no time at all they had Captured Igor and defeated his raiding party.

Now Igor was really a very nice Duke indeed (you don't have to count the raiding and the looting because everybody did it all the time; it would have looked Rather Odd if they didn't), and as soon as he was Taken Prisoner he behaved politely and asked to be taken to see the Prince of the Drevlians to pay his respects and offer his apologies. The Prince lived in a beautiful Palace with a very thick thatched roof. This was to keep out the cold Russian winter, and very cosy it was, too.

But as soon as he arrived at the Prince's palace he saw that things were Very Different indeed from the way in which he treated his own Important Prisoners. Instead of asking him to supper to talk things over, the Prince took one look at him and shouted:

"Take that man outside, Sergeant, and execute him forthwith!"

Igor was so surprised he did not really believe it, but the Sergeant and his men marched him outside and Executed him without further ado. '

When Olga heard what had happened she was most dreadfully sad because she loved Igor very much, and she felt very frightened of having to govern the Duchy all alone. (What is a Kingdom?) However, she ruled very well and very wisely for her age and all her people loved her.

But the Drevlians were extremely Proud of themselves over what they had done, and they thought that, after all, they must be very good soldiers indeed to have Captured the Duke of

Kiev. So the Prince called his Council together and said:

"We are doing very well since we got rid of the Duke, but it seems to me that if we capture the whole of his country, which joins ours, we shall be a very large and strong country indeed. Let us go and seize the Town of Kiev!"

"What about the Duchess?" said one of the Councilors.

"She's pretty fierce and Ruthless." (What does Ruth mean? Well, it means "Pity" as Lucy means "Light" and Joan means "God's Gift." So to be ruthless means to be pitiless, doesn't it?)

"What's a woman?" said the Prince. "I'm not afraid of a woman, are you?" and all the Councilors said no, they weren't.

"And another thing," said the Prince. "I will marry the Duchess Olga, and so our two countries will be even better joined together."

So, instead of sending an Army to besiege Kiev, the Prince sent twenty Ambassadors down the river in ten boats with beautiful sails and strong oarsmen and presents for Olga. When they reached Kiev they went in a procession to the Castle and asked to see the Duchess Olga.

Olga met them in her Throne room, sitting on her Throne and looking very beautiful.

The Ambassadors genuflected politely, and their Spokesman (who spoke for them all because it would be a Gabble if they all spoke at once) said:

"Your Grace, you know that our Mighty Prince has killed your fighting Duke Igor?"

Olga nodded.

"Well," said the Spokesman, "our Prince is a fine and rich man. He asks you to marry him so that our countries may be joined together to make one bigger and stronger country."

Olga was furiously angry at this message but she pretended not to be, and she said very politely:

"Sirs, I must have time to think it over. It is late now, but tomorrow you shall have all the honors you deserve. Go back to your boats for tonight, if you will, and rest. When my people come for you in the morning, make them carry you in their arms in your boats in a procession! Don't ride or walk. It will be Grander to ride in your boats."

So the Ambassadors bowed and left the castle, very pleased that they would be so grandly treated the next day.

"She's not so bad as we thought she might be," said one of them as he settled down in his boat for the night.

Meanwhile, Olga gathered together her people and they made a Plan. They dug ten enormous pits in the Courtyard in front of the Castle and when they had finished they went to bed quietly and rested.

Next day five hundred men marched down to the boats, leading twenty beautifully decorated horses.

"Good morning, my Lords Ambassadors!" they cried to the men on the boats. "We have come to take you in Procession to the Castle of Kiev! Here are your horses."

"No, we don't want horses!" said the Ambassadors. "They aren't good enough for us! Remember that we are really Conquerors, although we haven't had a battle!"

"Well, what would you like?" asked the Senior Officer (who knew quite well).

"You must carry us in our boats in a Procession to the Castle!"

"*Carry* you?" said the Senior Officer (who knew perfectly well). "Carry you in our arms?"

"Yes," said the Ambassadors.

"Alas," sighed the soldiers, "we are slaves! You great Drevlians have killed our Duke and now you are going to take our Duchess away! How sad a day for us!" (But they spoke with their tongues in their cheeks.)

As they came near the Palace, the Duchess Olga came out on her balcony above the courtyard to watch the grand procession of Ambassadors in their Boats. But as they came even nearer, the boats were thrown into the pits and the Ambassadors had their necks broken and they were buried under their boats.

Then, before the news could get back to the Drevlians, Olga sent some men that night to catch as many pigeons as they could that were nesting and roosting in the thatch of the Prince's Palace roof. "Be very quiet and careful," she said; "don't wake anyone, whatever you do."

Next evening the men came back with hundreds of pigeons in nets. Then Olga tied little twigs on to their tail feathers and dipped the ends into some stuff which would burn very slowly. Just at roosting time she lighted the sticks and let the pigeons free. At once they all flew back to their nests and holes in the thatch. Before you could say Jack Robinson the Whole Palace was blazing and the pigeons flew out again wondering what could have happened as soon as they arrived home! So the Drevlians lost their Prince and their Palace and a good deal more besides because the fire spread all over the place. The Councilor was quite right. The Duchess Olga *was* fierce and ruthless, but all that happened while she was still a Pagan.

So Olga ruled her people kindly and well. She made their Taxes as small as she could afford and she did her best to get good doctors for them from other countries who knew more about these things than the Russians did.

After a time some missionary priests came to preach to the people of Kiev (you remember that they were not Christian people?), and Olga listened to them carefully. After a great deal of thinking and asking questions, she became a Christian because she thought it was a wise and good religion. Some of the priests stayed in Kiev when the missionaries moved on, and a great many Russians were converted.

Olga was loved very much by her people and they used to give her presents of honey and furs, which was lovely for her. When she died she was called "The Dawn and the Star of Salvation for Russia" because she had done so much for the Christian Church. Russia became more and more Christian as time went on until it was called Holy Russia. But now, I expect you know, there is persecution there again and the Christians have a terribly difficult and hard time. I hope people remember to ask St. Olga about it. I am sure she still helps the Russian Christians, even in these hard days.

St. Olga's Special Day is June 11th and people all over the world are called after the Great Saint who used to be called the Pitiless Duchess of Kiev.

St. Alice

Once upon a time there was a Princess called Alice, and she had a Royal but Disreputable Family. (Disreputable is Dissipated in Appearance and Character.)

When she was sixteen Years old she married the King of Italy, and so she was the Queen of Italy, and she lived in Rome most of the time, and she often saw the Pope. But after only three years her husband, the King, died, and she was a Widow.

Now Alice had an Uncle Berengar, and he said to Alice: "Now, my dear, I have a Plan for your future. You can't be a Widow when you are only Nineteen. You must marry my son Prince Adalbert."

"But," said Queen Alice, "I can't marry my Cousin! It isn't allowed, and besides, I don't like him!"

"Nonsense, girl!" said Alice's Uncle Berengar. "No one hereabouts knows that he is your Cousin, so what's the Odds?"

"But God will know," said Alice. "And, after all, it's God's rule that Cousins mustn't marry."

"Stuff!" said Alice's Uncle Berengar. "You *must* marry him, because I want him to be the King of Italy!"

But Alice wouldn't, and then Uncle Berengar showed himself in his True Colors. He sent for Alice's Ladies-in-Waiting and told them to take away her Jewels and her Costly Raiment and her shoes and even to cut off her Hair! Then she had a

Sacking frock, and she was put in a Deep Dark dungeon under a castle on Lake Como.

But Alice had a lot of friends, and one of them was her old Palace Priest called Father John. When Father John heard what had happened to the Queen he was in a Great State.

"Poor girl!" he said. "I mean poor Her Majesty! I *must* go and see what I can do for the child; I mean for Queen Alice."

So he went to the castle by the lake and he looked at it carefully all the way round. Soon he saw a little Grating in the ground, and he peered in.

"Oh, Father John!" said a voice, "dear Father John, can you *possibly* get me out of this horrible place; it's got Black Beetles in it!"

"Well, my dear child, I mean Your Majesty," said old Father John, "I'll do what I can, but it won't be Too Easy, because I shall have to dig a Tunnel from a long way off and come up through your floor."

"Can I help?" asked Alice, a bit more cheerfully.

"Not with the Tunneling," said Father John, "because someone might see you. But you must pray for me all the time, and then no one will catch me at it."

So Alice asked God if He would *please* not let anyone see Father John tunneling. "Because I *do* want to get out of this Horrible place," she said to God. "But if you *want* me to stay here of course I will, and I won't even Mention the Black Beetles, even though they do give me the Cold Horrors." And often and often in the day she asked God the same thing, and whenever she woke up in the night she reminded Him, and she asked Our Lady to pray for Father John, too, and she did.

So every day old Father John tunneled and tunneled until he got right under Alice's floor, and then he began to tunnel upwards under Alice's floor, and sometimes Alice could hear Scratching and Bumping noises underneath. One day, under one of the stones of the floor came "Knock! Knock!" And Alice stared at the stone and very slowly it lifted up at the corner and there was Father John's round blue eye looking at her! She quickly lifted off the stone and Father John came out very Dusty and Cobwebby. He mopped his face with his handkerchief.

"Well, my dear, I mean Your Majesty," he said, "now how about getting out of this Ghastly Hole?"

"I would like to go now, really," said Alice. "It will soon be Dark."

So Alice popped down the hole, and they pulled the stone over the place (it made rather a scraping noise), and they hurried away down the tunnel. But an Unlucky thing happened.

The Dungeon Keeper just happened to be passing the door when he heard a Scraping Noise, and he stopped.

"I wonder what that Queen Alice is up to in there?" he said to himself, and he opened the door with his Jangling Key and looked inside. No Alice!

"Well!" said the Dungeon Keeper, "well, I *say*! Goodness me!" and he looked about, and he saw the loose stone. He shouted for the other Dungeon Keepers, and they all came, and they got down into the Tunnel and hurried after Alice and Father John!

After a few minutes Alice and Father John came out of the end of the tunnel into a cornfield, and they could hear the Dungeon Keepers coming after them, shouting and Jangling their Keys.

"Now, m'dear, I mean Your Majesty," said Father John, "I will go on along the path and the Dungeon Keepers will follow me. You stay among the corn, and they will pass you. If they catch me, I'll say I'm just going for a walk or something!"

So he went off down the path beside the cornfield, and Alice popped into the tall corn and stood as still as a mouse! She'd only just got settled when the Dungeon Keepers rushed out of the end of the tunnel, shouting and Jangling their Keys, and they ran down the path after Father John.

Alice carefully peered about. No one to be seen! So she

quietly went across the cornfield towards a town called Canossa, where there was a Fort. The Commander of the Fort was a man called Atto, and he was a very good friend of Queen Alice's, and she thought that perhaps she could stay with him until her luck changed. But Canossa (the town where the Fort was) was a long way off, and it was getting very Dark and Alice kept on walking and walking, and the ground got wetter and wetter, until she had no Idea where she was, and she was Lost! She thought that she had better keep on walking because (although she was lost) the farther she walked the farther she would be from the Dungeon by the lake!

But when it was Quite Dark a Terrible Thing happened! Suddenly the ground got much softer and wetter, and Alice's foot went Right In. Then her other foot went in past her knee, and she couldn't get it out! Alice was so frightened that she just stood quite still without moving, and she sank deeper and deeper, until both her legs were Right In.

"I'm in a Marsh!" she said to herself. "What *shall* I do? By the time it is the morning I shall have sunk so far that it will be past my Head and I shall be Drowned in Mud!"

The mud was very cold and clammy, and when Alice tried to move her feet it made horrible loud Sucking noises, and Frogs and things came plopping about, frightening Alice out of her Wits. (Your Wits are your natural Intelligence, or the Sense you were Born With. Do you know the story of Epaminondas who hadn't got the Sense he was Born with?)

After a long time Alice was as deep as her Middle, and she was freezing cold. But still she hadn't thought of what to do. I expect that by now you will have thought of her Guardian Angel, haven't you? But poor Alice, having Lost her Wits, never thought of anything at all.

Then God, who is always so Kind, was sorry for Alice, and He put a thought into her head and this was the thought:

"*What* about my Guardian Angel? Why didn't I think of him before? I must have lost my Wits!" And she said to her Guardian Angel:

"Please, my Good Angel, whom God has appointed to be my Guardian, watch over me during this night! I am so sorry that I forgot you, but I was in such a Fright that I couldn't think of anything at all."

And then she waited and waited for her Guardian Angel to help her. You see, however good a person is (and after all Alice was a Saint), they can't do *anything at all* without God. So Alice couldn't even think of her Guardian Angel until God gave her the thought. Did you know that if God stopped thinking about you for One Second you wouldn't be there at all? Neither would the trees in the garden, nor your dog or anything that is alive, because God is Life as well as Everything else.

After some time Alice saw a little Little Light moving about, and it came nearer and nearer, and went this way and that, until she began to hear little Splashing noises and Bumping noises, and then she heard a cough!

"Hello!" she shouted. "Please come this way, whoever you are! I am stuck in a Marsh!"

The light came nearer and nearer, and there was a Fisherman in a Boat!

"Whatever are you doing there, Miss?" he said in a Surprised voice. "You'll get your Death of Cold!"

And he pulled Alice out, all covered with slippery Mud, and got her into the boat.

"Lucky for you that I came this way, Miss," he said, and he covered Alice up with some nets, which was better than nothing. "I only come this way Tuesdays as a rule, and it's Friday today. I really don't know what made me alter my mind."

"It was my Guardian Angel," said Alice. "He was Watching Over me during the Night." And she rubbed off some of the mud with a piece of Fishing Net.

"Well, I never saw anything of him, if he did, Miss," said the Fisherman. "But it was very kind of him, I'm sure."

So Alice went home with the Fisherman, and the Fisherman's wife dried Alice and washed her clothes and put her to bed with a bowl of Hot Bread and Milk to keep out the cold. In the morning she *was* surprised to see that the poor muddy girl called Alice was really Queen Alice! She talked about it for years and years afterwards.

So many other things happened to Alice that there wouldn't be room in the book for anyone else if I told you any more. But when she got married again she had a Son, and when he grew up he married a Greek Princess who was Incredibly Beautiful, and who had a Feathered Harness for her horse and had hundreds of Jewels and Pearls, and wore her hair in a Golden Net. But she wasn't very nice to Alice, I must say.

Alice's Special Day is on December 16th, and anyone whose Birthday is on that day can have her for their Special Saint, but specially someone that I know whose name is Alice Mary.

St. Bonita

Once upon a time there was a Goose Girl who lived in the Auvergnes in France and her name was Bonita. Every day it was her work to lead fifty-seven geese out to the good pasture where the fine short grass grew, not too dry, not too wet. She never drove her geese, because all geese would rather follow than be driven. If you walk along in front of them, they follow after you in a long line, single-file, but if you drive them they bunch together and tread on each other's feet, and squawk.

Well, Bonita took all her geese out every day, as I said before, and she used to sit and knit or just daydream in the sun until it was time to take them home. She could not read (not many people could in those days), but her father had given her a picture book of Saints, and she often used to take it out with her. She could tell who each of the saints was by the little hints that the artist put in for people who could not read.

I am sure I remember telling you about them before, but I will remind you of one or two. St. Blaise with a Pig, St. Lucy with her Eyes on a plate (why?), St. Cecilia playing an Organ, St. Angela with a ladder going straight up out of the middle of a field, St. Philip Benizi with a Pope's crown on the ground by his feet, St. Frances with her Guardian Angel and a Pen. You can think of plenty more of them. Every saint has a Little Something so that you can tell who they all are.

Bonita always liked a picture of St. Julian. (There are a lot of St. Julians, but this one had his house by a wide River, and he used to ferry people across.) She used to think about St. Julian most of them all, living all by himself for a penance, and how he, as well as St. Christopher, looks after travelers. She used to talk to him about her geese.

One very wet summer Bonita was taking her geese out as usual, and she thought it would be a nice change for them if she took them down to the stream for a swim. It was a narrow little stream at the bottom of the valley, and she could easily paddle over or even jump across in some places. They hadn't been down there for some time because it was Rather far Away and there mightn't be time to get back if it Rained very hard. (It was a wet summer, you remember?) When she got halfway down the hill with the geese all strung out behind her she saw that the heavy rain had flooded the stream. It was quite half a mile wide in places. Very deep, it must have been, in a small valley. She quickly turned to take the geese back up the hill, but she was too late! The geese had seen the lovely new lake, and with loud Cacklings and Honkings they spread their wings and taxied down the hill and into the water. All fifty-seven of them. It *was* a nice change for them—they had never seen so much water. They dived and bathed and stood up flapping their wings. They stood on their heads and they zoomed about, half flying and half swimming. They loved it. Bonita couldn't think how she could ever get them all out again. If only she could get to the other side, she thought, she could at least stop them from getting out of the water on the Far Bank and wandering right away out of sight.

"Oh, what *can* I do?" she said to her friend St. Julian. "Do tell me what to do! I must get to the other side somehow. Could you help me, do you think?"

Suddenly there was a Great Wind, so strong that it lifted Bonita into the air and sailed her across the flood like a bird. She landed on her feet on the Far Side rather out of breath. And with the corner of her eye she *just* caught sight of her Guardian Angel before he disappeared!

"*Well*," said Bonita to herself, "that was sudden, and no mistake!" She shoved one or two geese who were coming ashore back into the water and then sat down to collect her wits. As she looked around she remembered that there was a little Chapel hereabouts, hidden among some trees. She had never been in it because it was usually too far away.

"I think I'll just go and say thank you to Our Lord and my Guardian Angel and St. Julian for sailing me over so beautifully," she thought. So she made sure no geese were coming in to land on the wrong side and then went to the chapel which was just behind her. She went in and made her prayer of thankyous. When she came out she was still too surprised to think quite straight, but she was much less breathless.

"I wonder who this Chapel is dedicated to," she said to herself. "I think I'd better find out and say thankyou to whoever it is, because it was nice to find a chapel so handy."

She went back inside the Chapel and looked around. And there, just inside the door, was a very big picture of St. Julian! The Chapel was dedicated to him. Wasn't that a good coincidence?

Bonita wondered how ever she was going to get the geese and herself back to the right side of the Flood. She waited and wondered until it was nearly Dark. Then she saw somebody far

away on the other side dragging something big and heavy. The man came right down to the edge of the water, and then she could just make out that it was her father, with a Boat.

He rowed across, and Bonita waved to him each time he turned his head to see where he was going. She met him at the edge of the water.

"Well, Bonita!" he said. "We wondered why you were so late. I went up the hill to look for you, but I couldn't find you."

"I thought the geese would like a swim," said Bonita. "I didn't know there was a flood."

"Neither did I," said her father, "until I came this way. How ever did you get over? You are perfectly Dry, even your Shoes!"

Bonita told him all about it as he rowed her back to the other side, and he said that wonders would never cease.

When they had got out of the boat and pulled it well up out of the water in case it Rose again, Bonita was still worrying about how she could get the geese away from the water and back to their warm sheds for the night. They were still enjoying themselves very much and she was sure they would rather stay out. But it wasn't safe because of the foxes.

"Ah," said her father, "your mother's got all that Planned Out. Here she comes, see!"

And Bonita's mother came down the hill carrying the big bucket with the geese's supper in it. Usually they had it in their sheds just before they were shut up for the night. She stood at the edge of the water and clattered the long iron spoon against the side of the bucket. Well, you can guess what happened. All the geese came gossiping and swimming over for their supper, and as they began to come out of the water she turned and walked slowly up the hill with all the geese cackling around her, stretching their long necks, trying to get a mouthful. Not until they were all safely in their sheds did Bonita's mother let them have their supper. By that time they had forgotten all about the lake, because their swim had made them so hungry.

St. Bonita's Special Day is October 16th. I made this story for all the people in America who are called Bonnie. In England I don't think we use that name at all. There's another French saint called St. Bona who would do very well, too, but I like St. Bonita best.

St. Margaret

Once upon a time there was a Queen of Scotland called Margaret and she was very Kind. And the King's name was Malcolm.

One of Queen Margaret's favorite things to do was to feed hungry people and to give clothes to people who hadn't got any. So that all the Prisoners and Beggars and Poor-and-Raggies used to be going to the back door of the Palace all day and every day. And every morning, just before Lunch, the Queen used to come out and see what they all wanted and give it to them, and King Malcolm used to help her.

One day, two men were having a drink in an Hotel and One said to the Other:

"Aren't we Lucky to have such a Nice King-and-Queen?"

"Why?" asked the other man, who was all Against Kings and Queens.

"Well," said the Nice man, "whoever goes to the Palace, Man, Woman or Child, Friend or Enemy, Rich or Poor, Ill or Well, Tired or Strong, they give them things to eat, or clothes or bandages or somewhere to sleep, or whatever it is that they want."

"Rubbish!" said the Nasty man, "I don't believe it. Have you *seen* them do it?"

"Well, no," said the Nice man, "I haven't actually *seen* them *do* it, but some Other People told me that they had seen them."

"Aha!" said the Nasty Man, "there you are! I expect the King-and-Queen *paid* those other people to say how Kind they were! Kings are never nice, nor are Queens."

"Well, if you don't believe me, go and see for yourself," said the Nice Man Rather Huffily.

"All right, don't be Cross with me," said the Nasty Man. "I'll go tomorrow. Have another drink?"

"Thank you. I don't mind if I do," said the Nice man. And he did.

The next morning the Nasty Man, who was Fairly Rich, dressed up as a Poor-and-Raggy. Then he made his face all dirty, and then he picked up a Sharp Heavy Stone and dropped it on his foot and made a nasty Bruise and Skin-up on it. He did this so that the King-and-Queen would be sorry for him if they really did come and see all the Poor People.

When he got to Dunfermline, which was where the Palace was, he saw a Crowd of Ill and Poor and Generally Dilapidated People outside the back door, and he waited with them.

When the Stable Clock struck Twelve the back door opened and out came a man and a woman in workmen's clothes, carrying baskets of food and things.

"There you are!" the Nasty Man thought to himself; "you see, the King-and-Queen don't Bother to do anything themselves, they just send their Shabbiest Servants." And he Stamped on the ground because he was so Angry, and he quite forgot it was the Sore foot that he was Stamping with until he had Stamped with it, and that made him more Angry than ever!

While he was doing this, the man and the woman were walking about and Looking After the People. They gave bread-and-butter and Cocoa to some, and new Shoes and Hats to others, and they Bandaged Up the ones with cuts and things.

Soon the man came to the Nasty Man.

"What can I do for you, my poor Friend?" he said.

"I'm no friend of yours!" said the Nasty Man rudely. "I don't have Servants for my friends! But if you want to know, I've hurt my foot." And he showed the man his Sore Foot, which felt much Worse since it had been Stamped with.

"Don't touch it!" he said. "I'd rather the woman did it, she might be more Careful than you. It hurts Very Much."

"All right," said the man. "Here are some Potted Meat Sandwiches. When you have eaten them the Queen will come and do your Foot."

The Nasty Man Stared! Then he said to a Poor-and-Raggy who was beside him:

"Who was that man I was just talking to?"

"It was King Malcolm, of course," said the Poor-and Raggy; "who did you think it was?"

"I thought that they wouldn't Bother to come themselves,"

said the Nasty Man in a Sorry Voice.

Soon Queen Margaret came and Knelt in front of him:

"Let me see your poor foot," she said, and she washed it and Bandaged it Up with some Pink Gauze and some White Bandage.

"There you are!" she said as she tied the Bandage. "Goodbye, and God Bless you!"

"Not till I've said I'm very Sorry, Your Majesty," said the Nasty Man, who wasn't so bad at Heart. "I always thought Kings-and-Queens were Grand and Haughty. I was very rude to King Malcolm when I didn't know who he was."

"That's all right," said Queen Margaret. "Are you that Man who was fighting against us Last Year?"

"Yes," said the Man-who-wasn't-Nasty-any-more, "but I hoped you didn't know that."

"Never mind," said Queen Margaret. "The King wants you to Stay the Night, now that you are here."

So the Man-who-wasn't-Nasty-any-more Stayed the Night, and when he went away next morning he couldn't help telling everybody how Specially Nice Queen Margaret and King Malcolm were! Not like before he went!

Queen Margaret did lots of other things, like riding over a River buckled on to a Horse, and things like that, but you can find them in another book. But one thing I will tell you, and that is that in Edinburgh, near the Castle, is a little Chapel, and it is Nine Hundred and Something Years Old. And it is called St. Margaret's Chapel, and it is the one she used to go to Church in. It has very small windows and very thick walls, so perhaps that is why it has Lasted so Long.

St. Margaret's Special Day is on June 10th usually. But some people in Scotland have it on November 16th as well, because she is so Special for them.

ST. MARGARET

Scotland was a happy land
When Margaret was Queen,
Poor folk were better cared for
Than they have often been.

So when she went to Heaven,
She was asked to mind
The poor souls leaving Purgatory,
Because she is so kind.

They come out very tattered,
And tired and sore.
She gives them tea and comforts them,
As she did before.

And combs their hair and washes
The smoky marks away,
And sends them into glory
A thousand a day.

St. Irene

(Now this Story isn't at all Exciting, but it is very Interesting, because it is about Two Plans. And at the end you will be able to choose which of the Two Plans you like best.)

Once upon a time there was a Princess of Hungary, and her name was Princess Irene, and she married a man called John the Beautiful, because he was so Handsome.

After their Honeymoon, and when they had settled down at home, Princess Irene and John the Beautiful were sitting in the Garden after breakfast. They were throwing bits of bread to the birds and talking about the different ways that they could Know and Love and Serve God in this world, and be happy with Him forever in the next world (which is Heaven).

"I do think that we ought to make some sort of a Plan," said Irene, and she threw an extra fat piece of bread to a Rather Shy bird.

"Well, we both love God more than anyone else," said John the Beautiful, "so I should think that to start with we could build a Chapel in the garden. Then we could live very near the Blessed Sacrament, and be able to go and visit Our Lord lots of times a day, so that He could help us with the Plan if we got in a Muddle."

"Yes, let's do that first," said Irene. "Some people," she said, "are Monks and Nuns and spend *all* their time for God, and have nothing at all for themselves."

"But *we* couldn't," said John the Beautiful, "because we are Married."

"Well, we could if we both wanted to and the Pope said we could," said Irene.

"But we don't want to," said John the Beautiful, "and God *likes* people to be married, and to live in their houses, and garden in their gardens, and have children in the nursery, and look after their dogs and things."

"But perhaps He would rather that they were Monks and Nuns," said Irene, "because it is so happy to be married that people might forget God."

"It couldn't really be like that," said John the Beautiful, "because God specially made Two Sacraments for the way we live. One of them is Marriage, so that people can use and enjoy all the things that God has invented for them, and have children so that they can know about God, too. The other one is Holy Orders, which is for Priests. And Nuns and things give up everything in the world for a Sacrifice, and spend all their time for God. People can choose which way they will live. God likes to have some of each."

"Oh, yes," said Princess Irene, "and the Two Sorts can't do without each other. The people with Holy Orders, like Priests, teach us and give us the Sacraments, and the Monks and Nuns pray for the people who forget to pray for themselves, so we couldn't get on without *them*."

"And the Marriage people," said John the Beautiful, "grow

the food and make the clothes and the machinery, and build the houses and the Churches and have the children, and all that, so of Course we couldn't do without *them*!"

"Well," said Irene, "we can serve God just as much when we are married, but not in the same way as the people in Holy Orders."

"Of course we can," said John the Beautiful. "God made the world and everything in it for us to enjoy. All the things in it remind us of Him, and so we go on loving Him more and more."

"Don't let us both have the same Plan," said Irene; "let's be different, and then we'll be able to tell each other how we get on."

"All right," said John the Beautiful, and so it was settled.

John's Plan was that he would Serve God by doing things for His people. (Because you remember that God said that if you do things for people because you love God, then God counts that as doing it for Him.) So John farmed his farms and gardened in his garden and sailed in his boat and rode his horses and did it all because God is Good. He gave his extra milk and corn to poor people who hadn't got any. And he grew extra vegetables and flowers and gave them to the Hospital, and he sailed his boat because God has made the Sea and the Wind and the Sun so strong that John thought that it just showed how Strong God must be. And that made him so happy that he used to sing louder than the Wind and the Waves. And he built the Chapel in the garden, so that he and Irene could go to Holy Communion every morning, and hear what God had to say to them.

All the people in the village loved John the Beautiful, and

they liked to see him riding by on his big horse, and they all ran out and waved to him as he passed, and John thought to himself:

"They can't all be running out just to see *me*. It must be my Big Shining Horse." And so he polished his harness and put shining Silver medals on it, and put Ribbons in his horse's mane, so that the people would have something to look at. Then he put on a Golden Silk Cloak and rode through the Village. All the people clapped and cheered, not because of the Horses and the Cloak, but because they loved John. But he never thought of that, because he was thinking about how good God is.

"Well!" said John when he got home, "that *was* a Success! I think I'd better put on splendid clothes every time I go out to see about Roofs and Drains and Extra Milk and things." And he did, and he went about Enjoying everything.

"It would be disappointing for God," he thought, "when He makes all these things and no one even Notices them. And I must say God has given me everything, because no one could have nicer neighbors than I have, and no one *could* have a nicer Wife than my Princess Irene."

Now Irene was Shy, and she didn't want to Serve God by serving her neighbors, because she never knew what to say to them, and so she made a different Plan.

"I know what I will do," she said. "I will spend all my Spare Time with God so as to make up to Him for all the people who forget Him. And I will collect all the Sacrifices I can, and give them to Him to try to make up for all that He has done for us."

So Irene used to wear Rather Plain clothes so that no one would notice her, and she used to Sew and Knit things for the

Poor-and-Raggies, and she used to send food and fruit and cake and soup and things to the Hospital, and all that. But no one ever knew who did the knitting and the sewing.

Irene was very busy in her house, because she had some children, and she made their clothes, and she made the jam and she stored the fruit, and all the time she gave all her work to God, and when she got tired she gave Him her tiredness for a Sacrifice. And always she thought how kind God was to give her such a nice Family.

"No one could have nicer children than I have," she said, "and no one *could* have such a good and Handsome Husband." And all through the day, whenever she had a minute to spare, she used to visit the Blessed Sacrament, and God told her things. But whenever John went Sailing, Irene went, too, because she loved the Sun and the Wind.

After supper John and Irene used to compare notes, and tell each other about the things that they had been doing.

"Your way is best, though," said Irene to John, "because you make so many people happy."

"No, *your* way is best," said John the Beautiful, "because all your ornaments are inside, and all the things that you do are secrets between you and God. Our Lord said that we ought to do it like that, and lay up Treasure in Heaven."

"Anyway, whosesoever way is the best, you are the nicest person in the world," said Princess Irene.

"No, you are!" said John the Beautiful, and they both laughed.

I wonder which Plan you like best? It doesn't matter which, because there have to be some of each.

St. Irene's Special Day is on August 13th, and anyone who

has her Birthday on that day, as well as all the Irenes, can have
her for their Special Saint.

✓ *St. Christine*

Once upon a time there was a girl called Christine and she
lived in Belgium with her two older sisters and they were
Orphans.

Now Christine was a great Trial to her sisters because she
was very venturesome and disobedient. To make things worse
she was quite an acrobat, and besides that she could make
her voice seem to come from any part of the room without
moving her mouth at all. (This is called Ventriloquism and
sometimes you can see people doing it on Television.) Her
sisters were rather ashamed of her Tomboy ways and they sent
her to look after the cattle to keep her out of the way.

There was a watermill near the place where the cows came
to drink, and Christine loved to let herself go down the narrow
channel and be whirled round by the big wooden wheel and
come up again in the foamy pool at the bottom. She must have
been very small and thin, because she never hurt herself. It was
a long time before anyone saw her doing this, but when they
did she was stopped at once because it was so dangerous.

"You only do it to draw attention to yourself," said her sisters.

"We are ashamed of you!"

"I *don't*," said Christine. "I do it because I like doing it. It's a lovely feeling when you whirl under the water round the wheel."

"It's a wonder you haven't been drowned or squashed," they said, "and if you do it again we will have to keep you locked up."

Christine was frightened at this, because above all things she loved to be free.

"If I am locked up, I might as well be in Purgatory," she thought. "I think that I should die of it."

This made her think of all the poor souls in Purgatory, who must wait until all the dirtiness of sin is cleaned away before they can go to Heaven.

"They must feel awful," thought Christine. "They are longing and longing to see God and they can't until their souls are perfectly clean." And she used to pray for the souls in Purgatory that their time there might be shorter and that they could go to God for ever.

As she grew older she thought more and more about Purgatory and she used to go without many things for the sake of the souls there.

"Let me do some of their suffering for them, dear Lord," she used to say. "Let me share with them and help them to get to Heaven quickly."

But although she gave up a lot of things for the Holy Souls and prayed a great deal, she was never Solemn or Staid. God had made her a cheerful and happy person and she was.

There was a Convent near the house where Christine and her sisters lived, and the nuns used to give Sylvia her meals there when her sisters were too cross to have anything to do with her. Once she gave the nuns a great shock by rolling herself up like a hedgehog and rolling along the passage, but they couldn't help laughing. And she used to play tricks on them by making her voice come out of dark corners. After they had got over their fright they used to laugh because it really was very clever to be able to do it. They loved Christine and she always obeyed the Reverend Mother, but very few other people.

Christine was great friends with all the children round about because she knew so many stories and tricks, but none of them could learn to make their voices come from somewhere else.

When she was old enough she left her cross sisters and lived in huts and sheds and farm buildings or wherever anyone would let her stay. But we don't know much about what she did until she was old.

When she was quite old she once saw the Baron of the Castle resting by the roadside with his soldiers. They had been marching home for days, and they were enjoying a picnic meal before marching the last few miles. Christine stopped and looked at the Baron, who was no better than he should be.

"What a very Handsome man you are, Sir!" she said.

"Aha!" laughed the soldiers. "Listen to the compliments! How do you like praise from such a raggy old woman, my Lord?"

"She isn't praising me, but God who made me," said the Baron. "I didn't make my own face!"

The soldiers stared in surprise. He was a bit surprised himself that he should have said such a thing.

"Quite right," said Christine as she turned away. "But you should love Him better than you do, for giving you such a beautiful face."

The Baron always understood Christine, and he saw through all her Acrobatics and Nonsense to her unselfish and loving soul. But he didn't mend his ways until a long time afterwards, and that was when he was dying of a wounded chest that he got in a battle with the French people.

He sent for a servant:

"Go and tell Christine that I want to see her, if she will come," he said.

"*Christine?*" said the servant in surprise. He thought his master must have lost his wits because of his wound. "But, my

Lord, she is a raggy old thing, you can't want to see *her*. People say she must be mad to live as she does."

"*She* isn't mad," said the Baron. "But I sometimes think that *we* are. Go and bring her to me."

So Christine came and sat with the Baron and they talked together about everything under the sun and about God and prayer and death. They talked all the afternoon, and then the Baron asked for a priest to come and he made his Confession and had the Last Sacraments. That evening he died and Christine prayed for him while he was in Purgatory.

When she was very old, the Reverend Mother of the Convent (whose name was Mother Beatrice) made her come and live in the Convent, where she would be warm and would have proper meals. She made up a little bed for Christine in her own room and looked after her very kindly till she died. On the day that she died a very Unusual thing happened and this is what it was:

In the evening Mother Beatrice asked Christine to tell her the secret of how she had learned to know and love God so well.

"Tell me, Christine. I am sure you know something that I do not. Tell me before you go. It will help us all to be better nuns."

Christine lay quite still with her eyes shut and did not answer, and Reverend Mother thought she was praying. So she went down to get her a hot drink for her supper. When she came back with it, Christine was dead.

"Christine!" said Reverend Mother Beatrice. "Why did you go without saying goodbye to all the Sisters who are your good friends? That was very unkind of you! Come back at once!

You have always obeyed me, and I tell you to come back." And she called the other nuns.

Christine opened her eyes again and said:

"Reverend Mother, you shouldn't have called me back from Heaven, it is a glorious place. But I have always obeyed you, so here I am."

Then she said Goodbye to all the nuns and asked Reverend Mother to come near. She whispered a Secret in her ear, and then she died again. We do not know what the secret was because Mother Beatrice never told anyone. Perhaps Christine told her not to.

St. Christine's Special Day is July 24th, and thousands of people are called after her. In Belgium they have a holiday on her Feast Day. Anyone whose name is Christina or Kirsty or Christian or Christabel can have her for their Saint.

√ St. Ida

Once upon a time there was a girl called Ida and she lived in Cologne in Germany. When she grew up she married a count whose name was Henry and went away with him to live in his castle in a place called Toggenburg. (I once had a goat who came from Toggenburg. She was brown and white and her name was Bobolink.)

Now Henry loved Ida very much, but he was a jealous man with an Impossible Temper. He was jealous of anyone who even spoke to Ida, and so she had a very lonely life for years, and then some extraordinary things happened to her.

One day, when Henry was out hunting and Ida was, as usual, all by herself, she thought she would remind herself of happier days. So she went up to her bedroom and took out all her Wedding Things, her lovely silk embroidered dress and the beautiful lace wedding veil and her little white shoes. She took them all out and laid them on her bed. Then she took out all her jewelry. (Henry had given her a lot in all the years they had been married.) And she cleaned and polished it all and set it out beside her wedding things. It made her homesick to look at it all, but it did look lovely. Then, just before she went down to lunch, she slipped off her Wedding Ring and put it on her white wedding prayerbook, which lay on her pillow. It just Completed the Picture.

After lunch there were quite a lot of household things to see to, and then Henry came home for his supper, rather hungry and tired. When she had soothed him down with a delicious meal and a comfortable chair and a blazing fire, she remembered all the things still spread out in her room. She thought she had better go and tidy up before they went to bed. So up she went to her room, shut the windows, drew the curtains, lighted the lamp and put away her jewelry in all its little cases. Then she started on the wedding things. She carefully folded her dress and veil and put away her gloves and slippers. Then, just as she was going to pick up her prayerbook, she noticed that her wedding ring wasn't there! She looked everywhere. She got out her dress and veil again and shook them, and she looked in her gloves and slippers. She looked to see if it had fallen behind the pillow or under the bed. It simply wasn't anywhere at all. She went downstairs again, but she didn't say anything to Henry, because of his Impossible Temper, and when the fire died down they went up to bed.

Well, time went on and Henry didn't notice that her wedding ring was missing and Ida didn't mention it in case she found it again. She wore another ring so that her finger didn't feel so bare.

One day, her Groom who looked after her horses and whose name was Otto was walking through the forest when he saw a large untidy nest. It was a jackdaw's nest half in and half out of a hole in a tree. He climbed up to see if the eggs had hatched, but they hadn't. But there, under three pretty eggs, was a Wedding Ring! Of course he didn't know whose it was. He did not even know that Ida had lost hers. So he put it on his little finger with rather a tight squeeze, climbed down the tree and went back to the Castle. At supper in the big kitchen, Otto told all the Castle servants about the nest, and he showed them the ring.

"Those jackdaws will steal anything that glitters," he said. "But this looks like real solid gold."

Now Henry's Groom, Franz, *did* recognize the Ring, because it had a deep scratch on it. He didn't like Ida and he didn't like any of her servants. He thought that things had been far better long ago, before Henry got married. In those days he could have everything his own way, but nowadays, what with Ida and her servants in the Castle, things were not at all the same. He was a cross man and always out to make trouble, so he told his master Henry at once that Otto was wearing Ida's

wedding ring.

Henry went into one of his Impossible Rages and sent for Otto.

"Show me your hands!" he shouted

Otto, wondering what it was all about, held out his hands.

"That's my wife's wedding ring!" roared Henry.

"Is it, Sir?" said Otto. "How very lucky! I found it this afternoon, in a nest!"

"That I *don't* believe!" Henry shouted again, and before Otto could get out of the way he drew his sword and killed him. Then, without stopping for a second, he rushed up to Ida's room and picked her up and threw her out of the window into a deep ravine that was at the bottom of the cliff the castle stood on. It was quite three hundred feet down, which is a very long way to be flying through the air.

Well, Ida's guardian angel must have been on the lookout, because the trees at the bottom of the ravine saved her from being killed. But she was so frightened that she simply daren't go back to the Castle. She had no idea at all why Henry was so angry. So after wandering about a bit she found a cave near the stream at the bottom of the ravine, and there she lived for years. Mostly she ate blaeberries (some people call them blueberries and others call them whortleberries and some others call them bilberries. I call them blaeberries. I wonder what you call them? Anyway they are all the same thing.) When the blaeberries were over there were wild parsnips and blackberries and crab apples to roast beside her fire. In the Spring there were birds' eggs too, but she knew it was wrong to take the eggs, so she only took one from each nest when she was really *very* hungry. After all, she had to eat something.

And every day she prayed for Henry and his Impossible Temper.

"He couldn't really help it, dear Lord," she said very often. "Really he couldn't. He is a man with a Terrible Temper and sometimes he loses it altogether."

That was all very well. But look what his Temper had made him do. He had killed Otto, and it wasn't his doing that he hadn't killed Ida as well. But she never mentioned that kind of thing to God. She still loved her husband, but she really dared not go back to him if he was likely to behave in the same sort of way again. She used to watch in the forest to see if she could see him out hunting, but she never did. And she wondered if Otto might find her when he was out exercising her horses. She didn't know he was dead.

When Henry recovered the temper he had lost he was most dreadfully upset at what he had done. He thought, of course, that he had killed Ida when he threw her out of the window. After a time he found he couldn't bear to live in the Castle any more because everything in it reminded him of his wickedness and of his dear wife. Because, in spite of what he had done to her, he did love her. He still had not found out what a Trouble-maker his servant Franz was, and he took him traveling all over Europe to try to forget his Misery. But you can't run away from yourself, and Henry's misery traveled with him. At last he came home, but he went out hunting all day and every day to make himself too tired to lie awake at night.

After five years had gone by one of the old Huntsmen twisted his foot in the forest. He went down to the ravine below the castle to bathe it in the cold stream before he tied it up to walk home. He sat down on a rock near a cave, and he was quietly holding his foot in the water when he saw someone watching him from the bushes. Being a Huntsman and used to wild animals, he kept very still, so as not to frighten whoever it was, and he watched out of the corner of his eye. Soon the person moved and crept towards the cave behind him. He pretended not to see anything, but he did see a thin, ragged woman with long hair. And she was wearing a piece of torn blue silk among the rags.

"That's the Countess Ida's dress," he thought. "I am sure it is the same. It's a very unusual kind of blue." He tied up his foot and got up quietly and walked away, and he never once looked over his shoulder, because he was a very good Huntsman.

As soon as he got back to the Castle he went straight to Henry.

"Sir, I do believe that the Lady Ida is still alive," he said.

"Nonsense!" said Henry "She couldn't be after such a fall. Anyway she would have come back."

"It doesn't sound possible I know, Sir," said the Huntsman, "but I do really think it might be."

Henry didn't think it *could* be true, but he did very much hope that it might be. He still loved Ida and was wretchedly unhappy about all that he had done. At last he went down to the ravine all alone, just in case it was true. And there he saw Ida in her rags, coming out of her cave, and at the same time she saw him. They fell into each other's arms and were too happy even to speak to each other.

Henry took her home, and after a bath and some clean clothes Ida felt more like her old self. But she had lived alone for so long that she never became used to talking very much again.

But all the same, she and Henry were very happy.

And God had answered all her years of prayers for Henry, and all her years of Patience and Forgiveness weren't wasted, because he never *quite* lost his temper again.

Ida lived with him in their castle until he died, and then, because she was still a very quiet person who had learned to know and love God when she was in her cave, she went to a convent and was a nun until she was very old, and died too.

St. Ida's Special Day is May 30th, and very few people in England are called after her, but plenty of Germans and Italians are, and Americans too. I made this story specially for a girl named Frances who lives in Pittsburgh and who wanted it for her sister Ida.

St. Elizabeth of Hungary

Once upon a time there was a Princess called Elizabeth and she was Four Years Old. She lived in Hungary, but she had to go to another place called Thuringia, because when she grew up she was going to marry Prince Ludwig of Thuringia and be Princess Elizabeth of Thuringia.

Elizabeth was very pleased and excited at going such a long way all by herself, but her Mother, the Queen of Hungary, was sad to lose her only little girl so soon. However, she was very Brave, and she gave Elizabeth some new clothes and new toys and a Velvet Coat, and a Silver Mug with her name on it.

Now Thuringia was more than a Hundred Miles from Hungary and Elizabeth was much too little to ride all the way on horseback like everybody else did, so what do you suppose she went in? A Silver Cradle! It was hung between two horses. One was called Lac (which means Milk) because he was white, and the other was called Mel (which means Honey) because he was pale brown. It was rather like a Hammock, and Elizabeth sat inside. She had Blue Silk pillows and a Red Velvet cover with E for Elizabeth on it, and she had a little Gold crown on her head.

Behind Lac and Mel followed twelve other horses, all carrying things. One carried Elizabeth's Silver Bath; another Jewels; and another Silk and Satin to make her clothes when she got older. Sometimes Lac went a little faster than Mel, and that made the Cradle swing, and Elizabeth loved it!

When they arrived at Thuringia it was Long After Bedtime, and as soon as she had had a quick supper of milk and biscuits she was put to bed. Prince Ludwig's mother, Queen Sophia, slept with her the first night, in case she was frightened, but after that she slept with Princess Agnes, who was Four Years Old, too, and was Prince Ludwig's little sister.

Elizabeth, when she grew older, used to read a lot to herself about Our Lord, and she Loved Him very much, but Queen Sophia and Agnes did not know Him very well.

One day (it was the 15th of August, a day when we all go to Church) the Queen told the two Princesses to put on their Best Rich Dresses and their Crowns and to go to Mass with her. There were other Kings and Queens with crowns on there, and

Queen Sophia took Elizabeth and Agnes to the Very Front seat, and sat there all Stiff and Proud between them.

After a little while Elizabeth took off her crown and knelt down. Queen Sophia was so angry that she said quite loud: "What *are* you doing, Elizabeth? Kings and Queens don't kneel, they are too Important, and put on your crown at *once!*"

"I am very sorry," said Elizabeth, "but how can I sit and be Grand and Proud when Our Lord is here, and how can I keep on my Golden Crown when He only has a Crown of Thorns? He is much more Important than us because we *are* only People, even if we are Kings and Queens."

Queen Sophia got Very Red, but she didn't say anything, and she kept her crown on and went on being Grand and Proud, because she had forgotten that Our Lord was so *much* more Important than Kings and Queens with Crowns On

After Elizabeth was grown up she married Queen Sophia's son, Prince Ludwig, and she loved him and he was very kind to her and gave her a Rosary made of Coral, and a Penknife with E for Elizabeth on it. But Queen Sophia didn't like her because she made her feel Ashamed when she always would take off her crown in Church.

One day Elizabeth had been out to see an old man who was ill in the village. She had taken him two Red Blankets because he had not enough bed-clothes, and some bread and some Honey for his sore Throat, and some Cocoa. He loved cocoa because it Reminded him of Chocolates. She was just coming back along the road, rather Late for Dinner and wondering what Queen Sophia would say, when she saw a man lying by the hedge. She went and looked at him to see if he was all right, because people who lie beside roads have sometimes been Run

Over or something, and then she saw that he had Leprosy very badly. Now in those days Leprosy was supposed to be a very Catching Illness and Elizabeth was afraid she might catch it and give it to her children, so she did not touch him for a minute, while she stood and thought; and this is what she thought:

"What shall I do? Because if I give Leprosy to my children it will be a Dreadful Thing, and besides they will give it to everybody else. But I can't Possibly leave this very Ill Man here, because he ought to be in bed. *And*, as he doesn't seem to have a bed of his own, I ought to take him home with me."

In the end she took him home to the Palace, leaning on her arm, and put him to bed in Prince Ludwig's bed because she knew that the servants would be very Angry if she put the raggy old man in one of their beds because of Leprosy being so Catching.

While she was downstairs, seeing about hot water bottles and things, Queen Sophia went into Prince Ludwig's room to put some of his things away—he was rather untidy—and she saw the Ill Man in the bed! At first she was very frightened, because, of course, she thought he must be a Burglar hiding; but the man, who was very glad to be so comfily in bed, smiled at her and said:

"Princess Elizabeth said I could be in this bed because I haven't got a bed of my own, wasn't it Kind of her? She said she was coming back in a minute."

Queen Sophia was Furiously Angry, because of Leprosy being so Catching, and she went and called Prince Ludwig, who was downstairs waiting for dinner, and she made him come upstairs to see.

"Just *look* what Elizabeth has done now!" she cried. "She has brought a Leper here and has put him in your Bed! Do you hear me? In your *Bed!*"

Prince Ludwig looked down at the poor man.

"It is Our Lord Himself," he said quietly, and the old man disappeared!

Our Lord sometimes pretends to be someone else to the people who love Him best, to see if they are really as kind to other people as they say they would be. If they Knew it was Our Lord of *course* they would do anything for Him, but sometimes we can't be Bothered to do things for Ordinary People even though He did say that doing things for them was the same as doing them for Him.

Another very Interesting Thing happened to Elizabeth. It was a very cold winter, and the Village People's corn had not grown properly in the summer before, so they had nothing to eat. Now there was a lot of corn in the Palace Granary, but not enough for Everybody, so Prince Ludwig said that it was no use giving it to Only a Few because it would not be Fair on the Others, and so he told Elizabeth not to give away any at all. But there were some Special People in the village who never had very much to eat anyway, even when there wasn't a Famine, so that now there *was* one they were nearly Starving. So Elizabeth took some of the Palace corn to give them. (Kings and Queens often seem to feed Poor People in the winter when there isn't any corn. Like Joseph did, and Good King Wenceslas did when he Looked Out and saw a Poor Man Gathering Winter Fuel.)

Anyway, Elizabeth was carrying some corn in a big bundle and hoping that no one would see her, when she suddenly met Queen Sophia and Prince Ludwig! Elizabeth was very frightened, because you remember that she had been told *not* to give any corn away. So she said to Our Lord:

"Please don't let them see what is in my Bundle, because then they won't let me have any more, and those poor people will Die of Hunger."

But Queen Sophia said:

"What have you got there, Elizabeth?"

"Roses," said Elizabeth.

"*Roses!*" said Queen Sophia. "In the middle of winter? I don't believe it!" And then she turned to Prince Ludwig and said: "I believe she's got some of the Palace corn when you said she wasn't to."

"Oh," said Prince Ludwig, "I am sure she wouldn't do that. What *have* you got, Elizabeth?"

Poor Elizabeth was more frightened than ever, so that she couldn't even speak. Queen Sophia took hold of her bundle and gave it a Pull to make her drop it, and Elizabeth let go, and down on to the Snow tumbled a great bunch of Roses!

Our Lord did quite a lot of other things for Elizabeth, and she spent all her time doing things for Him, and she built a Hospital for all her Ill People, and it is still called the Hospital of St. Elizabeth.

Her Special Day is the 19th of November, and she still has Hospitals built for her.

St. Clare

Once upon a time there was a girl called Clare who lived in Assisi at the same time that St. Francis was starting the Franciscans. Her family was quite rich and her father was a Nobleman. Clare was very shy, and she only felt really at home with her two sisters, Agnes and Beatrice. All the family were very interested in what Francis was doing and they very often talked about it, and so did everybody else.

"I do wish I could go and help him," said Clare. "There are so many things that women could do. There's Nursing and Looking After Orphans and Teaching Catechism and all that. Men aren't really meant to do those kind of things, are they?"

"But women can't be Friars," said Agnes. (Because Friar means Brother. What is the French for brother?) "And," said Agnes, "there don't seem to be any convents for nuns whose Most Important Rule is to be poor now so as be rich in Heaven."

"But nuns are never really Rich," said Beatrice, "because of their three vows."

"No," said Clare, "but when they go to be nuns they give the convent all their Worldly Goods, and so in the end they all have enough money to buy things for everybody. They buy books and paints and embroidery silk and medicine for poor people and all that."

"Franciscans have nothing at all except the things that people give them," said Agnes. "The brothers have to beg for *everything*, even bread. But women can't do that."

"I know they can't," said Clare, "but I wonder why not?"

She wondered about this for a long time, and she used to ask God what He wanted her to do and whether He thought that Women Franciscans were Impossible. But God didn't answer.

When she was eighteen years old Clare went to Church on Palm Sunday with her father and mother and Agnes and Beatrice. All the time she prayed that God would tell her about asking Francis if she could join him in his work. When the time came for everyone to go up to the altar and receive their palms Clare felt too shy to join the crowd. She sat in her place and watched the people coming and going, and she wished she felt brave enough to go up and get her palm.

The Bishop saw her sitting there, and he knew how shy she was. So, very kindly, when all the other people had their Palms, he came down the Church to where Clare was sitting and gave her her Palm and blessed her, and went back to the altar.

Clare was quite sure that God had answered her at last in this way.

"I must be very poor," she thought. "I must be so poor that I mustn't even ask for a Palm on Palm Sunday. I must wait until I am given it or else go without." And she thanked God for His kind way of answering her prayer.

That evening, wearing her rich silk dress and her pearl earrings and necklace, she went to see Francis. She offered him her jewels to sell for his poor and begged him to let her be a Franciscan.

"I will do absolutely anything you say, if only you will let me," she said.

Well, Francis did not really think it would be a Good Plan because there were not any Women Franciscans at all. But he remembered the parable about the man who kept on asking his neighbor for some bread in the middle of the night. Do you remember how, in the end, the neighbor got up out of bed and went downstairs and found some bread for his friend? So in the end Francis said:

"Well, all right, Clare, you can be a Franciscan if you really want to so much, but you can't live with us. You will have to go and be a Franciscan all by yourself in the Benedictine Convent near your own home."

"Oh, but *Francis!*" said Clare. "I would be a Benedictine then and not a Franciscan at all! *Please* don't send me there!"

But Francis said, rather sternly:

"Clare, you have just said that you would do *absolutely anything* at all if only I would let you join us. And here you are, grumbling away at the very first thing I tell you to do. Go along now, and if you Prove your Worth I will see what can be done."

So Clare went to the Benedictines, who did not really want someone living in the middle of them who wanted to be Another Kind of nun. They thought that a few days of prayer and fasting and sleeping on a hard bed would soon cure this rich girl of her Queer Ideas and that she would go home. But they were wrong.

Clare remembered what Francis had told her, and she did her very best to obey the Benedictines in every way. Very soon her Sister Agnes joined her and, a little later, Beatrice. The r parents thought that they were Quite Mad and that they wou d grow out of it. But they were wrong, too.

At that time Francis and his Friars were mending a fallen-down Church, and when, after some months, it was finished, he went to see Clare.

"Now, Sister," he said, "you have been quite good and obedient all this time, and meanwhile I have been to see the Pope about you. He says that you may start a convent of Women Franciscans and that they must observe *all* our Rules of Poverty, except going out to beg. Your job will be to pray night and day for people who Will not or Cannot or Do not pray enough for themselves. You must also pray for all missionary priests, because life is extra difficult for them." Then he smiled at Clare and said, "Well, to start you off we will give you the Church that we have just finished mending."

"Oh, thank you, Francis!" said Clare. "You *are* kind. I do hope I will be a good Franciscan."

So Clare and her two sisters, Agnes and Beatrice, started their Convent by building huts for themselves round their church. Soon a few of their friends joined them, and then more and more. Clare, who became the Reverend Mother when everything was in going order, was very fierce with her nuns about being Poor.

"We must have *nothing* except what we may be given," she said. "If we possess nothing at all, then we will have no worries about money or cooking or bills and things, and so we will have more time to pray for all those people. That is our First Job and comes before anything else."

The nuns were even poorer than the Friars, who at least were allowed to go out and beg. Very often they nearly starved, and people called them the Poor Clares, and they still do. I know some who live in Bayswater in London, and there are eighteen or nineteen more convents of Poor Clares in England and hundreds more all over the world now. They are really very poor indeed, and they are very cheerful and happy, and what we would all do without their prayers for us, every night and day, only God can know.

One thing Clare wouldn't have, and that was any of her nuns Overdoing it.

"If you fast *too* much," she said, "you will get ill, and then you will not be able to take your turn at praying in the night, and that is your *work,* that is what you are a nun *for.* You can't please yourself and neglect your work. No one can. Also, if you get *too* cold by having no bedclothes at all, you will never be able to get back to sleep again when you come back from praying in the cold chapel in the night. And if you can't sleep, you can't work. You must always remember that it is very hard work being a Poor Clare."

A very interesting thing happened when Clare had been Reverend Mother for a long time. The Pope and the German Emperor, whose name was Frederick, couldn't agree over something or other, and in the end the Pope Excommunicated Frederick and said that he couldn't be Emperor any more and that the German people must choose another Emperor.

Now in case you don't know, let me tell you that being excommunicated is one of the worst things that can happen to anyone, if not the Very Worst. The excommunicated person is not allowed to have *any* of the Sacraments, no Confession or Holy Communion or *anything.* Ex is Latin for Out of, and Communication is sharing with others or having something in *Common* with them. So that *Communion* is a sharing or belonging and Holy Communion is a sharing and belonging with

God. So the excommunicated person may not share any of the Church's things or belong any more to the *Community*. (What does Communism mean? Or Communal? Or Exit? Or Exile?)

Anyway, Frederick was Excommunicated from the Church, and he was so upset about it that he went to war with the Pope, and it was called the War of the Guelphs (the Pope's side) and the Ghibellines (Frederick's side).

At one time the Ghibellines were winning, and they came into Italy and began to attack the town of Assisi where Francis and Clare lived. And there was a great deal of burning and looting and robbing. As the war came nearer and nearer to the Poor Clare convent the nuns were more and more frightened. But they didn't tell Clare what was happening because she was ill in bed. At last they could actually see the Ghibellines coming towards the high convent wall, and they lost their nerve and went to Clare.

"Oh, Mother Clare, please! We don't know what to do!" they said. "The Ghibellines are here, and they will want to use the convent as a Barracks, and they will kill us all. What *shall* we do?" And they crowded round Clare's bed and told her that now the soldiers already had ladders against the walls and would be inside at Any Moment.

Clare was feeling very ill, but she got up at once and hurried to the Chapel.

"Dear God," she said, "please don't forget all my poor nuns, they can't fight and they'll all be killed. Please, unless You really want us to die, will You save them?" And God said to Clare:

"Yes, I will save them. They are doing so much good with their prayers Day and Night. You can never know how many souls are saved because of you and your nuns. But I know."

"Oh, thank You, dear Lord," said Clare. "And could You possibly save the people of Assisi who have been so good to us and who have given us food?"

"Go and speak to the soldiers," said God, "and I will go with you."

So Clare took the Blessed Sacrament from the altar and carried It carefully in a little gold box called a Pyx. She took It to the arch above the big gates. And all the time she was carrying the Pyx she was thanking God for being with them. When she saw the soldiers peering over the walls from the tops of their ladders, she was frightened and couldn't think what to say to them. (Do you remember how shy she used to be?) So she just held up the Pyx in front of them and stood quite still.

Suddenly all the soldiers stopped shouting. They stared at the Pyx and at Clare. Then, without a word, they quietly took down their ladders and marched away from Assisi, and that was the last the town and its people saw of them.

God did so many things for Clare that a whole book would be needed to get them all in. But I will tell you one more thing.

This happened inside the Convent. One of the nuns, called Sister Andrea (which is the girl's name for Andrew, like Joseph and Josephine) had broken one of the Rules and had not told Clare, as she ought to have done. She just went on as if nothing had happened. She thought that God wouldn't notice a little thing like that. But God always does notice, and very soon Sister Andrea had such a very sore throat that she couldn't speak at all, let alone pray with the other nuns when they were in Chapel. But she didn't say anything about it. Her throat was so bad one night that she thought she was going to die, and she wished Mother Clare would come round, as she did sometimes, and then she could confess to her about the Broken Rule. Clare didn't come because she was ill herself and in the infirmary, but she had a dream about Sister Andrea and she said to the Sister Infirmarian:

"Sister, would you very kindly take Sister Andrea a soft-boiled egg and tell her to eat it very slowly? It will make her throat feel better, and then she must come and see me."

"A soft-boiled *egg*, Mother Clare?" said the Sister Infirmarian. "In the middle of the night? Anyway, I didn't even know she had a sort throat."

"Neither did I," said Clare, "until a minute ago."

So Sister Andrea ate her egg very slowly, and her throat did feel a bit better. Then she got out of bed and went to see Clare in the Infirmary and told her about the Broken Rule. Clare scolded her, but not very much, because God had already given her such a Sore Throat. But Sister Andrea became one of the best nuns in the Convent after that.

St. Clare's special day is August 12th, and anyone called Clare or Clara can have her for their special saint. But not Clarissa, because there is a St. Clarissa for them.

I really wrote this story for someone whose other name is Morag, but she might be rather old for it by now.

St. Isabel

Once upon a time there was a girl called Isabel and she was a French Princess and her Father was the King of France and her Mother was the Queen of France. She had seven brothers and no sisters and she used to go to School in a convent called Longchamps near Paris. When Isabel and the next brother to her were quite young, they heard about "First Fruits" and they loved the idea.

Do you know what "First Fruits" are? Well, in case you don't, I'll just tell you. Quite a lot of people give away, for

God's sake, the first thing they make, or do, or grow. The first ripe apple in the Garden they might give away to someone who hasn't got an apple tree. Or the very first week's wages they ever earn they might put in the poor box. Or the very first piece of sewing or knitting that they finish well. Or the price of the first puppy or calf they ever sell. Have you been to a Harvest Thanksgiving in a Church? Well, everyone brings something that God has grown for them, fruit or corn or vegetables, or perhaps a specially baked loaf of bread made from their own wheat, or something. Then all these things are given away to Hospitals and Almshouses or somewhere.

Anyway, Isabel and her brother Louis loved First Fruits and they always gave away anything they could think of. They made themselves a Motto, which they were always saying to each other, and because they were French children it was a French Motto, and this is what it was:

"Les Prémices appartiennent à Dieu," which means "First Fruits belong to God."

One day Isabel found that she could sew quite well now, and so she thought she would make her First real Thing.

"What shall I make?" she wondered. "It mustn't be too big or take too long or I might get tired of it and make it badly. I know, I will make a little linen cap for a baby, and if I put ribbons on it, it could be a bonnet." So she took a piece of fine linen out of her work basket and began to sew. She sewed all the afternoon in the Palace Garden, and the Queen's ladies-in-waiting sat around with their embroidery and gossiped among themselves while they kept Half an Eye on the Queen's children.

After a while Louis came to see what Isabel was doing.

"What are you making, Isabel?" he asked her. "It doesn't really look like anything, does it?"

"It does if you hold it like this," said Isabel. "It is going to be a cap or a bonnet, it depends on whether I put ribbons on it or not."

"Oh, it *is* like a cap!" said Louis. "Let me try it on, Isabel."

"All right, only mind the needle," said Isabel, and she gave him her piece of sewing.

"Look!" said Louis. "It just fits me! Can I please have it for a nightcap, Isabel? Then you needn't put ribbons on it. I *do* want a nightcap!"

"But I can't give it to you because of the Motto," said Isabel. "It is my first real Thing that I've made."

"Oh dear!" said Louis. "But of *course* you must give it away. I would have liked it so much! Will you make me another one, Isabel?"

"Yes, I will," said Isabel, "and if it hadn't been for the Motto you could have had this one with Pleasure."

"Thank you," said Louis, and he went back to play with his six brothers and Isabel sat sewing busily until she finished the little cap. She didn't make it into a bonnet after all.

Now two of the Queen's ladies-in-waiting had heard Isabel and Louis talking about their First Fruits motto and they thought how kind they were although they were still so very Young. So when the little cap had been given away to a poor woman who had a baby, they went to see her.

"Good morning, ladies," said the poor woman.

"Good morning," said the Queen's ladies-in-waiting. "We wondered if you really want Princess Isabel's little cap very much?"

"Well, I do rather," said the poor woman. "You see, my little boy just fits it. Why do you ask me?"

So the Queen's ladies-in-waiting told her all about Isabel and Louis and their Motto. "And," they said, "we rather thought we would like to keep the little cap ourselves because we are very fond of the Queen's children."

"I quite understand," said the poor woman, "but what shall I put on my little boy's head?"

"Oh, we didn't want you to *give* it back," said the Queen's ladies-in-waiting; "we will buy it from you for quite a lot of money. Enough to buy clothes for all of your children and you and your husband as well."

"If that is the case," said the poor woman, "you may have it at once," and she took it off her little boy's head and wrapped it in a parcel and gave it to them then and there.

The Queen's ladies-in-waiting gave her a large Sum of Money and took the little cap back to the palace with them.

"We will keep it always," they said, "because we do love Isabel, and because she is so sweet she might be a Saint one day and then we would have a Relic."

And they kept it all their lives, wrapped up with a little note to say what it was and who had made it. When they died the people who were tidying up their things found it and read the note.

"The best thing to do with it is to give it to the Princess's school at Longchamps," they said. "After all, the nuns there taught her to sew."

And they did, and do you know that the little cap is still there in the Convent for people to see although it is Seven Hundred Years Old? Because the Queen's ladies-in-waiting were right and Isabel was a Saint. So was her brother Louis, after he was the King of France.

St. Isabel's Special Day is on August 31st, and people of all countries are called after her in every kind of language.

St. Gillian

Once upon a time there was a girl called Gillian and she had an Uncle whose name was Alexis and he was a Servite and a friend of St. Philip Benizi. She was an Italian girl and so her mother called her Juliana, which is Italian for Gillian. St. Joan of Arc's mother called her Jeanne, which is French for Joan, and St. Francis was called Francesco at home.

One day when Gillian was nearly grown up her Uncle Alexis asked her what she was going to be.

"I think that I'll be a Servite like you and all the others," said Gillian.

Uncle Alexis laughed. "You can't be a Servite," he said. "Only men are Servites, there aren't any Nuns!" Then he thought to himself: "But what a good idea though; perhaps she could start a new Order of Servite nuns."

Gillian said that she did not want to be a Benedictine or a Franciscan or a Dominican or any other kind of nun, only a Servite because Uncle Alexis had told her so much about them and they always went to a Servite Church on Sundays.

So Uncle Alexis talked it over with the other Servites and it was agreed that Gillian should be the first Servite Nun, and she was.

I am not going to tell you all the things that Gillian did in her life after she started her new order and made her new Convent with Servite Nuns in it, but I will tell you the most Interesting and Important thing of all. This thing happened at the end of her life.

But before I tell you this I must tell you about the Habit that the Servite Nuns have, because the Important thing has to do with it. Some time before, when the Servite Order for men was started, Our Lady told the seven first Servites that she specially wanted them to remember her Seven Sorrows. (Do you remember the Seven Sorrows of Our Lady? Shall I just remind you?)

They were all the sad things that happened to her in her life, the sort of things that would have made her cry.

The First time was when she took her Baby, who was Our Lord, to be presented to God the Father in the Temple. The old priest there, whose name was Simeon, told her that such sad things would happen in her life that they would feel like swords in her soul. This made her sad and frightened because she did not know what he meant.

The Second sorrow was when she had to escape with her Baby into Egypt, with St. Joseph, in the middle of the night because of Herod's soldiers. It was sad for her to leave her home and her friends and go to a Foreign Country without any luggage.

The Third sorrow was when she lost Jesus for three whole

days in a strange crowded town when He was only Twelve. It was very worrying for her because she thought that He might have been run over or something.

The Fourth sorrow was, I think, the worst one for her. It was when she met Our Lord carrying His Cross through the streets of Jerusalem, with the crowds all staring and laughing at Him. It must have been dreadful for her not to have been able to help Him.

The Fifth sorrow was when she stood with St. John and watched her Son being crucified, not because *He* did anything wrong but because we do.

The Sixth sorrow was when Our Lord was dead and the Disciples took Him down from the Cross for her.

And the Seventh sorrow was when her Son was buried in the cave belonging to St. Joseph of Arimathea.

I have reminded you of Our Lady's sorrows so that you will know about the Servite Nuns' Habit. When Our Lady came and told the Seven Friends to start the Servite Order and to remember her Seven Sorrows, she was dressed in black and white. Mostly in Black because black is a Sad Color. And the Seven Friends remembered how Our Lady was dressed, and Gillian's Habit was made exactly the same. The Servite Nuns still have that same Habit except for One Thing. And that is the story I am going to tell you that is so Important and Interesting.

When Gillian was fairly old and had been the Mother Prioress for some time, she had a very bad Illness of the Throat and went to bed. She couldn't even get up for Sunday Mass and so the priest used to bring her Holy Communion in bed, in the same way as people in Hospitals have it. Well, poor

Gillian got worse and the doctor said that she couldn't possibly get better. The Nuns were sorry that their Mother Prioress was going to leave them, but she herself was delighted.

"I feel better already," she said, "because I'll be seeing Our Lord soon now. I have been waiting and waiting to see Him all my life."

Now her Illness of the Throat got so bad that she couldn't swallow and so she couldn't have Holy Communion any more, and Gillian was very upset about it. She loved the Blessed Sacrament and all day she looked forward to the next morning and the time that the priest would come. She prayed that her swallowing would get better, but it didn't.

"But I can't go on all this time without You," she said to God. "Why do You go away from me just at the end of my life, when I need You so badly?" But still she couldn't swallow.

When the priest came to see her she said:

"Do you think, Father, that if I may not have Holy Communion you could bring the Blessed Sacrament here so that I could see it?"

"Yes," said the priest, "and I will pray that your throat will be a little better so that I can give you Holy Communion."

When he came back Gillian was delighted and glad.

"Thank You, God, for coming to me when I cannot go to You," she said. Then she said to the priest:

"Father, do you think that you could put the Blessed Sacrament on my chest near my heart for a minute? It would be instead of having Holy Communion."

"No," said the priest. "I don't think that it would be allowed."

"*Please*," said Gillian. "It would be very miserable to die without Our Lord. At least He would be close to me. I think

I'm going to die very soon now."

So in the end the priest was so sorry for Gillian that he put a little piece of white linen on her chest when she was lying in bed, and he put the Blessed Sacrament on it. As soon as it touched her, a Wonderful Thing happened! It disappeared! And at the same time Gillian smiled very happily and left her poor ill body behind and went away with God.

At first the priest was very worried because he thought that the Host might have slipped off the little square of white linen and got lost somewhere. But it hadn't. It had gone right through into Gillian because she couldn't swallow, and there was a little round mark with a Cross on it on her chest just over her heart, exactly the same size as the Host!

And that was a wonderfully kind miracle for God to do for Gillian because she wanted Holy Communion more than anything in the world and so He gave it to her Himself.

And now for the One Thing that is different in the Nuns' Habit. If you look at a Servite Nun, you will see that just over her heart on her Black Habit is a small round silver Host because of the way that God let Gillian have Holy Communion.

St. Gillian's Special Day is on June 19th, and although not very many people are actually called Juliana itself, Julia and Julie and Juliet are all different ways of saying it. I think more people are called Gillian in England and America because Gillian is English for Juliana.

There is another name that can belong to this story. Can you guess what it is? Well, it is Dolores because of Our Lady's Seven Sorrows. (What is the French for pain or sorrow? What is the Latin word?)

St. Katherine

Once upon a time there was a lady called Katherine, and she lived with her maid Mabel, but I don't know where they lived.

One day at Breakfast Katherine said:

"You know, Mabel, I had a very Peculiar Dream last night."

"Did you, Madam?" said Mabel, and she brought some more Toast.

"Yes," said Katherine. "I dreamed that we must sell this house and go and live in a Town where the Church Bells ring by themselves!"

"Dear me, Madam!" said Mabel, and she brought some more Butter.

"So we will sell this house at once," said Katherine.

"Very good, Madam," said Mabel, "and which is the Town with the Church Bells?"

"I've no idea," said Katherine, "the Dream didn't say. We'll just have to find it."

"Well, it's all the same to me, Madam," said Mabel, and she picked up Katherine's table napkin.

So they Sold Up the house and packed up their things and started off. And whenever they came to a Town they went and stood by the Church and Listened. But the Church Bells never rang by themselves. There were always some Bell Ringers inside. Or else it was the Church Clock, which is not at all the

Same Thing.

At last they came to Hereford. When they got to the Church they stopped and Listened as usual, but they only heard the Clock striking Half Past Six. (Which didn't Count.)

"I'll tell you what," said Katherine in a Tired Voice; "we'll go to one more Town and then we'll Rest for a few days."

"That suits me, Madam," said Mabel, and so they started off for Ledbury, which was about fifteen miles away. As they went, the Sky got Blacker and the Wind got up and the Rain came down and the Lightning flashed and the Thunder roared and there was a Storm! When at last they got to Ledbury they were Drenched. The wind howled and whistled round the corners and all the windows in the Town rattled and the curtains flapped and the smoke blew down the chimneys *and* . . . the Church Tower rocked in the wind AND THE BELLS RANG BY THEMSELVES!

So they both thanked God with all their hearts that they had found the Town·that they were looking for and that at last they could stop their Search. Then they went into an Hotel and dried themselves and had an Excellent Supper and a Good Night's Rest.

The next day Katherine went round about looking for a House to buy, and by lunch time she had found the Very One. It was not too small and not too big and it had an Orchard and a Paddock and good Stables. Just what she wanted! So she hurried back to the Hotel to tell Mabel, and to collect their things, and they settled in that very day.

Well, as time went on Katherine made lots of friends in Ledbury. Rich ones and Poor ones. The Rich ones came to Tea with her and asked her to Dinner, and the Poor-and-Raggies came and had Dinner with her and asked her for things to Take Away with them for their Relations who couldn't come. And they asked her for Medicine and Bandages, too, because Doctors were very Far and Few in those days. And she tidied up the Hospital and gave all the Ill People new Blankets and things. And everything that they asked for, Katherine gave them, and they all Blessed her for a Good Woman. Which she was.

The thing that she liked doing best, when she wasn't dealing with Poor-and-Raggies, was riding on her Mare, whose name was Gadfly. But one day Gadfly had a very nice Foal called Toby, and then, of course, Katherine couldn't ride for a while because Gadfly had to stay at home to look after her Foal. So instead, Katherine asked all her friends to Tea on Thursday to see the new Foal, and they all said that they'd like to come very much.

So, on Thursday morning Katherine went to an earlier Mass than usual so as to Get Things Ready. But when she came back for Breakfast there wasn't any! And Mabel wasn't there either. Poor Katherine with her Tea-Party and all! However, she set to and got everything done and the Cakes made and the Sandwiches cut, and all the time she wondered what *could* have happened to Mabel.

Well, in the afternoon all the Guests began to arrive, and when they'd all had Tea Katherine said:

"Now let's go to the Stables and see Toby!"

So they all trooped out and down through the garden to the Stables, and Katherine went in Front because no one else knew the way.

They all followed her into the Stables, and at the second

loosebox from the end Katherine stopped.

"There!" she said, and looked through the bars.

Nothing!

Katherine stared. Nothing? How could there be nothing when it was Gadfly's own Loosebox? All the Guests crowded round and Craned their Necks and chattered and opened the loosebox door and Stared.

"Where's the Foal?" they asked Katherine.

"*I* don't know!" said Katherine. "I can't make it out!"

So they all went back to the house, and after they had talked about it they Came to the Conclusion that Gadfly and Toby had been Stolen. Then they all went home and left Katherine to think what to do about it.

Well, Katherine was very Fussed for two reasons. One, that Gadfly and Toby were Stolen. And two, that Mabel was Lost.

So she went to the Church that was quite nearby and she knelt down and she said:

"Please, God, will You help me to find Gadfly and Toby? I *think* they have been Stolen, but You *know* what has happened. I don't know where to start looking for them, so, as the ground is wet and Muddy, will You help me to find their Footprints? And please, Dear Lord, what *has* happened to Mabel? I am so worried about her. May her Guardian Angel please be Specially Careful of her while she is Lost? Because she is Rather Silly." Then Katherine went and lit a Candle at Our Lady's Altar and she said:

"Dear Our Lady, would you please pray for Gadfly and Toby and Mabel while I go out and look for them? I'll leave this Candle here so that whenever you see it you will Remember me."

Then she went back to the Stables. Sure enough, she saw Gadfly's hoof prints at once, and beside them some smaller ones that belonged to Toby. And beside them both she saw some little round Heel marks that must have belonged to the Thief! She followed them easily until thy came to a Stream.

"There!" she thought, "the Thief was too clever for me! I can't tell which way they have gone because they have been walking in the Stream!"

She stooped down and looked at the stones in the Stream.

"Goodness me!" she said in a Surprised Voice. And what do you suppose had happened?

Lots of the Stones had Hoof marks and Heel marks dented in them! God had answered Katherine's prayer in a very good

way indeed. Because the marks couldn't Wash Off however long they stayed in the Stream. In fact, though it is more than Five Hundred Years ago they *still* haven't Washed Off!

So Katherine went along and along the River, and soon she saw somebody in front of her leading a Mare. And a Foal was following them, and they were all three walking in the water. She hurried after them. She could go Faster along the Bank than they could along the stones at the bottom of the Stream. And when she got nearer who do you suppose the Thief was? Yes, Mabel!

Mabel couldn't think how Katherine could have found her so quickly until she saw the Stones. Then she was very sorry and Ashamed, and she said she couldn't *think* what made her do it.

"I know what made you do it, though," said Katherine.

"What did?" said Mabel.

"You forgot God," said Katherine, "and so, when the Devil put that Idea into your head, you forgot the Devil, too. So you just thought it was your Own Idea, and you never bothered to think whether it was a Bad one or a Good One. Were you going to sell the Horses?"

"Yes, I was," said Mabel, "and I'm sure I'm very Sorry for it, Madam, I won't do it again." And they all went home. (Mabel must have been *very* Silly, you know, because why on Earth didn't she Ride Gadfly and let Toby run behind, instead of Leading her along the Stony bed of the Stream, and having to get so Wet? However, perhaps it was just as well, because Katherine couldn't have found them nearly so quickly if she hadn't been walking.)

About those Stones. If you go and look in the River Sapey,

near Ledbury, you will find some of the Stones still there, with Gadfly's big Hoof marks and Toby's smaller Hoof marks and Mabel's little round Heel marks on them. And the Hospital there is called St. Katherine's Hospital because of the New Blankets and things.

St. Katherine's Special Day is November 25th. And anyone called Kathleen or Kate or Kitty or any of those Names can have her for their Saint. (Unless they belong to St. Catherine of Siena, of course.) Especially those People who have their Birthdays on that day, and also all the people who live in Ledbury.

St. Catherine
of Siena

Once upon a time there was a Family who lived in Siena in Italy and their name was Benincasa (which is Italian for Good-in-the-House). Now you needn't laugh and say "What a funny name!" as you did just now, because we have just as funny names in England, or perhaps even Funnier. What about Good-enough? Or Bucket? Or Summerhay? Or Godtobed? Or Catchpole? Or Christmas? Or Hunnybun? Or Lambkin? Or Dearlove? Or Bumpus? Or Pennyfeather? Or Birdikin? You can think of heaps of others for yourself.

Well, all this about names isn't anything to do with the Story, and if you hadn't Interrupted by laughing at Good-in-the-House, we'd have finished by now!

Well, Mr. Benincasa's name was Giacomo (which is Italian for James), and Mrs. Benincasa's name was Lapa (which doesn't mean anything in English).

Giacomo had a big Dyer's shop and he was Rich and he invented beautiful New Colors and he dyed Silks and Velvets for the Noblemen to buy.

The Benincasas had Twenty-five Children, and the youngest was called Catherine.

Now although all the Twenty-five Children weren't at home at once, you can imagine that no one had much time for Catherine, and she used to play by herself a lot.

Her Favorite Place to play was on the Stairs. There she used to run up and down; to the Shop; to the Window; to the Kitchen; and to her own Private Bedroom. She loved her own Room. It was very small and gray with the Window very High Up. But it had a Red Brick Floor which Catherine thought was Beautiful. (When you go to Siena you can see her Room and the Stairs and all.)

Anyway, Catherine loved the Stairs. She used to sit and Read on them; and Hop up them; and Jump down them. And she used them instead of a Rosary sometimes; one Hail Mary for each Step!

The other place that Catherine loved was the Dominican Church. The Dominican Church in Siena is on a Hill, and it has heaps of Steps going up to the Door and people sit on them to eat their Lunch so as not to be late for Office! (I did it once and so will you one day!)

Catherine was very fond of her Father, and her Father was very fond of Catherine, although he was a Very Stern Man sometimes.

One day Catherine was sitting on the Stairs when she heard a Great Commotion going on in the Kitchen!

"I want the Very Best Wine for Lunch. Two friends are coming!" she heard her Father saying. "Go, Vittoria, and fetch some at once! My very *Special* Wine!"

Catherine heard Vittoria (who was one of her Sisters) hurry down to the Cellar with the Big Jug, and then she heard her hurry up again!

"There isn't any, Father!" she said in a Frightened Voice. "Nothing comes out of the Tap!"

"*Isn't* any?" shouted her Father. "You Stupid child! No one should have Touched it except me! It *must* be there!"

Catherine felt all Cold Inside! That very morning she had given the Wine to a Poor Family! She had wanted to do the best she could for them, and so she had given them the Special Wine!

She went into the Kitchen, her Heart Thumping with Fright!

"I'll go down and get it, Father," she said, taking the Big Jug from Vittoria's hand. "Vittoria has been up and down so often today!"

"Well, mind you bring up Plenty," said her Father, "it *can't* have gone!"

Catherine went slowly down the long Cellar Stairs with the Big Jug, and as she went she said:

"Please, Our Lord, don't forget me now! You know about the Wine and I *had* to give the Poor people the best we'd got!

I could not give them Cheap Wine just because they are poor! And now Father is Upset because he wants it for his friend. *Please* do something!"

By this time Catherine had reached the Cask that held the Special Wine. (A Cask is a Barrel.) There was a little Tap at the bottom of the Cask and Catherine put the Big Jug under it and Turned it On. Wine poured out and filled the jug in No Time!

"*Thank You,* Our Lord!" said Catherine as she climbed up the Cellar Stairs with the Big Jug. "Thank You *very* much!"

Vittoria was Most Astonished, but she didn't say anything because Catherine made a Face at her not to.

When Catherine was older she was a Dominican Tertiary. (Tertiaries don't have to live in a Convent as Nuns do. They dress Ordinarily and say Office and things, but they usually live at home.) And she used to work all day in the Hospital because there weren't any Proper Nurses in those times.

There was one Very-Ill-Bred woman called Cecca in the Hospital, and she had Leprosy, so no one wanted to go near her. Until Catherine started working there no one made Cecca's bed or brushed her hair or anything, and they pushed her Food to her on a plate with a Long Stick because of being afraid of catching Leprosy.

Catherine was very sorry for Cecca, and so she washed her and brought her a New Nightie and brushed her hair and made her bed with Nice Clean Sheets. And then she brought her her Tea in a Round Brown Pot on a Blue Tray.

"Now," she said, smiling, "do you feel more Comfy, poor Cecca?"

"No," grumbled cross old Cecca.

"Have I forgotten something?" asked Catherine.

"You never gave me a New Ribbon for my Pigtail," said Cecca. "I *want* a New Ribbon!"

"I *am* sorry!" said Catherine. "I'll bring you one tomorrow."

"You'd better," grumbled Cecca. She blew her Tea to cool it and splashed it on her Clean Sheet. "*Now* look what you've made me do!" she cried angrily, and she Banged her cup back on the tray and Cracked it.

Well, Catherine looked after Cecca for weeks and weeks, and never a Kind Word did Cecca say! She was Rude and Cross and Grumbling and Impatient, but Catherine was never cross back because Cecca was so Ill and had a Pain. At last Cecca stopped being so Tiresome, but her Leprosy got worse and worse.

Catherine's mother was Distracted!

"Really, Catherine, you *mustn't* go on Nursing that old woman!" she said. "You will catch Leprosy Yourself, and that would be Tragic!"

"But if I don't, no one else will," said Catherine, "and she can't help having Leprosy. You know, Mummy, you'd be Miserable if you weren't allowed to nurse *me* if *I* got it."

"That's not the same thing at all," said Mrs. Benincasa. "You are my Daughter!"

"Well, Cecca's Somebody's Daughter!" said Catherine.

So her Mother didn't say any more, and everybody said how Kind and Charitable Catherine was.

But in Spite of All Precautions, one day Catherine got Leprosy in her hands. At once all the people who had praised her began to say things like:

"There you are! What did you expect?"

and:

"Of course, if you *will* go into dirty old Hospitals and look after Lepers you mustn't Grumble if you catch Leprosy!"

"I'm not Grumbling," said Catherine. "It can't be Helped, that's all!" and she went on looking after Cecca. But she slept in the Hospital and not at Home, so that no one there would catch Leprosy from her.

At last poor old Cecca died, and Catherine went to her Funeral, and then a Wonderful thing happened!

Just as the Priest said the Very Last words, Catherine's hands stopped having Leprosy and looked strong and well again! And Our Lord said to her:

"There, Catherine! You have done so much for Me that I thought I'd do something for you in return!"

Catherine was very Wise when she was older, and she helped the Pope when his enemies were getting too Strong, and he took her Advice, and when she died people made up a Hymn for her.

When you go to Siena (as you may, one day) you will certainly hear somebody singing it. Errand boys whistle it as they Deliver the Groceries, and children sing it on their way to School, and people sing it in Church after Benediction. It is very like the Vesper Hymn that we have in Lent.

St. Catherine's Special Day is April 30th, and if your name is Katherine, or Kathleen or Kitty or Kate, it counts.

St. Joan of Arc

Once upon a time there was a girl called Joan and she lived in France. She used to look after her Father's Sheep, and every day she would take them out to a Grassy Place, and while they were eating the grass she would get her Knitting out of the Workbag that she had for Christmas, and she would Knit and talk to God.

God and Joan were extra great Friends, because Joan Really Loved Him, not only just Said she did, as some people do.

Well, in those days, the King of France had died, but his Son, Prince Charles, hadn't been Crowned yet because there hadn't been time. Prince Charles had got himself into Rather a Mess with his Government and things and he had lost Nearly All his Kingdom, so everyone was Rather Bothered about it.

One day Joan was sitting Knitting some bedsocks and watching the Sheep choosing what grass they would eat, when some Very Beautiful People came and stood in front of her.

"Who are you, please?" asked Joan, getting up quickly. Her knitting wool Rolled away, and one of the sheep kept smelling it.

"We are St. Catherine and St. Margaret and St. Michael," said the Beautiful People, "and we've got a Message for you from God."

"What Message?" asked Joan, feeling Rather Small and Unimportant to be talking to Three Saints at Once.

"We must tell you how to Save France from her Enemies and to make Prince Charles safe and get him Properly Crowned King," they said, and they told her what to do.

Joan was very Bothered. She couldn't believe that she was Grand or Important Enough to Save France, so she waited to see what would happen next.

After a day or two St. Catherine came and said:

"Joan, why aren't you doing anything about Prince Charles? It's time you started, you know."

"Must I really?" asked Joan. "It's Rather Frightening to go to the Prince's Palace and Save him from his Enemies."

"Yes, you must go, or he'll Lose his Throne," said St. Catherine.

So Joan went to the Palace, as quickly as she could.

"Can I see Prince Charles?" she said to the Door Keeper.

"What for?" said the Door Keeper.

"I've got a Message for him," said Joan.

"Who from?" asked the Door Keeper.

"God," said Joan.

"Go away and don't be Silly," said the Door Keeper, and he shut the Door in her face! Poor Joan! She tried again at Another Door with another Door Keeper. This time the other Door Keeper went and told the Prince. When he came back, Joan said:

"What did he say?"

"He said: 'Go away and don't be Silly,'" said the Door Keeper, and he shut the Door in Joan's face!

Well, Joan Kept On asking to see the Prince until at last they took her to him. He was sitting on his Throne, all very

Grand and Important in his Royal Robes, but the Crown was on a cushion beside him, because he hadn't been Properly crowned yet.

"What's all this nonsense?" said Prince Charles, tapping the arm of his Throne with his Rings.

"God says that I can help you to Save France and then you can be Properly Crowned King at Rheims," said Joan.

"Rubbish!" said Prince Charles.

"But God says so, and St. Catherine and St. Margaret and St. Michael came and *Told* me!" said Joan.

"*If* God is helping you, do you Know what I was doing a Year Ago Last Monday?" said the Prince. He was trying to Set a Trap for Joan (which is what people do for Birds and Rabbits).

God told Joan and she said:

"Yes, you were spending some Money that didn't belong to you."

Charles *was* Surprised! He didn't think that anybody knew about that. He forgot that God knew.

"All right," he said, "I'll give you a Suit of Armor and a Shield and a Big White Horse, and you can Lead my Army into Battle."

The first thing that Joan did was to make all the soldiers go to Confession, because most of them had lots of Mortal Sins. Then she led the Army into Battle, in a place called Orleans, and it Won! It was the first time they had won for Simply Ages, and they all Cheered Joan. (I expect they won because they were in a State of Grace.)

Every time that Joan Led the Army, on her Big White Horse, they always Won, and at last she Saved France and

the Prince was Properly Crowned King at Rheims. Of course,
they won because St. Michael-who-is-Good-at-Battles kept telling her what to do. (You remember, Holy Michael Archangel,
defend us in the Day of Battle?) And St. Margaret and St.
Catherine kept bringing her Messages from God. She didn't
always see them: sometimes she only heard their voices.

Well, as soon as Charles was Safely Crowned, he really didn't
care what became of Joan. He stopped being Nice to her and
sent her to fight some Other Enemies at Compiègne to get
her out of the way. It was an Enormous Battle and Joan got
Wounded and Taken Prisoner.

Now, if King Charles had liked, he could Easily have Saved
her, but he Just Didn't Bother, and so she was put in a Very
Dark and Horrible Prison.

After she had been there for Ages, a Perfectly Horrible man
called Cauchon said:

"Let's get Rid of Joan Altogether. All the People love her
and they might try and set her Free, and that would Lead
to a Riot." (A Riot is when people Rush about and Burn
Things.)

"But she hasn't done anything wrong, so we can't Kill her,"
said one of his Friends.

"We can Make Something Up," said Horrible Cauchon.
"Let's say that it was the Devil who taught her to Save King
Charles and not God, and see what she says."

So they got Joan out of Prison. She was very Thin and Ill
because of being Wounded and Starved and being in the Dark
all the time.

"What about these Voices, that you say were St. Michael and
things?" said Cauchon. "They couldn't have been. It must have

been the Devil."

Joan was Shocked. "They couldn't have been the Devil because they said who they were, and they were Nice and the Devil is Nasty. Besides God *said* they were Saints."

"God wouldn't talk to *you*," said Cauchon, "you aren't Important Enough."

"But He does talk to me," said Joan.

"You are a Witch and you talk to the Devil," said Cauchon, "and Witches have to be Burned Alive unless they Confess that they *are* witches."

"I can't confess I'm a Witch," said poor Joan, "because I'm *not* and the Voices *were* from God."

"They were from the Devil," said Horrible Cauchon, Staring at her.

"Well, can I please ask the Pope about it?" asked Joan, "because whatever he says is sure to be right."

"Yes," said Cauchon; "write him a letter and I'll have it sent at once."

So Joan wrote to the Pope—at least, a soldier wrote for her and put down what she said, because she couldn't write, and they gave the letter to Cauchon to post. (She couldn't post it herself because of being in Prison.) But abominable Cauchon never sent it to the Pope at all. He just threw it in the Fire and wrote an answer himself and took it to Joan, after a few days, so as to make her think it had come from Rome.

"Here's the Pope's answer to your letter," he said. "He says that your Voices were from the Devil and not God, so you must be Burned."

"Well, if the Pope says so he must be right," said poor Joan, "but I really did think it was God."

So a Big Bonfire was got ready in the Market Place, to Burn Joan. And the next morning some Soldiers came to her in Prison.

"This afternoon you will have to be Burned, Joan," they said, "so don't go to sleep or anything."

"Please, can I go to Confession first?" asked Joan, who hadn't been allowed to see a Priest all the time she was in Prison.

"No, of course not," said one of the Soldiers rudely. "Witches can't go to Confession."

"Well, *please* can I have Holy Communion, then?" said poor Joan.

"*No!*" said the Soldier, and he laughed and slammed the door.

Joan prayed to be Brave. She hadn't even got a Crucifix to look at, because Cauchon had taken hers away; he said Witches weren't allowed Crucifixes.

But Our Lord sent a Priest who gave her Holy Communion and heard her confession first, before the Soldiers came and took her to the Market Place. There was a huge Pile of Wood and Sticks with a big Post in the middle. They tied Joan to the Post and lit the Sticks. Then one of the Soldiers felt very sorry for her, so he took two of the Sticks and held them in the shape of a Cross for her to look at, because he hadn't got a Crucifix.

When Joan was nearly Burned up, our Lord came and took her to Heaven.

"I took you quickly," He said, "because you have had such a Dreadful Time, what with Prison and being Wounded and everything, without being Burned for a Long time as well."

"Thank you very much," said Joan. "It was Really you giving me Messages, wasn't it?"

"Of course it was," said Our Lord. "I'm glad you didn't Change your Mind because now you are a Very Important Martyr instead of a Poor Shepherd Girl."

"Am I really?" said Joan. "How lovely!"

When the Pope found out what had been happening nearly twenty years afterwards he was Very Very Angry, and he made a Proclamation. And this was the Proclamation:

THAT JOAN WAS *NOT* A WITCH AND THAT HER VOICES *WERE* FROM GOD.

And a Cross was put up in the Market Place in Rouen where she was burned.

And that is the Story of Joan of Arc, who is sometimes called the Maid of Orleans because of the First Big Battle that she won there.

St. Joan's Special Day is May 30th, and lots of people all Over the World are called after her. Even me.

St. Frances

Once upon a ~~time there~~ was a Rich Lady called Frances, and she was Italian and she lived in Rome.

Frances did not like being Rich, very much, "Because," she

said, "Why should *I* be Rich, when Our Lady was Poor?" So, although she lived in a Grand House and her three children were dressed in Velvet, and her husband Lorenzo (which is Italian for Laurence) had Gold Lace on his clothes and she had Twenty-three servants, she used to put on working clothes and go and fetch the Firewood, and milk the Cows, and feed the Chickens and things in their Farm that they had just outside the Town. And she gave away nearly all the money that her husband Lorenzo gave her to the Poor.

Now there was a Special thing about Frances, and it was this:

She could see her Guardian Angel! She was always talking to her Guardian Angel and she told him what she was going to do and things, and she would ask him to Wake her up in Time for Mass, and he always did.

You know, it must be very dull for our poor Guardian Angels when we never take any notice of them except when we say: "Oh, my Good Angel whom God has appointed to be my Guardian, watch over me during this night," when we go to bed! Supposing that all your life you *had* to be with one person wherever he went, and all he *ever* said to you was: "Just keep an Eye on my things while I am asleep, will you?" Wouldn't it be dull? Suppose that *you* never said anything except that to *your* Guardian Angel, and you lived until you were One Hundred? I should think he'd be very glad when you died and he got another Job!

Anyway, Frances and her Guardian Angel were such great friends that God let her see him, and that made it Nicer Still. No one else saw him, though.

Well, one day Frances went to the little Chapel that was in

her house and began to say her Office, as Priests do, and Nuns do, and lots of Ordinary People do, too. She had just got to Halfway through Matins (which is one of the things like Vespers and Compline only in the morning), when into the Chapel came the Parlormaid called Vittoria (which is Italian for Victoria), and she said:

"I'm sorry to disturb you, Madam, but there's a Poor-and-Raggy come to the door and he wants to see you."

Frances shut her book and went downstairs. She gave the Poor-and-Raggy some sandwiches and Bandaged Up his sore finger. When he had gone she went back to the Chapel and started Matins (what's French for Morning?) all over again from the beginning, because she did not like leaving off in the Middle.

She had just got to exactly the same place as before when a voice by the door said:

"Excuse me, Madam, but could I have a Word with you?"

It was Maria the Cook! (Maria is Italian for Mary.)

"Did you want the chicken for Lunch or Dinner, Madam?" she asked, "and is there anyone coming to Lunch? I forget what you said. And may I please have some more Raisins, we've Quite Run Out. And, Madam, would you mind coming down and seeing that piece of Beef? The butcher ought to know better than to send such Stuff."

So Frances shut her book again and went downstairs. When she had Sorted Out everything in the Kitchen she went up and started Matins again for the third time! She had just got to the Very Same Place again when she heard her husband Lorenzo calling her:

"Frances! Where are you? Here is Giuseppe" (which is

Italian for Joseph) "with the new Sheep Dog, and he has brought a Fine Pheasant with him!"

Frances shut her book and went downstairs to her husband Lorenzo. When she had done all she could for Lorenzo and Giuseppe, and had said what a Lovely new Sheep Dog it was, and had said that they would have the Pheasant for Sunday Lunch and all that, she went up to the Chapel again!

Just as she had got to the same place *again* she heard:

"Mummy! *Mummy!* Mummy, *do* come! That little Green Pig that you gave me last night has lost all its legs!" It was Battisto (short for John the Baptist), her youngest little Boy, who wanted her.

Poor Frances got up again, shut her book and said to Our Lord:

"I *am* so sorry, Dear Lord, to keep *on* stopping, but You see how it is."

"That's all right," said Our Lord. "You can easily go on talking to Me while you are bustling about in the house."

So Frances mended the Green Pig and went back to the Chapel. And there she saw her Guardian Angel writing on the Front Page of her prayer book (the white page where your name is usually written), and she went and looked over his shoulder to see what he was writing. And there, in beautiful Shining Gold Letters were these words:

"Propterea benedixit te Deus in aeternum."

Which means: "Therefore God has blessed you for ever."

And those were the very Words that Frances kept going to say when she was interrupted all those times!

"Why has God blessed me?" Frances asked the Angel. "I thought He mightn't like me going away and leaving Him so often."

"Because you were *so* Patient and didn't tell the Others that you minded being Interrupted," said the Angel, and he put a period after his writing.

St. Frances' Special Day is on March 9th. Anyone called Francesca counts. And whom do you suppose the Other Special Day in this Story belongs to? Everybody's Guardian Angels, of course! And that is on October 2nd. And don't forget your poor Guardian Angel, will you?

ST. FRANCES OF ROME

That you can be a saint,
In quite a rich home,
Is shown by the case
Of St. Frances of Rome.

She had plenty of children,
A husband, a cook,
A household to manage,
A housekeeping book—

And they kept her so busy
Both up and downstairs,
She couldn't think when
To get on with her prayers.

She no sooner was kneeling
Than someone would call—
She thought she would never
Get finished at all.

First her husband must see her,
Then up came the cook,
Then a little boy shouting
To please come and look—

Then a friend with a very
Long story to tell,
And a dozen poor people
With troubles as well.

And she never lost patience,
Or said "Not at home,"
And that's why we call her
Saint Frances of Rome

St. Rita

Once upon a time there was a woman called Rita and she lived in Italy in a very nice house and garden with her Husband whose name was Benedetto, which is Italian for Benedict. They were very happy and they had two little boys called Martino (which is Italian for Martin) and Giuseppe (which is Italian for Joseph). But actually Rita called them Tino and Beppe for short. As well as the boys, Rita and Benedetto had two black dogs living with them and their names were Nero and Sombra.

Tino and Beppe grew big and strong, and they went to school. And every day Nero and his wife Sombra went together to the school to fetch them home to tea, and then all six of them would settle down happily by the Fire (if it was winter) or in the Garden (if it was Summer). I don't know what they did in the Spring and Autumn. I suppose it would depend on the weather, don't you? Rita loved making homemade jam and jelly and bottled fruit and cakes and bread and cheese and butter, and you can be very sure her husband and sons enjoyed their mealtimes as much as you or I would. (And so did Nero and Sombra.)

Well, time went on and the boys grew up until they were sixteen and seventeen years old. Then there came an Epidemic in Italy and nearly everyone caught it. (An Epidemic is when a great many people all get the same disease at once. Sometimes nearly everybody gets Influenza at the same time and the doctors are Run Off their Feet.)

The first to catch the Epidemic in Rita's family were the boys. Benedetto and Rita sat up every night with them because they were so ill and feverish. They made them hot lemon drinks and cold orange drinks and did everything they possibly could, but first Beppe died and then, four days afterwards, Tino died. Rita and Benedetto were so sad that they couldn't really believe they had lost the boys. They went to Church and asked the priest to pray for them and to say Masses for them, but even then it didn't seem really true. It was like a long awful dream that never stopped. The house felt empty, and the dogs (who were the grandchildren of Nero and Sombra) wandered about, and there was too much quiet. Then, about ten days later, Benedetto woke up one morning and said:

"Rita, I don't feel very well today."

"All right, darling," said Rita. "Stay in bed and I'll bring you up your breakfast on a Tray." And she went down to the sunny kitchen, quite glad to have something to do instead of just missing the boys. She set a very nice tray with a green cup and saucer and a green plate and she made a hot drink and she set out some homemade butter and marmalade and toasted some homemade bread. It all looked quite delicious, but Benedetto wasn't really very hungry, though he did his best to eat just to please Rita, who had taken so much trouble for him. By the evening he felt worse, and by the next morning they knew that he had caught the Epidemic too. Rita nursed him all day and all night, and one evening he seemed a little better. He talked with Rita about their home and the boys and the garden and the dogs, and he said how much he loved Rita and how good and unselfish she was. Then he settled down and Rita kissed him good-night and he went to sleep, and he never woke up again.

Poor Rita could not believe that anyone could feel so lonely. She knew, of course, that Benedetto and the boys were all right and that it was lovely for them to be all together with God, who had taken them away.

"I expect it was because they were so nice that God wanted them in Heaven," she thought, "but I do *wish* He had taken me too. Perhaps I am not nice enough. I think that *must* be why."

At last she sold her house and her things and gave the dogs to her sister to look after. Then she went to an Augustinian Convent to be a nun until she died and could join Benedetto and the boys. She always thought that she had been left behind because she wasn't good enough for Heaven. The Reverend Mother told her very kindly that God had wanted her to be a nun so that she could help other people by her prayers and her patience. But she still secretly thought that it was because she wasn't good enough.

Once when she was praying she asked God if He would let her feel some of the pain He had felt from His Crown of Thorns.

"I would understand so much better, dear Lord," she said, "if You would only let me Feel as well as Know. My imagination is not really very good." As she was praying, she felt a terribly Sharp Pain in her forehead. Later on, when she looked to see what was hurting her, she found she had a bleeding sore place there. It was there for months and months, and it never healed up but always looked new, no matter what the Sister Infirmarian put on it. The Reverend Mother wasn't very pleased about it. She said that Rita was Showing Off and that nuns must never be Singular. (Singular is being the only one to do or be anything instead of being exactly like everyone else.)

Well, one day several of the nuns were going to Rome to see St. Peter's and to get the Pope's blessing. Rita had never been to Rome and she asked the Reverend Mother if she might be one of the ones to go.

"If the Pope blessed me," she said, "it might help me to be nicer, and then God might let me go to Him and be with Benedetto and the boys."

"Oh no," said the Reverend Mother, "you can't go to Rome with that great mark on your forehead. People would stare at you. If you *must* be conspicuous, then you must stay at home."

Rita was rather sad, because she had never thought, even once, of being Singular and Conspicuous. That night when she went to bed she put some ointment on the wound and prayed for it to go away so that she might be allowed to go to Rome and perhaps learn to be Nicer.

"I know that I asked You to let me have it," she said to God, "but I *do* want to go to Rome. Unless, of course, You would really Rather I stayed here."

Next morning there wasn't a mark to be seen on Rita's forehead. Reverend Mother said she was glad Rita had Stopped All that Nonsense and that now she could go to Rome with the others. Rita was delighted. She and the other nuns spent a week in Rome and saw the Pope (who blessed them in the Name of the Father and the Son and the Holy Ghost). Then they saw all the things that everybody sees in Rome, catacombs and all. They came back with many stories to tell the others, and Rita told and listened with the rest. Next morning the mark on her forehead was back and it never went away again. Reverend Mother said she might have done it on purpose, so as to get to Rome. Which wasn't very kind, whichever way you look at it. And anyway, it wasn't True. But perhaps Reverend Mother was only Trying Rita's Patience to help to make her soul stronger.

When Rita was quite old she caught a very bad Chesty Cold and Cough one Christmas time. The nuns were very good to her and nursed her kindly in the Infirmary.

"Are you quite comfortable, Sister?" they asked her one day, when she was Very Ill. "Is there anything at all that you would like?"

"Yes, Sister," said Rita. "I would very much like a Rose and a Fig from the garden if you think you could spare any."

The nuns thought that Rita's temperature had made her wits wander. How could they get her Roses and Figs in the middle of Winter?

"Poor Sister Rita has forgotten what time of year it is," they said, shaking their heads sadly. But later in the day one of them went into the garden for something else, and there, in the snow, she saw a big red Rose and two ripe Figs for Rita. Almost better than Summer ones, they were.

St. Rita's Special Day is May 22nd, and very many people are called after her because she was such a very nice person and she had such a lot to put up with. And in spite of it all she was always patient and sweet-tempered, which people often are not when they have Too Much to put up with. I'm sure I shouldn't be, would you?

St. Veronica

Once upon a time there was a Horse Dealer who was an Honest Man. Whenever he had a horse to sell that was not quite Perfect (perhaps it had a Hard Mouth, or was a bit Nappy, or Shied, or was Galled or something), then he always Mentioned it to the customer in case he might not want a horse like that. Well, this horse dealer was very poor, because he didn't sell many horses, and he had a Daughter called Veronica.

Veronica was a very nice girl, but she couldn't read or write, because her father was too poor for her to go to school, and so she used to go out Weeding to earn a little money. Weeding is rather a tiring job, but Veronica liked it because it was nice and peaceful, and gave her time to think about God. The more she thought, the more she wanted to be a Nun, and at last one day she said to her Mother:

"Mummy, I *do* want to be a Nun. Do you think I could?"

"No, darling," said her Mother, "you couldn't because you can't read or write, and we can't Afford to send you to School." And she went on getting the supper ready.

Poor Veronica was very Disappointed. And every night she used to go to bed early with her candle (they hadn't got any other kind of light), and she used to try to learn her Letters and how to Write.

But it is very difficult to learn your letters if there is no one to help you. I am sure that you find it quite hard enough even though there is always someone to ask.

One night she worked at her reading and writing until her candle burned out and she put her head on the table and cried!

"Ill *never* know my letters!" she sobbed sadly, and she rubbed her eyes. "And if I don't I can never read or write, and then I can never be a Nun!" And she rubbed her nose.

All of a Sudden the room got light again without the candle, and there was Our Lady, looking at the Letters.

"You Never mind, Veronica," said Our Lady, "you don't have to know all these letters. Now, I'll help you! You only need to know Three Letters, a White Letter, and a Black Letter, and a Red Letter."

"I didn't know that letters had Colors," said Veronica, sniffing and drying her eyes.

"These have," said Our Lady. "Now Listen. The White Letter is TRUTH. You must *tell* the Truth and *think* the truth and *do* the truth. That's easy, isn't it?"

"Yes," said Veronica in an Interested voice.

"The Black Letter is CONTENT. You must be contented wherever God puts you, and never take Offence if He gives you a Humble job. If He wants you to Weed then you must want to Weed and not want to be an Industrial Magnate or something. If God wants you to be a Nun, you'll be one, never fear."

"Yes," said Veronica, nodding her head up and down.

"Now the Red Letter," said Our Lady. "The Red Letter is for Our Lord's PASSION. You must learn how to think about all the things that Our Lord did, but especially about all the terrible things that happened to Him before He died for us all. Learn all you can about these three Letters and the others will come in time." And she went away.

Veronica learned the Three Letters for a long time, and then she went to a Convent and asked the Reverend Mother if she could please be a Nun.

"Well," said the Reverend Mother, "but you won't be able to do much, will you, if you can't read or write?"

"No," said Veronica sadly, "I wouldn't be much help, I'm afraid." And she turned to go away again. Just as she got to the door the Reverend Mother said:

"Veronica, if you were a Nun here would you go into the streets and Beg for us?" Veronica stopped.

"Beg in the Streets?" she thought. "We have always been poor, but we have never done that!" And she was just going to say very Politely to the Reverend Mother that she really didn't think that she *could,* when she remembered the Black Letter (do you?) and she said:

"Yes, Reverend Mother, I would certainly Beg for you if you told me to."

And so Veronica at last had the thing that she had wanted for so long, and she was a Nun. And every day she used to go out into the Streets and beg from door to door. Sometimes people gave her something, but more often they said:

"What, you Cadging round here again? Some people don't know what to do with their time!" And they would Slam the door and leave Veronica outside.

And when that happened Veronica would remember the Black Letter and try next door.

Now because of the Colored Letters Veronica began to know a great deal about God, but she was very Shy about letting the other Nuns know about the kind of things that God did for her, in case they thought she was Boasting (which is blowing your Own Trumpet).

One day, on the Feast of Corpus Christi, all the Nuns were at Mass. The priest had just got to the part where he lifts up the Host for everybody to see (called the Elevation), when a wonderful thing happened. There at the Altar was the Baby Jesus with Three Angels! Veronica stared and stared, and she was so happy to see such a thing that she smiled an enormous Smile. After Mass, when they were all coming out of the Chapel, she said to one of the other Nuns:

"Wasn't that a Wonderful Thing?"

"What was?" said the other Nun.

"Didn't you see the Baby Jesus?" said Veronica in a Surprised voice.

"No," said the other Nun, staring at her, "did you?"

But Veronica got Shy and rather red and Embarrassed, and she didn't say any more. She knew that God had let her be the only one to see Him.

Veronica was very sad because she couldn't sing Office with the other Nuns (because of not being able to read and write), and she kept telling God how sorry she was to be so stupid. One evening she was sitting in her room while all the other

Nuns were singing Vespers and Compline, and she looked at her Office book, and she tried to read it but she couldn't.

"You sing it with me," said a voice just behind her, "and you will find that it isn't so difficult after all!"

Veronica turned round. She was very surprised, because she thought that all the others were in Chapel and that she was alone. But it wasn't another Nun at all; it was her Guardian Angel! And they both sang Vespers and Compline, and Veronica did find that it wasn't so difficult as she had thought that it was.

After that her Guardian Angel came every evening; and once, when she was ill, the Nun who looked after the ill ones saw a light under Veronica's door.

"That naughty Sister Veronica!" said the Nun. "She ought to be asleep, with that Bad Cold she's got!" And she went to Veronica's room to turn out the light. But when she got there she heard Singing!

"Well now!" she thought, "Sister Veronica doesn't know how to sing Vespers. I wonder who can be in there with her?" and she opened the door very quietly. There was Veronica, sitting up in bed and singing Vespers. But the Nun who was looking after her couldn't see the Guardian Angel, and she shut the door carefully again.

"I don't know what to make of it at all," she said to herself as she made some Bread and Milk for Veronica's supper. "It's all Very Queer."

St. Veronica's Special Day is on January 13th. There are some other Veronicas, but I told you about this one because her father was a Horse Dealer.

St. Joan of Valois

Once upon a time there was a King of France called Louis XI, and his wife's name was Queen Charlotte and they had one child who was a daughter called Princess Anne. The King and Queen very much wanted to have a son and call him Prince Charles after his mother. (Charles is the boy's name that goes with Charlotte and Caroline and all those.) So they prayed and prayed for another baby and God answered their prayer, but when the baby came it was another girl. The King was furious and said it was All the Queen's Fault. Which of course it wasn't, and the baby was Christened Joan.

In those days people used to engage their babies to each other and then wait until they grew older and could get married. They got married very young indeed, to our way of thinking—really quite little. So, as the custom was, Joan was engaged to be married to the little son of the Duke of Orleans. (What do you know about another Joan and Orleans? Anything? Nothing?) When Joan was one week old she was sent away to the Duchess of Orleans to grow up with her family for the first part of her life. She was very happy there, and the Duchess treated her just like her own daughter.

When she was four years old her father the King sent for Princess Joan to come home so that he could see what she was like and how she was getting on. When she arrived with the

Duchess, her mother the Queen welcomed her little daughter with love and kindness. But her father took one look at her and said:

"She is uglier than I had thought possible!" And he pushed her away. The Duchess picked her up and kissed her.

Joan was very small indeed, and she had a crooked back and the sweetest and loveliest face anyone had seen for a very long time. The Duchess of Orleans told the Queen that she was as Good as Gold and was the Kindest little girl she had ever known. And never in her life had she grumbled when her back hurt her.

"Does it hurt her much?" asked the Queen.

"Sometimes it does," said the Duchess.

"Poor little thing," said the Queen. "I do think she is so sweet, don't you? It *is* a shame about her back."

"I love her," said the Duchess.

Queen Charlotte cried sadly over her daughter and gave her a little Princess's Apartment all for herself in the Palace, and some people to look after her. The Duchess went home and left Joan there, to wait till she was old enough to marry her son.

Joan was very lonely, poor little girl, because her sister Anne, who was much older, had married a Count and gone away to live in his castle in Dinan, which is a town in Brittany. And although all this happened more than 450 years ago the cattle is still there and I have seen it and been inside it. It is called Le Chateau de la Princesse Anne.

The lady who looked after Joan was horrid, and Joan used to go to the Palace Chapel for comfort.

"I am safe here," she thought, "and God and Our Lady are

so kind, they won't mind me being so small."

She spent more and more time playing by herself in the Chapel until the King said that she *must* stay in her own rooms and that it was Forbidden for her to go to the Chapel except on Sundays with everyone else.

"It isn't natural," he said to the Queen, "for a child to spend all day in a Chapel."

When Joan was six years old the Queen had another baby, and this time it was the son they had waited for so long, and they called him Charles. Joan loved the new baby, and when he grew older he was her greatest friend and protector. At first the King wanted to keep them apart, because he couldn't bear to see Joan. But he was so proud of his son and loved him so much that he let him do as he liked, which was lovely for Joan.

As soon as the new baby had been Baptized the King made a great Procession from the Palace to the Cathedral of Notre Dame to give thanks to God for the birth of a Prince who would one day be King. The Queen and Princess Joan were there and all the Nobles and Ladies of the Palace. It was a beautiful day and the sun shone on the silks and satins of all the cloaks and dresses and the harness of the horses. Blue and green and red and silver and yellow. The King and Queen and Joan had their crowns on because it was a State Occasion.

Joan, who was only six, went by herself to the Lady Chapel in the Cathedral, and she knelt down and took off her little golden crown and offered it to Our Lady. She put it down at the foot of her statue.

"Its a special thankyou from me, Our Lady," she said, "because now I have a brother. When he is older perhaps he will look after me. I do love having a brother."

(I expect that is why Prince Charles was so good to her later on.)

When she had finished her prayer she heard a Kind Voice say:

"Thank you, Joan. When you are older you shall found an Order in my Honor."

At the time she didn't know what this could mean, because she knew she was to be married to the son of her dear Duchess of Orleans, so how could she have time to found an Order? But she always remembered about it.

Her father, King Louis, was more and more unkind to her as time went on.

"Princesses *must* be beautiful," he said to the Queen, "and just look at your daughter—a Hunchback!"

"She has a beautiful face and a beautiful nature," said the Queen, "and I love her."

"Well, I don't," said the King. "I think she's Awful."

One day when he had lost his temper about something else he remembered Joan in her Princess's apartment, and before anyone could think what he was going to do, he rushed into her room waving his sword and tried to kill her! Luckily one of his nobles who had come running behind him caught hold of his arm and, instead of killing Joan, the sword made a great cut right down her arm. She had a scar for the rest of her life. After this the King left her alone. Even *he* was ashamed of what he had done to his daughter, so he tried to pretend he hadn't got one. Which was much better for Joan.

When she was fourteen years old Joan was married to the young Duke of Orleans. The King (you remember?) had arranged this when she was born because he wanted a Right Hand Man who was also a Relative. But the Duke didn't like Joan much (actually he didn't know her very well) and he did not like to be seen with her, or even to be with her at home, because she was so small. So Joan lived in her own part of the castle and kept house for him beautifully. All the people of the Duke's court loved her, and so did the people of Orleans.

"Her heart is as lovely as her face," they said. "She is as good as gold and she smiles like a happy angel."

Well, time went on and the King died and Joan's brother Prince Charles was King of France instead, but he was still too young to be King by himself. So his older sister, Princess Anne, came from her castle in Brittany to help him. Joan's husband thought *he* ought to be the King's adviser (or Regent, as it is called), and he started a war with King Charles about it. Joan was wonderful at trying to make peace between her Husband and her Brother. Twice she got her husband pardoned when he was taken prisoner by going to Charles about it. She found it very difficult to know whose Side she was on.

"Do forgive him, Charles," she said. "He is your Enemy, I know, but he is my Husband, too."

And King Charles, who loved his sister Joan, did forgive him. Twice.

Then, when he was only twenty-eight, Charles suddenly died and the Duke of Orleans was King, and Joan was the Queen of France. As soon as the new King had settled down, he sent for Joan.

"Now I am King," he said. "You are the Queen."

"Yes, I know," said Queen Joan.

"Well," said the King, "—er," and he pulled at his collar and got rather red in the face. "Well, I don't think you would like all the Pomp and Circumstance of being a Queen, would you? The Processions and Banquets and all that?"

"I wouldn't mind," said Joan. "If I am a Queen I shall have to live like that, even if I did mind."

"I was thinking," said the King, "that we don't really know each other very well. We've hardly seen each other since our wedding, what with one thing and another. And you know, we never asked to marry each other, it was all arranged for us without our having a chance to say if we wanted to or not. So one way and another, I thought we might ask the Pope if our marriage really counted. If he says it doesn't, then I could marry a proper Queen who will enjoy Pomp and Circumstance and you could do just what you like."

He was very hot and nervous because he was afraid Joan would be offended and make a fuss and perhaps even say that she would rather be Queen and stay in the Palace. But Joan, although she was rather hurt in her feelings, did understand how the King felt. So she said:

"Very well, perhaps that would be best. But if I am not married to you, what do you think I had better do?"

The King was so relieved that she had been so nice about it that he said he would give her two Duchies if the Pope said they were not married. And he did. So Joan was Duchess of two Duchies instead of being the Queen of France. (What is a Kingdom? And an Empire? And a Bishopric?)

She lived in the Duchy of Pontoise and she used all the Income that she had from the Duchy of Berry for all sorts of Charities and Kindnesses. When she was much older she remembered what Our Lady had said to her when she was six years old. (Do *you* remember? It was in the Cathedral after the Procession in honor of her brother Charles' christening?) Well, what Our Lady said was:

"Thank you, Joan. When you are older you shall found an Order in my honor."

(Founding an Order, or a school or anything, is beginning it or starting it. Important people often lay the Foundation Stone of grand new buildings. What about Profound, which means deep? And De Profundis? And there are the foundations of a church, aren't there? A great many schools pray for their Founders and Benefactors every day. And so they should. Ask somebody else to explain Benefactors if you don't know what they are. Otherwise we shall forget this is a story about

St. Joan and begin to write a dictionary, and what would you do then?)

So Joan founded the Order of the Annunciation, and she is the Patron Saint of all Cripples and Hunchbacks, and she is a very sweet person to know about. She is often called by her surname as well as her Christian name, so that she doesn't get mixed up with the other St. Joan. French surnames often have "de" in front of them, and Queen Joan's name was de Valois. St. Joan of Orleans name was d'Arc, and there was St. Francis de Paul, wasn't there?

St. Joan of Valois' Special Day is February 4th, and hundreds and thousands of people all over the world can have her for their saint. Different countries spell or say Joan in different ways. The Scots say Janet or Jean, the French say Jane or Jeanne, the English say Joan or Janice or Jane, the Italians say Giovanna, and I expect you can think of plenty more. So all these people as well as those whose birthdays are on February 4th can have her for their saint. And very lucky they are too.

St. Teresa

Once upon a time there was a little girl called Teresa and she lived in the town of Avila in Spain. She was seven years old and her favorite Thing to do was reading, and whenever she read

ng she always wanted to go and do it herself. She
brothers and sisters, and one of the brothers, called
loved reading too, but he didn't always want to *do*
as well. So Teresa and Rodriguez used to read To-
never they could, and their Favorite Book was about
because of the Pictures. It was a very big and heavy
on every page was a beautiful painted picture. There
was one of St. Lawrence being Roasted on a Gridiron for being
a Christian, and one of St. Longinus getting Ready for Battle,
and one of little St. Hugh walking along the Dark Street in
the Un-Christians' Town, and there were heaps of others too.

One day Teresa and Rodriguez were lying on the floor in the
nursery with the Big Book when Teresa said:

"I wish *we* could be Martyrs, because then we could go
straight to Heaven instead of waiting till we get old and die."

"If you are a Martyr you have to be killed because you are a
Christian," said Rodriguez, "and no one will kill *us* because
they are Christians themselves." And he went on looking at a
Picture of some Fierce Lions and some Christian Martyrs with
all the Roman Citizens looking on and cheering and waving
flags and the Band Playing. Really, being a Martyr must be
Most Exciting!

"If we could only get to Morocco the Moors would chop off
our heads *Immediately*," said Teresa; "Christians are their
Worst Thing."

"It's rather a long way for us to go," said Rodriguez, who
would rather have stayed in the nursery with the Book.

"Well, will you go if I do?" asked Teresa.

"I suppose I shall have to," said Rodriguez, who didn't want
Teresa to be a Martyr and get to Heaven first!

So, after lunch, while they were having their Rest (and all the Grown-ups were too, because of it being so hot in Spain), Teresa had a Good Idea.

"Quick!" she said, "Come on, Rodriguez, before Nurse comes up from the Kitchen!"

And they ran out of the nursery and out of the garden on to the Hot and Dusty Highroad. They walked and they walked and they walked and they walked. Rodriguez got tired and dragged his feet, and the dust flew up in a great cloud and made him sneeze. He *hated* going to Morocco, but Teresa said she wasn't tired, and he didn't want her to be a Martyr and not him.

When their Nurse came up out of the Kitchen and saw the Children's beds empty she ran to their Mother, who was still having her Rest.

"Are the children with you, Madam?" she asked.

"No, Nurse, I thought they were with you," said their Mother, and they started looking All Over the House.

"You look upstairs and I'll look downstairs," said the Mother, and she looked in the Hall and in the Dining-room and in the Library and behind the Drawing-room sofa and under the Kitchen table. No one there!

"Bother the children!" said the Children's Mother.

Nurse looked under all the beds, in the Bath, in the Wardrobes and on top of the cupboard in the Nursery. No one there!

"Oh! deary, deary, what *has* become of them?" said Nurse.

"The only thing to do," said their Mother, "is to wait until Uncle Juan comes Home in Time for Tea, and then he can go out on his Swift Horse and find them." And they started getting Tea ready so that Uncle Juan would not have to wait.

When Uncle Juan was riding along on the Swift Horse so as to be Home in Time for Tea he saw a Cloud of Dust coming along the road to meet him!

"Dear me," he thought, "I do hope it isn't Moors, they might cut off my head." So he rode his horse into a field and hid behind a hedge and waited for the Cloud of Dust to go past in case there were Moors in it.

As it came nearer and nearer, Uncle Juan said to himself: "It looks rather small for Moors, perhaps it's a Wolf!" So he waited some more. He wasn't actually *frightened,* but he hadn't got his Sharp Sword with him, and its Absence might have led to Awkward Complications.

When the Cloud of Dust came up to him a Voice came out of it! Uncle Juan got such a fright that he nearly jumped Right Out of his skin. He just managed to keep inside it by pressing down the top of his head.

This is what the Voice said:

"*Need* we be Martyrs *today,* Teresa? Couldn't we p'raps be them tomorrow instead?"

And there were Rodriguez and Teresa still walking along the Hot and Dusty Highroad!

"What *are* you two doing here all alone?" asked Uncle Juan.

"We're being Martyrs," said poor Rodriguez sadly.

"No, *going* to be Martyrs," said Teresa, "in Morocco. Our heads'll be cut off and then we'll be in Heaven. We're walking there."

"But what about the sea?" asked Uncle Juan. "How will you get across?"

"*Is* there any sea?" said Teresa. "I never knew that. *Bother!* Well, we can be Hermits in the garden instead." (Hermits are people who live all alone in little huts and sometimes turn into Saints.)

Rodriguez was very pleased that the sea was in the way. He had not really wanted to be a Martyr, but only because Teresa did.

"Can I ride on your horse, going home?" he said.

"Can *I*?" said Teresa.

So Uncle Juan put Rodriguez up on the saddle in front of him and Teresa up behind him and they trotted home grandly on the Swift Horse.

Their Mother was Rather Cross when they got home, but when they told her about being Martyrs she said it was an Excellent Plan but Impracticable, and being Hermits was the Same Thing, only Better.

So after Tea they went out into the garden to build Hermits' Cells, but whenever the walls got a little bit high they fell down again and Rodriguez said Hermits was a Silly Idea and he would rather be a Soldier when he grew up. And when he did grow up he *was* a Very Fine Soldier who went to fight in South America, but Teresa invented a New Kind of Nun. And this is how she did it.

There were already some nuns and friars who dressed in brown, with white cloaks. They were called Carmelites, after Our Lady of Mount Carmel. Teresa liked the Carmelites because a lot of Hermits lived on Mount Carmel, and she still *rather* wanted to be a Hermit. But she thought that they ought to be Sterner and Poorer. So she didn't let her sort of Carmelite have any Stockings and made them have Harder Rules to keep.

So if any of you live near a Carmelite Church or Convent and you see the Fathers dressed in brown and white you can remember about Teresa and the Stockings.

St. Teresa's Special Day is on October 15th, and I expect lots of people's Birthdays are on that day.

St. Angela

Once upon a time there was a little girl called Angela, and when she was ten years old her father and her mother both died and a kind Uncle took Angela and her elder sister home with him to look after. Now Angela's father and mother had brought up their children properly and they all knew their catechism and all that and the kind Uncle went on with telling them all about God, the Sacraments and all those things. Now Angela was very unlucky, because when she was twelve her sister died very suddenly in the night without having the Last Sacraments or Confession or anything.

Angela was terribly worried.

"Supposing she had a mortal sin," she said; "she hadn't been to Confession for two or three weeks, oh! *supposing* she had a mortal sin?" And she asked God every day to let her know if it was All Right.

Her kind Uncle got quite anxious about her. "I'm sure it's all right, Angela," he said; "she was a good little girl and God knows that she didn't have time for the Last Sacraments." But

Angela still worried about her sister until she made herself quite ill.

"You do look Thin and Mingy, Angela," said her kind Uncle, "and now that it is haymaking time at my farm in the country, I'm going to send you there for a good holiday in the fresh country air. Now mind you come back with fresh round rosy cheeks!" and he gave Angela an apple to eat on the journey. But Angela went on asking God about her sister and in spite of the country air she looked Mingier than ever, and the farmer's wife was at her wit's end to know what to do with her.

One day Angela was walking slowly along the side of a hay-field in the sun when she saw a Misty Patch in front of her, with the sun shining through it.

"Well," she thought, "that's funny! I've never seen a Misty Patch like that in the middle of a hot Summer's day. In the Autumn, yes, but the Summer, no." And she went towards the Mist to see where it was coming from.

When she got there she thought she saw her Sister in the mist and the sister smiled and nodded her head and said:

"I'm quite all right, Angela!"

Angela was so delighted that she laughed and sang and ran quickly back to the house and told the farmer's wife.

"There now," said the farmer's wife, "the good God was sorry for your pale face and sent her to show you that you needn't worry any more!"

"Wasn't it kind of Him though?" said Angela.

"It was that," said the farmer's wife, dishing up the dinner. "Now come and eat a proper meal dearie, and get those roses back in your cheeks!"

And you know, from that day, Angela got better, and by the

time she went home to her kind Uncle's house she had round pink cheeks instead of the pale ones.

When she grew up Angela was surprised to find that very few of the children living near her in the town knew anything at all about God or the Church.

"But it's terrible!" she said to some friends who had come to tea with her; "we were taught all those things when we were tiny little girls, and these children are quite big and some of them have never even heard of Our Lord."

The friends were all rather Concerned too, and after they had gone home Angela went out for a walk by herself to think out a Plan of what she could do about the Town Children. As she walked through a grass field she saw an Extraordinary Thing.

She saw a wide golden ladder like stairs sticking straight up out of the field high up into the blue sky, and up the ladder were going all sorts of girls. Tall and short, old and young, dark and fair, fat and thin, rich and poor, but they were all laughing and singing as they hurried up the ladder. And as she stood staring at this wonderful sight she heard someone say: "Angela, these are all your girls that you are going to collect for God!"

Angela was so interested that the very next day she visited her friends and they decided to collect the little girls that played in the streets and teach them in homemade schools. They weren't real schools of course, because each friend took a few girls home and taught them there; one taught history and one arithmetic and one geography and all that, but they *all* taught Catechism. When they had finished in the mornings the friends visited hospitals and prisons to find girls there and they taught them too. At first no one noticed them much, but the little girls used to talk at home and sometimes their mothers used to go with them and soon they always went with them and a lot of them wished that they had learned all this before.

One night when she was asleep Our Lord came to Angela and spoke to her.

Angela sat up and rubbed her eyes.

"Who is it?" she said.

"It's Me, Angela," said Our Lord.

"Oh! how kind You are, dear God," said Angela; "all my life I've wanted to see You, but of course, I never thought I *really* would," and she went on looking and looking at Our Lord, in case He went away.

"Angela, when are you going to make a new sort of nun out of all your friends and yourself?" said Our Lord. "I think it is time you did."

So Angela told the Pope what Our Lord had said and then she came home and told her friends, and they made a New Kind of Nun whose work was to make Schools for Girls. Now all the friends (who were Nuns now) wanted to call the Order after Angela, but Angela said, "No, I am not important enough to have an Order called after me. But shall I tell you what I think? Do you remember St. Ursula with all her eleven thousand girls?"

"Yes," said the nuns, "we remember quite well." (Do *you*?)

"Well," said Angela, "I would like to call the new Order after her, because she had all those girls long before we did."

And all the nuns thought that would be an Excellent Idea, and so they were called the Company of St. Ursula, or the Ursulines, as we call them for short. And I expect a good many of you go to Ursuline schools, don't you?

St. Angela's Special Day is on May 31st, and anyone called Angelina or Angelica or Angeline counts, because they are all one and the Same name.

St. Rose

Once upon a time there was a Very Small Baby who lived in a town called Lima, which is in Peru, which is in South America. She *was* going to be christened Isabel as her Father wanted her to be, but her Mother said that she was so pretty that her Face was like a Rose Petal, so she must be called Rose.

"Well, I do call that a silly reason," said her Father. "She might be all Wrinkled and Ugly when she grows up, like a Toadstool, and then think how people will laugh if her name is Rose!"

"Well I *want* her called Rose," said the Baby's Mother, and to Save Further Trouble, the Baby was christened Rose Isabel.

When Rose grew up she became a Very Special Friend of Our Lord's, and her Favorite Things to do were Gardening and Sewing. All day she worked in her Garden, and she grew heaps of Roses because Our Lady loves them and because, when they are dead, they are all Stiff and Thorny, and that reminded her of Our Lord's Crown of Thorns.

She used to fast a lot, and that used to make her Pale and Thin, so that her Mother was always saying:

"Rose, you are looking Rather Mingy. Are you sure you eat enough, darling? I'm sure you'd be better for Three Good Meals a Day. Now, you *must* eat this Steak and Kidney Pudding, I had it Specially Made for you!"

Now, Rose loved her Mother, and she didn't like her to be So Worried, and so she sometimes ate what she was told to eat, and that made *her* worried because of not Fasting. So, one day, she said to Our Lord:

"Please may I fast and not Look Mingy? Because Mummy gets Worried if I'm Pale."

And so Our Lord made it so that Rose always had nice Rosy Cheeks, however much she fasted, and so everybody was happy and not worried.

Rose looked after a lot of Ill People in the town and she made clothes for Poor People, and she gave food to Hungry People, and no one bothered about her much, except some of the People she looked after.

Now, because all her Work kept making her late for meals and things, and because she never had time to pray when her Family was fussing about Parties, Rose thought that she had better go and live in a Little Shed that was in the Garden. It was really Very Small Indeed and had only one room, and it was Rather Dark and there were Hundreds of Mosquitoes there, so that poor Rose had a Miserable Time. She couldn't pray properly when she was being Bitten all the time, so she asked God if she could Make a Bargain with them, and He said she could.

So Rose said:

"Listen, all you Mosquitoes! If *you* never bite *me* any more, *I'll* never squash *you* any more."

And they didn't so she didn't, and Things were more Peaceful after that. And the Mosquitoes kept away Unwelcome Visitors.

Well, Rose went on with her work for God, and as she got older and older she loved Our Lord more and more, until at last He let her go to Heaven so that it would be easier for her to talk to Him, and *then* an Exciting Thing Happened!

As soon as she had gone to Heaven, people began to say to each other:

"You know that Rose? Well, she made all my Children's Clothes for me for the Love of God instead of for Money!"

Or:

"Did you know Rose? Well, she gave all those Beggars her food, and often had nothing herself." And things like that.

Then someone said:

"What about her being a Saint? Do you suppose she was?"

And then they all said:

"Let's ask the Pope to make her one!"

So some of them Sailed Across the Sea to the Pope and told him all about Rose and her Kindnesses and how she loved Our Lord so much that she did all her Work for Him.

The Pope was Very Surprised.

"But there aren't any American Saints!" he said.

"We know that, Your Holiness," said All the People, "but Rose was Very Special, so couldn't she be one?"

"It seems Funny to think of an American Saint," said the Pope; "you might as well say it could Rain Roses! It's just as likely!"

As soon as he'd said that, there was a beautiful Smell! Just like Roses, it was. (As a Matter of Fact it *was* Roses, coming from Heaven because the Pope said they couldn't, only, as they'd such a long way to come, the Smell got there first!)

Then came the Roses themselves! Red ones and Pink ones and White ones and Yellow ones and all the Other Colored

ones, raining down as the Pope said they couldn't! All the people cheered! They *knew* that Rose ought to be called a Saint, and there was God showing everyone that He thought so, too.

The Pope scratched his head and thought. He had never *heard* of such an idea as an American Saint. But all the time, the Roses kept on falling and falling; they were getting Quite Deep now, nearly up to his Knees!

"I suppose there *could* be one!" he thought, "But I don't Hold with it."

Now the Roses were up to his Waist, and they were falling

faster than ever, and at last they reached his Neck, and he was afraid they would Bury him Entirely!

"All right," he said, "I'll make her a Saint, and now send someone to pick up all those Roses!"

As soon as he'd said it the Roses stopped falling and All the People went back Across the Sea to Lima to tell the Others how God had made the Pope make Saint Rose.

St. Rose's Special Day is August 30th, when there are plenty of Roses about, and she was the First American Saint. Lots and Lots of People are called after her, and if their names are Rosa or Rosina or Rosamund or something, it Counts.

ST. ROSE

St. Rose in Heaven is in charge
Of all Our Lady's Roses,
It gives her rather more to do
Than anyone supposes.

The rose-trees reach for miles and miles
All over lovely flowers,
And every one that opens
Is a good deed of ours.

St. Rose she always sings at work,
Our Lady loves to hear her,
And thinks of good excuses
To go down and be near her.

"St. Rose," she asks, "what is in flower?"
"Why, Ma'am, there are so many!
This one's because of Jane who gave
A raggy man her penny.

"And this big red one is because
Of a little boy called Jack.
I hear you love him very much
And he always loves you back

"But I must be about my work
And water this with grace,
I mustn't let a bush go dry,
Or I shall lose my place!"

She gets her water-pot, and sings,
And makes the garden glisten,
And still Our Lady finds excuse
To linger there and listen.

St. Jane

Once upon a time there was a little girl and her name was Jane
Frances and she was French. (Have you got two names?)

When Jane was very little her Mother died and her father
found her a very kind governess who looked after her and took
her for walks and gave her lessons. Jane liked her lessons (some
do and some don't), and she learned a lot about God and the
Catechism and all that as well as History and Arithmetic.

One day, when Jane was five, a Protestant gentleman came
to lunch with her father and Jane went down when they were

just finishing so as to eat a piece of sugar dipped in coffee. While she was slowly sucking her sugar she listened to what the two men were saying.

"Well," said the Protestant gentleman, "no doubt Catholics have a great many rules to keep and I think that some of their ideas are quite good, but one thing I'll *never* believe. How can you believe that Jesus Christ is actually in the Blessed Sacrament? It is pure nonsense!"

Jane looked at her father who was looking rather Stern, and then, because she was so shocked she said:

"But Our Lord said that He *was* in the Blessed Sacrament. If you don't believe Him, then you must think that He is a liar, and you couldn't think that!"

The Protestant gentleman laughed.

"I must say," he said to Jane's father, "your Church has got a good champion there!" Then he looked at Jane. "Come here, my dear, here's a piece of toffee for you because you have the courage of your opinions."

Jane took the toffee and said, "Thank you, Sir," and then she put the toffee in the fire.

"What's the matter with it?" said the Protestant gentleman, looking a bit ruffled.

"There's nothing wrong with the *toffee,*" said Jane, "but I don't want anything of yours, please, if you talk about God like that."

"Now run upstairs, Jane," said her father, and she did, but she never forgot the Protestant gentleman.

When she grew up Jane was engaged to be married to a very Handsome and Rich young man called Charles and she was very happy.

One day, at Corpus Christi (what do those words mean?), Jane said to her Rich young man:

"Let's go out and see the Procession of the Blessed Sacrament."

"All right," said the Rich young man, "and let's take some sandwiches and apples in our pockets so that we can have a picnic afterwards and not come home for tea." So that is what they did, and out they went.

Now I expect you know that in Catholic countries like Spain and Poland and Italy and France and parts of Germany and Austria, there are Processions when it is the Feast of the Blessed Sacrament. People make Altars at places in the town, usually in the Market Place and perhaps in the biggest street. The people put as many flowers as they can all round about, and everyone brings some from their own gardens and so there are always plenty. Then after Benediction in the Church in the afternoon, the priest carries the Blessed Sacrament right out of the Church followed by the Choir and any other priests who may be there, all singing. Then all the people in the church follow them and that makes the Procession.

Well, the Procession goes through the town and whenever it reaches one of the Flowery Altars it stops while the priest gives a short Benediction to all the people who are waiting there and then they all go on to the Next Place, and end up back in the Church again. And all the people along the roads kneel down as the Blessed Sacrament passes by.

But in England we are not a Catholic country, although there are a lot of Catholics here, so our Corpus Christi processions are just round the Church or, if there is a Convent anywhere about we very often have them round the Convent garden so as to have outside Altars.

Jane and her Rich young man were living in France, so they went out into the streets and found a Flowery Altar. There they waited for the Procession.

Soon they could hear Singing, and all the people looked at the ground to see if there was a smooth place to kneel on and not stones or mud or anything.

Then the Procession came. First the little boy with the incense and then the priest very carefully carrying the Blessed Sacrament, and then the other priests and the choir and all the people who had joined on to the Procession.

Everyone round about knelt down, and so did Jane, and they had Benediction and everyone kept very still and quiet. After Benediction Jane looked round for her Rich Young Man and there he was standing up and leaning against a tree, with his hat on, looking at his packet of sandwiches!

"*Charles!*" said Jane, when she had got to him in the crowd. "Charles, what is the matter, don't you feel well or what?"

"Why?" asked Charles, "I feel quite well, do I look Pale?"

"No," said Jane, "but you didn't kneel and you kept your hat on when the Blessed Sacrament was there."

"Why not?" asked Charles.

Jane was Flabbergasted. "Why not?" she said. "But you should take your hat off politely to anyone else, and yet you are Rude and Ill mannered to God Himself!"

"Ah, but I never bother with all that," said Charles. "After all, I'm not a Catholic, so why should I?"

"Even Protestants can have Good Manners," said Jane, "and I never knew that you weren't a Catholic. Why didn't you say so before?"

"Because I thought you mightn't marry me if I did," said Charles; "but you will, Won't you?"

"No," said Jane, "I *couldn't,* because we don't think the same things and we wouldn't be happy."

"Well stop being a Catholic then," said Charles; "then it will be all right."

"Don't be silly," said Jane. "Now I must go home. Don't come with me."

So Jane went home and on her way she stopped for a minute at the Church to tell Our Lord how sorry she was that Charles had been so Ill mannered.

But Jane did get married later on to a very nice man called Monsieur le Baron de Chantal and his name was Christopher and he lived in a Castle, so Jane was Madame la Baronne de Chantal and she was very happy.

There were such a lot of poor people living near the Castle that Jane asked Christopher if she might have a huge meal cooked once a day so that anyone who was a Bit Short could come and have a Free Meal.

"Yes, of course you may," said the Baron; "I don't know why I didn't think of it before."

So every day at Noon (when is that?) Jane and any Helpers who liked used to go out on to a wide Terrace with enormous Saucepan things with Dinner in them and the Poor People used to queue up for their helping because that has always been a good way of keeping a Crowd in Order. But one day Jane thought she saw the same woman twice.

"Surely I gave her some dinner a few minutes ago," she thought, "because I remember that she didn't like carrots. So she watched the people carefully and she saw a good many of the same people twice! And what do you suppose that they were doing? After they had had their Helping (and a good big one it was) they ate it quickly and then went round the back of the castle and joined on to the queue again. As soon as Jane saw what was happening she stopped and said:

"Oh, but that is not Fair!"

"Why?" said the man who was holding out his plate. "There is plenty more dinner."

"It is too Easy for you," said Jane; "you can't have everything that you want as easily as that. Do you know that if I want something from God sometimes I have to beg and beg for weeks before He lets me have it. Even then, sometimes He doesn't so that I have to make do with what I have."

"But you've got plenty for yourself," said the man; "not like me."

"Yes, I am lucky," said Jane, "but I haven't enough for all of you as well unless I work for it."

So the man, who hadn't thought of that, felt rather ashamed and said that he'd go and rake up some of the dead leaves in Jane's garden if she liked. Jane said Thank you and so he did.

Once a very Queer thing happened. Jane was out for a walk with her dog and she had on her thick shoes and an old coat. She went along a lane full of trees with red and yellow leaves with the sun on them, and the pale blue sky was behind them and she was thinking what good color schemes God invents when round a corner came three Poor and Raggy men. They stopped in front of Jane and one of them took off his hat politely and asked her could she give them a little money because they had nowhere to sleep and the nights were getting rather chilly.

"Yes, of course," said Jane, and then she remembered that

she had not got her purse with her because she was only taking the dog for a walk. "I am so sorry," she said. "I haven't any money with me."

"Never mind, Lady," said one of the men. "But it will be cold sleeping out tonight."

Jane was very fussed.

"But you mustn't do that," she said. "I know! Here, take my ring, it is worth quite a lot of money and you will be able to sleep indoors for months. My husband gave it to me for my birthday." Jane sighed because she liked the ring very much.

"Thank you kindly, Lady," said the man. "We won't forget you." And all the three men Disappeared.

Jane stared.

"The sun must be in my eyes," she said to herself, and she looked again but there was no one there.

When she told the Baron he was very surprised too, and in the end they decided that the three men must have been Angels. It certainly looks like it, doesn't it?

After a time the Baron died and Jane was very lonely. So she spent all her time Visiting the ill poor people round about. She took them fruit and milk and eggs. She used to make their beds and tidy them up and give them their dinners and make up the fire so that they would not catch cold by getting out of bed to do all those things for themselves. In the end she invented a new kind of Nun. They were called the Order of the Visitation of the Blessed Virgin Mary because they Visited the ill people in their houses. I know two girls called Ellen Mary and Alice Mary and they have got a Great Aunt who is a Visitation Nun.

St. Jane's Special Day is on December 13th, and if you remember that her other name was Frances there must be thousands of people who could have her for their Special Saint.

St. Bernadette

Once upon a time there was a little girl who had an Aunt called Aunt Bernarde. So her Mother called her Bernadette, which means Little Bernarde, after the Aunt. (Just like Cigar*ette* means Little Cigar, and Kitchen*ette* means Little Kitchen.)

Bernadette lived with her mother and her father and her sister, whose name was 'Toinette (which means Little Antony, after St. Francis' friend). They were very, very poor, and had only one room in their house, and Bernadette always had a Bad Cough.

Well, one morning, after breakfast, Bernadette noticed that there was no more wood for the fire (it was a very cold day in February), and she said to her mother:

"Shall I go out and find some more wood? Or we won't be able to cook the dinner."

And her mother said:

"Thank you, dear, but I'll go because of your Cough. It is too cold for you."

Just when they were settling who should go, there came a knock at the door: Rat! tat! tat!

"Come in!" said Bernadette's mother, and a little girl called Jeanne (French for Joan) came in with her baby brother, who was Only Two, to play with 'Toinette.

"Let's *all* go and find some wood. I know a Special Place," said 'Toinette, who didn't want to stay indoors because she would have to help to wash up the breakfast things. So they all went out with a big basket, and Bernadette took some lozenges for her Cough. On the way to 'Toinette's Special Place they left Jeanne's little brother at his house, because he was such a bother and wanted to be carried.

'Toinette's Special Place was the other side of a stream, where there wasn't a bridge, and just across the stream was a big Cave with a big Rock beside it. 'Toinette and Jeanne paddled across, and the water was so cold that their feet nearly froze and made them cry. Bernadette daren't cross. It was so cold, and besides, she had a Cough. She tried to find some stepping-stones, but she couldn't. The others went farther and farther away, picking up sticks, and soon poor Bernadette was Left Alone.

It *was* so cold! Bernadette looked across the stream and thought:

"If only I could go in that Cave the wind mightn't be so cold."

She went to the edge of the stream and began to take off her shoes, but she coughed so much that she couldn't balance on one foot while she unfastened the other. So *she* began to cry, too! Then she thought she would say her Rosary until the others came back. So she knelt down, but her fingers were so cold that she couldn't feel the beads, and she had to look all the time to see where she had got up to. After a little while she looked up to see if 'Toinette and Jeanne were coming back yet, and there, right in front of her, was the Most Surprising Thing that had ever happened to her!

Right on top of the big rock by the cave there stood a Beautiful Lady! She wasn't holding on, and the wind wasn't blowing her things about as it was Bernadette's. She smiled. Bernadette rubbed her eyes and looked again. How *could* the Lady have climbed up there without her noticing? And who could she be? She had on a long white dress, and a blue sash, and a white veil over her hair, and she was holding a gold Rosary with white beads. It looked as if she was saying it with Bernadette. When she saw the Rosary, Bernadette remembered that she had stopped in the middle of hers, and she thought that perhaps the Lady had come to say it with her. Only why did she stand in such a funny place? Why didn't she come and kneel with Bernadette? The Lady smiled at her again, and she suddenly felt quite warm and happy instead of cold and miserable. She forgot that 'Toinette and Jeanne had Left her Behind, so she went on saying her Rosary, and the Lady looked as if she were saying it too, but Bernadette only heard her saying the "Our Father" and the "Glory be" parts.

"What *are* you doing? What are you saying your prayers out here for?" said a voice behind her. Bernadette jumped. The others had come back without her noticing them.

"What are you looking at? Why are you looking so pleased? *I* can't see anything," said Jeanne.

"Look at that Lady up on the Rock," said Bernadette. "Who is she?"

"There isn't anybody, you've been asleep, Lazy, while we've been picking up the sticks," said 'Toinette. "Come along home, my feet are cold."

When they got home, 'Toinette told her mother what Bernadette had been doing, and her mother said it was a Dream. But it wasn't.

Next day Bernadette said she was going to the cave again to see if the Lady would come back. Aunt Bernarde and her mother said that they would go too. So they started off. Now, to get to the stream they had to go down a very steep and narrow and stony path. Bernadette could run down it, but Aunt Bernarde and her mother had to hold on to the side and go down slowly.

"I was saying my Rosary last time," said Bernadette when they had caught her up. "I think I had better say it again this time."

So she knelt down in the muddy field, near the edge of the stream.

"There she is!" she said.

But Aunt Bernarde and the mother couldn't see anyone. Bernadette thought this was very funny, but she didn't bother much because she was hoping that the Lady would tell her who she was.

"Would you please tell me who you are?" asked Bernadette. She was rather frightened, but her mother and Aunt Bernarde kept on whispering to her to ask. Besides, the Lady looked very kind, so perhaps she wouldn't mind being asked.

"I want you to come here, to see me, every day for a fortnight," said the Lady, "and then I'll tell you something Very Important." Then she disappeared.

Aunt Bernarde and Bernadette's mother were Rather Cross because they had not seen the Lady, so when Bernadette told her mother what the Lady had said about going there every day for a fortnight, she said:

"Of *course* you can't come here every day! It is much too cold, and your Cough will get worse. You are a very Naughty Little Girl, pretending to see a Lady like that, and making Aunt Bernarde and me come all the way down that steep path for nothing!"

Poor Bernadette cried again! It wasn't fair of people, and she couldn't think why no one else saw the Lady when there she was, all the time, as plain as plain. But she did wish the Lady had said who she was, because *everyone* said:

"Who *is* she, Bernadette?" and when she said, "I don't know," they *always* said, "Well, then, it can't be anyone at all." Which was silly of them, because you often see people without knowing who they are.

When Bernadette's father heard about it he was sorry for

her, and he said:

"Well, I don't see why she shouldn't go, if she puts her shawl on, and doesn't make her Cough worse."

So every day Bernadette tidied up the Room that was the Whole House; put some more wood on the fire; swept up the floor; put on her shawl; and went out down the very steep path to the stream in front of the Cave. And every day more and more people followed her to see what would happen, until there were Crowds and Crowds; but none of them ever saw the Lady except Bernadette. But they went on going because they hoped they might, although they thought that Bernadette was Only Pretending all the time.

One of the days, when Bernadette was kneeling by the stream, the Lady came and said:

"Cross the stream and come into the Cave, I want to tell you something."

Bernadette crossed the stream (it didn't feel a bit cold after all) and went in, and the Lady said:

"Kneel on the ground." Bernadette knelt down and waited to see what would happen next.

"Dig a little hole in the ground with your fingers," said the Lady, "and you will see something Surprising."

Bernadette scratched up the ground and made a little hole. She stopped and looked at it, and saw that it filled itself with water!

"Make it a little bigger," said the Lady. Bernadette did. More water came, and made the hole Brimful. More came, and the hole Overflowed and began to trickle along the floor of the Cave towards the field outside.

"Now wash in it," said the Lady. Bernadette washed her

face and hands, and found that it did not make her a bit cold. She suddenly felt very well and happy, and her Cough stopped making her chest hurt.

Now, all the people waiting outside couldn't think *what* Bernadette was doing in the Cave all this time, and they were getting Rather Cross, waiting in the cold, when suddenly someone said:

"Look!" They all looked and they saw the water coming out of the Cave like a very thin stream. As they looked it got bigger and bigger, and wider and wider, until it was a very wide one flowing across the field into the other stream. (The one that Bernadette didn't dare to cross the first day she saw the Lady.) Everyone was looking at the New Stream when Bernadette came out of the Cave. She didn't notice them, and went straight home. She didn't tell anyone how the New Stream came, or what the Lady had said to her.

That evening, when they were having supper, there came another knock at the door. Rat! tat! tat!

"Come in!" said Aunt Bernarde, and Fifteen people came in! Outside the door there were about Twenty more!

"Oh dear!" said Bernadette's mother. "What *do* they all want? We haven't got enough chairs! Here, Bernadette! 'Toinette! Get up and give your chairs to the ladies! What are you thinking about? Where are your manners?

But Bernadette and 'Toinette had been sitting with their mouths open, they were so Surprised! *Never* had they had so many visitors! Not even at Easter, when everybody went and visited everybody else.

"We want to know," said a Fat Lady with a Red Face, "what the Lady said to Bernadette in the Cave when she made the

New Stream." She sat down very hard on 'Toinette's chair, and one of the legs cracked.

"*Do* be careful," said Bernadette's mother, "that chair isn't very strong!"

"It's strong enough for *me*," said the Fat Red Lady, putting her hat straight. "Now Bernadette! Tell us *all* about it!"

"I can't tell you *anything*," said poor Bernadette, "except that she said that everybody must do penance because they aren't good enough, and that they must come and pray by the New Stream. She wants us to build a Church there, to pray in."

"Is *that* all?" said a Thin Cross Lady with a Sharp Nose. "We knew the Penance part before, we have it in Sermons! Catch *me* praying in a nasty damp field; getting my death of cold!"

"*And* building a Church, above all!" said a Stout Man with gray hair and a Gold Watch Chain. "Where are they going to get the money from, I'd like to know? *I* can't give anything!"

"She told me something else, very Special and Important," said Bernadette, "but she said that I mustn't tell anybody."

Of course everybody tried to find out what the Special and Important thing was, and they were all Very Angry when Bernadette wouldn't tell them.

The next day the Priest told Bernadette that she really *must* ask the Lady again who she was. Because how could they build her a Church when they did not know whom they were building it for? So everyone went down the steep path to see if, perhaps, they could *hear* the Lady, even if they couldn't *see* her.

They found some Ill People already there, who had heard about Bernadette's Cough being much better. They had been washing themselves in the New Stream, and some of them got quite better at once.

After Bernadette had been saying her Rosary for a little while the Lady came, as usual, to the top of the Rock. Bernadette suddenly felt Very Brave, and, looking up at the Lady, she said:

"Would you mind very much if you told me who you are? Everybody keeps *on* asking me, and I never know what to say." But the Lady only smiled.

"*Please* tell me," said Bernadette. But the Lady only smiled again, and she didn't answer.

"Dear Lady, do tell me!" said Bernadette. Then the Lady said, very quietly:

"I am the Immaculate Conception." And she disappeared.

Now Bernadette did not know what this meant at all. So she went to the priest and told him what the Lady had said, and asked him if *he* knew. The priest did, and he was very sorry he had not believed Bernadette before. Because "The Immaculate Conception" is another, and very long, name for Our Lady! And there she had been, all the time, every day for a fortnight, and everybody could have gone to love her and pray to her, and they hadn't even *seen* her, because they hadn't believed it *could* be, and they had said that Bernadette was Only Pretending all the time.

(*Now* do you see why the Lady didn't say the "Hail Mary" part of the Rosary? Because then she'd have been talking to herself, wouldn't she?)

Then the priest said:

"Now, Bernadette, you *simply must* tell me what Our Lady said to you, because it is very Important for me to Know. The Bishop will ask me."

But Bernadette said:

"I am very sorry, Father, but I can't tell you. She said I *mustn't* tell anyone."

"But," said the priest, "supposing the Pope asked you, you'd *have* to tell *him*."

"I wouldn't have to," said Bernadette, "because she said not to tell *any* one, and the Pope *is* someone."

So no one ever knew what Bernadette's Special Important Secret was.

Well, people still go to pray at the Church by the Rock (because they did build one after all), and heaps and crowds of people from All Over the World go and wash in the New Stream, and lots of them get better. You have heard of people going to Lourdes, haven't you? Well, that is where the New Stream is. Our Lady still goes there, too, but she doesn't let people see her any more. The only one who ever saw her was Bernadette. Perhaps no one else was nice enough to be allowed to.

St. Bernadette's Special Day is April 16th, and many people are called after her. Of course, there is another very Important Day belonging to this story. Whose do you suppose? Our Lady of Lourdes, of course, on February 11th, the day that Bernadette first saw her.

Anne de Guigne

This is a story about a little girl called Anne who used to live with her Mother in France. Now she lives in Heaven and helps people quite a lot, but her mother still lives at their home with all her other children.

Well, when Anne was Four her father was killed in the War, as lots of people's fathers were, and her mother was so sad that Anne cried, she was so sorry for her.

"Why was he killed? Do you know, Mummy?" she asked.

"He gave his life so that we should be safe," said her mother. "It was a Sacrifice. If our soldiers didn't go and fight and be killed, the enemy would come and Take us all Prisoners."

That made Anne think of the great Sacrifice that Our Lord made for us when He was Crucified. A Sacrifice is when you give something you like to somebody else. And the more you like the thing, the bigger the Sacrifice. Our Lord's was a very Special Sacrifice because He was killed in a very Horrible Way so that we could go to Heaven. And He *needn't* have done it like that because He is God and could have done it in a way much nicer for Himself. Or He needn't have Bothered about us at all, but just had Heaven all nice for Himself and His Angels. But He wanted us to be His Special People because He loves us, so He made the biggest Sacrifice He could and let His enemies scourge Him and bully Him, and even crucify Him. He needn't *even* have come and been a Man, because that wasn't very nice for God, was it, if you think of it?

Anyway, Anne suddenly thought that if Our Lord had sacrificed so much for her, she ought to do something back. We always want to do something nice for people who do nice things for us, don't we?

"I can't give Him a Sacrifice like He gave me," she said to herself, "but if I do lots and lots of little ones, perhaps they will Add Up into One Big One."

So, when she remembered, she used to do things for Our Lord. If she bumped her head on the corner of the table she used to say that Our Lord could have it in return for what He had given her; or if her brother Jacques took away her Special toy Wheelbarrow *just* when she was going to use it, she used to give it up to him so as to add to her Secret Store of Sacrifices. Or if chocolates were handed round, she used to try and be forgotten, and all sorts of things like that. And she remembered more and more as she got older, so that by the time she was Nine she was doing them all the time, only she didn't Tell Anybody what she was doing.

You know if you are told to do something you often don't want to do it? But if you like the person who tells you to, you *like* doing it? Well, Anne loved Our Lord, and because she *really* loved Him (like you love Mummy) and kept on doing things for Him to add to her Sacrifices, He used to talk to her. When she went to Holy Communion He told her all sorts of things, and He did everything that she asked Him to. Her Special Thing to Do, when she wasn't playing in the Nursery or doing Lessons, was to find out about someone who Stole things, or who wouldn't ever go to Church or something. Then she would tell Our Lord about it and ask Him to make it all right. Then she would run and ask someone:

"Has he stopped stealing yet?" and, if he hadn't, she said:

"Well, I'll go and pray some more, and then he will." And she did pray, and he did stop, always! Because Our Lord always does extra things for the people who do things for Him.

One thing that Our Lord told Anne was His Favorite Word. What do you suppose it was? Everybody knows it. Guess! It is quite a short one. It is "Yes." It is a funny one to have for a favorite, isn't it? The thing is, you see, whatever anyone says, or wants you to do, you say "Yes." Even if you Hate doing it. The more you hate it, the bigger your sacrifice to add to your Special Pile of Sacrifices. And Our Lord or your Guardian Angel counts each time you say it, and at the end we'll all see who has the most.

Well, by the time she was Ten Anne had got quite a lot of people to remember to love God by praying for them, and she got so good at it that God thought she'd be better in Heaven, nearer Him. And then she'd be able to get still more people, because everybody would know where she was and could ask her to do things for them more easily. So one day she had a very bad Headache. Anne was pleased about that because she said she liked being like Our Lord and His Crown of Thorns. But the headache got much worse and after a few days Our Lady came and took her away to Heaven.

When she had been there about a week, an old man in the village near her home got very ill. Anne's mother went to see him. He knew that he was dying, but he said that he didn't like God, he never *had* liked Him, and he wasn't *going* to like Him, however much He had done for him, so there!

"Oh dear!" thought Anne's mother, "I wish Anne was here. It is *just* the sort of thing she could have asked Our Lord about."

Then she thought:

"Well, after all, Anne is still my little girl, even if she has gone to Heaven, and she must do as she is told." So she said, "Anne, you really *must* see about this old man. Ask Our Lord to make him sensible before he dies."

And the old man turned over in bed and said:

"Well, after all, I was Stupid about not liking God, and I am sorry I said all that."

Hadn't Anne been quick about it?

Then Everybody began to ask Anne to do things for them, just as they used to while she was at home, and she still does because she has never forgotten Our Lord's favorite word.

Not very long ago Anne's sister Marinette got "flu," and was Very Ill in Bed with a Temperature. Anne's mother and the Doctor thought that she was going to die. So they asked Anne to ask Our Lord not to take Marinette away too, if He didn't mind, because it would be so lonely without her. As soon as they had finished asking, Marinette sat up and said she felt hungry and was Much Better, Thank you! Anne had said "Yes" again.

Now, there is one thing that you mightn't know about when you start Collecting Unselfishnesses, and it is this: Did you know that there is a sort of Unselfishness that is Selfish? I know it sounds all wrong, but it is when people Grab *all* the Not Very Nice things to do, and that doesn't give anyone else a chance of being Unselfish too. They might be collecting "Yes's" just as hard as you are, and you are spoiling it for them!

Anne hasn't got a Special Day yet, but her Mother is collecting all the things that she does from Heaven, and when she has got enough she will send them to the Pope, and then perhaps he will say which day she can have. So anyone called Anne can have Our Lady's Mother's Special Day, because she was Anne too; it is July 26th.